Outcome Harvesting

A volume in
Evaluation and Society
Jennifer C. Greene and Stewart I. Donaldson, *Series Editors*

Outcome Harvesting

Principles, Steps, and Evaluation Applications

Ricardo Wilson-Grau

INFORMATION AGE PUBLISHING, INC.
Charlotte, NC • www.infoagepub.com

Library of Congress Cataloging-in-Publication Data

A CIP record for this book is available from the Library of Congress
http://www.loc.gov

ISBN: 978-1-64113-389-0 (Paperback)
    978-1-64113-393-7 (Hardcover)
    978-1-64113-394-4 (ebook)

Copyright © 2019 Information Age Publishing Inc.

All rights reserved. No part of this publication may be reproduced, stored in a retrieval system, or transmitted, in any form or by any means, electronic, mechanical, photocopying, microfilming, recording or otherwise, without written permission from the publisher.

Printed in the United States of America

I dedicate this book to the dozens of primary users and co-evaluators with whom I have worked in developing Outcome Harvesting.

Contents

Foreword xi

Preface xv

1 **The Basics** 1
    The Essence 1
    The Outcome Harvesting Steps and Process 8
    Outcome Harvesting Exemplar 10
    The Guiding Principles 13
    Principles Applicability Rubrics 15
    Nature of the Outcome Harvesting Data 16
    The Professional Parameters 18
    The Common Thread of Complexity-Awareness 21
    Facilitator, Coach, and Mentor 23
    In Summary 25
    Notes 26
    References 26

2 **Step 1—Design of an Outcome Harvest** 29
    Who Will Use the Outcome Harvest? 31
    What Are the Principal Uses? 33
    What Do the Users Need to Know? 34
    Necessary Information 38
    Primary and Secondary Sources and How to Engage Them 42

Requirements of Time, Human, and Financial Resources.......... 44
Design Summary.. 49
Notes 50
References 50

3 Review Documentation and Draft Potential Outcome Statements 51
Organizing the Collection of Data.. 52
Extracting Outcome Data From Documentation 54
Practical Considerations 60
In Summary... 61

4 Engage With Human Sources to Formulate Outcome Statements 63
Gentle, Rigorous Ping-Ponging 65
Setting Up the Ping-Pong Table So Everyone Wins 67
First Ping—Facilitator Coach as Colleague 71
Second Ping—Facilitator Coach as Expert................................... 73
Last Ping—Facilitator Coach as Decision Maker 78
Facilitator Coach as Innovator.. 81
In Summary... 84
Note 85
References 85

5 Step 4: Substantiate the Outcome Statements............................87
The Substantiation Options.. 89
How to Substantiate for Maximum, Useful Credibility 93
The Substantiation Process... 95
The Cost of Substantiation 101
In Summary... 101
References 102

6 Step 5: Analyze and Interpret the Outcome Data.......................103
From Mainly Facilitator to Primarily Evaluator.......................... 104
Analysis—Usefully Organizing the Mass of Outcome Data...... 104
Interpretation—Using Outcome Data to Answer the
  Harvest Questions... 112
In Summary... 126
Notes 127
References 127

Contents ■ ix

7 Step 6: Post-Harvest Support for Use 129
    Support for Use of Harvest Findings 132
    Support for Uses of the Outcome Harvesting Process 136
    Use of the Outcome Harvesting Methodology 139
    The Challenges of Use, Non-Use, Misuse, Overuse, and
        Abuse of Outcome Harvesting 140
    In Summary 145
    Notes 147
    References 147

8 Outcome Harvesting's Process Principles 149
    I. Facilitate Usefulness Throughout the Evaluation 150
    II. Nurture Appropriate Participation 155
    III. Coach Human Sources to Formulate Outcome
        Statements 158
    IV. Strive for Less Because It Will Be More Useful 159
    V. Learn Outcome Harvesting Experientially 162
    In Summary 166
    Note 166
    References 167

9 Outcome Harvesting's Content Principles 169
    VI. Harvest Social Change Outcomes 170
    VII. Formulate an Outcome as an Observable Change 174
    VIII. Establish Plausible Influence of the Intervention 178
    IX. Rigorously Aim for Credible-Enough Outcomes 183
    The Principles in Summary 185
    References 187

A History of Outcome Harvesting 2002–2017 189

**B Developing Terms of Reference to Commission an
   Outcome Harvest** 201

C GUIDE for Outcome Harvesting Principles 205

    Glossary 211
    About the Author 219
    Index 221

Foreword

Outcome Harvesting. Pause for the opening applause. That's what a Foreword does, like the introduction of a keynote speaker, the Foreword invites anticipatory applause. If Steve Jobs was still with us, he would lead the applause because he, as a consummate innovator, understood, appreciated, and applauded innovation—and Outcome Harvesting (OH) is an important evaluation innovation.

Ricardo Wilson-Grau is the innovator. Innovation involves taking things that already exist, adapting them, combining them, and applying them in new ways. This is what Steve Jobs did with the innovation of the computer mouse. He didn't invent the mouse. And contrary to some accounts, he didn't steal the mouse from Xerox ("Steve Jobs," n.d.). He took technological parts and ideas discovered by others, improved and integrated them, and created something strikingly new, phenomenally useful, and easily adoptable. The roller, the one-button mechanism, the hand-fitting design, the surface-adaptable movement, the connection to the cursor, the low cost, and easy learning curve, in combination, constituted a breakthrough innovation. The mouse was a hardware innovation. Outcome Harvesting is a conceptual, methodological, and analytical innovation: *software for the evaluation mind.*

In this book, Ricardo will take you through the history of his innovation, take you inside the opportunities and thought processes that led to his breakthrough insights, unveil and illuminate the nine OH principles, and guide you through the six steps of OH. The book is rich with examples, applications, options, and creative possibilities. As with any great innovation, like the computer mouse, the elegance, sophistication, inspiration, and integration of OH are hidden in the simplicity and utility of the result. But I think you deserve to see and appreciate, all in one place and one illustration, the elements Ricardo has so creatively combined. These elements are scattered throughout the book and appear and reappear in various chapters. But here, for the first time, as preparation for your journey into OH, the separate component parts are revealed.

Before that unveiling, I should mention that I've had the privilege of observing OH evolve into the full-fledged, conceptually coherent, methodologically rigorous, and uniquely useful evaluation approach presented and explained in this book. I have known Ricardo since he began creating this innovation. I featured OH as a practical and actionable evaluation application in my qualitative methods book (Patton, 2015, p. 180). He was among the small group of developmental evaluators who offered advice in the form of a sidebar in *Developmental Evaluation* (Patton, 2011, p. 106). He co-authored a chapter on OH in *Developmental Evaluation Exemplars* (Patton, McKegg, & Wehipeihana, 2016, Chapter 10). He contributed an original chapter on OH principles to my recent book on *Principles-Focused Evaluation: The GUIDE* (Patton, 2018, Chapter 32). We have presented together and conducted workshops at several international evaluation conferences. Through our presentations together, his writings, his contributions to my books, and through lengthy discussions over the years about all aspects of evaluation, I have reveled in the emergence of OH as a valuable evaluation innovation.

So now, on to the unveiling of the elements Ricardo has so creatively combined. You must read the book to see how they interact and are integrated, but what follows will give you a glimpse of what is in store. By my count, being conservative, OH draws on, improves, and integrates at least 20 identifiable evaluation elements, approaches, and concepts into one elegant and useful innovation as illustrated in Figure F.1.

Enjoy learning about how Ricardo has masterfully put all these elements together. Enjoy learning about and then using OH.

—**Michael Quinn Patton**
Utilization-Focused Evaluation
Saint Paul, Minnesota

Foreword ▪ xiii

Figure F.1 Outcome Harvesting's 20 evaluation elements, approaches, and concepts.

References

Patton, M. Q. (2011). *Developmental evaluation: Applying complexity concepts to enhance innovation and use.* New York, NY: Guilford Press.

Patton, M. Q. (2015). *Qualitative research and evaluation methods* (4th ed.). Thousand Oaks, CA: SAGE.

Patton, M. Q, McKegg, K., & N. Wehipeihana, N. (Eds.). (2016). *Developmental evaluation exemplars: Principles in practice.* New York, NY: Guilford Press.

Patton. M. Q. (2018) *Principles-focused evaluation: The GUIDE.* New York, NY: Guilford.

Steve Jobs and the Truth About Innovation. (n.d.). Retrieved from the ZURB website: https://zurb.com/blog/steve-jobs-and-xerox-the-truth-about-inno

Preface

Since 2002, and full time since 2007, I have worked with colleagues, both co-evaluators and the commissioners of over 50 evaluations, to develop Outcome Harvesting (OH) to enhance accountability and learning for projects, programs, or organizations contributing to social change in Africa, Asia, Europe, Latin America, North America, and Oceania. If you are one of the world-wide members of the 188+ voluntary organizations for professional evaluation, and the staff of national, regional, and supranational organizations that commission evaluations, you will find in the book an alternative to many prevailing approaches to monitoring and evaluation.

In the past 4–5 years OH has become mainstream. I have witnessed how too often practitioners on both the supply and demand side misunderstand or misuse the approach. I recognized that I am responsible for not explaining the principles that underlie OH. I know that as with anything new that is shared widely in the spirit of the creative commons, it is impossible to control the quality of OH. Nonetheless, I do feel a duty to do whatever I can to influence the quality. In 2016 I set up www.outcomeharvesting.net to support the development of a community of practitioners: It received an average of 101 visitors a day in 2017. That year I began the Outcome Harvesting Forum, a discussion group where the lessons being learned worldwide about how to adapt this alternative approach to monitoring and evaluation are shared, challenged, and advanced. By the beginning of 2018, there were almost 300 members from over 40 countries passively or actively participating in this discussion group.

Consequently, I decided to write this book because I believe if the underlying principles are explicit, then all practitioners together can contribute to maintain the integrity of OH as we develop and transform it.

Bob Williams, my good friend and colleague and an award-winning systems thinker, author, and evaluator, points out to me that I am facing the succession problem.

> You are the first generation user. You have a substantially more sophisticated understanding of Outcome Harvesting, its dynamics and the necessary things to do than the vast majority of people who use it. I trust your use of Outcome Harvesting. But I don't trust those who learn from you to the same extent. Certainly, if the discussion group evidence is anything to go by. I call these people second generation users... you have been able to influence their thoughts and minds. But the future of OH depends on third generation users—and that's where the problems start. At the same time, 2nd and 3rd generations can innovate and improve method(ologie)s as well as fundamentally misunderstand the core principles. Most innovation and improvement are a process of trade-offs and in the best cases complete reinvention.... (B. Williams, personal correspondence, July 10, 2017)

Thus, with this book, coupled with my other efforts, I intend to minimize the risk of misunderstanding and misuse of the approach and influence the quality of use of OH.

In addition to sharing my experiences with the steps and the principles, I also intend to reveal the personal as well as professional reasons behind my choices so that you can have a point of reference with which to better understand them. I developed my knowledge and abilities as an evaluator, in general, and in OH, in particular, through a very hands-on, inductive process. Furthermore, I believe that whatever success I have had in my late-life career as an evaluator is due to being able to build on my prior experience. In addition to working from a young age and being involved in development in Latin America and globally all my adult life, this experience includes a quarter of a century as a manager of development and social change projects, programs, and organizations and a decade and a half in a staff position as a senior advisor at Novib, one of the four major development cooperation actors in the Netherlands and currently the Dutch Oxfam. Therefore, in my explanations of OH, I will weave in the life experiences that I have found enabled me to develop the approach. I believe that this experiential grounding may help you to sort out the roots of your own preferences to use, or not, the OH steps and principles as I explain them.

I am occasionally asked why I did not build on my development management experience to enter into mainstream evaluation practice. I believe the answer is that I am predisposed to be an unconventional evaluator because all my life I have tended to do things to change the fit instead of fitting in.

Living on Long Island, in New York state, I began working for pocket money when I was 10 years old. As an adolescent, I sold things door-to-door when my peers were staying after school for sports or art activities or working in minimum wage jobs at local stores. As a young man, I sold Colliers encyclopedias on pure commission and made so much money that I did not know how to spend it. From 1963 to 1965, I was one of the first U.S. Peace Corps volunteers, working community development with the agrarian reform institute in a frontier region of the Amazon basin in my maternal grandparents' native Colombia. I then went to finish my university education at the Universidad de Puerto Rico where the language of instruction is Spanish and I was one of a handful of foreign students. I paid my way working as the director of circulation in the largest magazine publishing house in the Caribbean.

Upon graduation in 1969, my wife, 6-month old son, and I moved to Guatemala where I managed a volunteer program of conscientious objectors for the American Friends Service Committee (AFSC) program; I then developed a "barefoot doctors" pilot project in rural health for the AFSC with the national Universidad de San Carlos in that country. For 7 years I served as the director of the Latin American Program of Friends World College, an experimental university whose experiential education aimed to produce citizens of the world, no less. In the 1980s I managed Inforpress Centroamericana, a political and economic news agency during revolution and counter-revolution in Central America. We migrated to the Netherlands where I was a senior manager with Greenpeace International based in the Netherlands and ran the campaign against toxics, briefly because, at 50 years of age, it was the first time I failed at doing a job.

I left management forever and in 1993 became an advisor to Novib, today the Dutch Oxfam, and one of the four historical development funding agencies in the Netherlands. All of this was before I became a full-time evaluator in 2007.

Since OH and all of my thinking and knowledge about it emerged from my practical consulting experiences, I will profusely exemplify. Because of confidentiality, however, the only experiences I can share by name are those that are in the public domain. These are the minority. For the majority of my applications of OH, I will only be able to refer to them anonymously.

What is in a Name?

The evaluations I did in the first years focused on the results of international social change networks and the effectiveness of development funders' own programs. My co-evaluators, our commissioners, and I gradually developed the six steps for evaluating innovative social change and development to unearth the results of processes that were laced through with uncertainty and dynamism. This too is the circumstance of the agricultural innovation that most family farmers (not those practicing industrialized farming but also not hunters and gathers) have to constantly engage in to be more productive while preserving their natural resources and their environment, and coping with the stresses on land, water, and biodiversity and the uncertainties of climate. The term Outcome *Harvesting* comes directly out of my experience with farming.

As we began to articulate these six steps, frequently I was reminded of living and working with farmers as a young man as a U.S. Peace Corps volunteer in Colombia. It was in El Caquetá to which campesinos were fleeing the civil war, known as La Violencia, ravaging the settled areas of the country. In this frontier territory, the transplanted farmers staked out claims to land in virgin jungle and farmed in a new environment—physically and biologically, but also socially, economically, politically, and culturally. There for 2 years, I experienced the challenges of farmers introducing new (to them) crops, in unknown terrain and environments, and without tried and true cultivation methods.

The steps in the harvesting stage of an agricultural innovation (planning the harvest, gathering of the mature crop, processing, transportation, storage, and marketing) compare to the six steps of OH. Furthermore, the pre-cultivation and cultivation stages of agricultural innovation also offer a metaphor for the planning and implementation of social change interventions operating in unpredictable, dynamic circumstances. As the UN's Food and Agriculture Organization (FAO) says, these family farming circumstances "leads to things being done differently in unpredictable ways... and acknowledges the complexity and nonlinear nature of the attempted change and introduces new factors (socio-economic, cultural, institutional, and political)" (FAO, 2012). These challenges were similar to those faced by the networks and development funders I was evaluating. Furthermore, the pre-cultivation and cultivation stages of agricultural innovation also offered a metaphor for the planning and implementation of social change interventions operating in uncertain, dynamic circumstances.

Thus, the image of "harvesting" the "crops" of a social change intervention and then working backwards to understand how the project, program, or organization had cultivated those "crops," seemed to me then, and seems to me now, to convey very well the Outcome Harvesting approach to the evaluation of the outcomes of innovative interventions. All this said, I am hesitant to carry the harvesting metaphor any further.

Colleagues Who Contributed to the Book

While I have been the constant actor in the development of Outcome Harvesting, the approach to monitoring and evaluation is the fruit of working with over 40 colleagues as *co-evaluators*[1] and almost as many primary users and commissioners.[2] All were new to Outcome Harvesting and a number have gone on to focus their work on outcome evaluation, either as internal staff responsible for monitoring and evaluation or as external evaluators. They all have therefore indirectly contributed to the book.

Beta Readers

Three of these colleagues have contributed directly as readers of both the first and second drafts of the book. The first was Bob Williams, who I quoted above. Bob is based in Wellington, New Zealand, and he and I have known each other for 10 years, initially through our participation in international evaluation conferences. More recently, he and I worked together on two other projects. One was as developmental evaluators for a global ecohealth initiative and another was on a resource panel for a complexity-aware monitoring and evaluation project for USAID. Outcome Harvesting was a secondary dimension to both these multi-annual projects. Bob's comments and suggestions on the first draft of this book were critical in helping me restructure the content. He also helped me see the need for innumerable changes to make the book more intelligible to people without Outcome Harvesting experience. During the review of the second draft, his comments and suggestions were not only helpful to me but also stimulated discussion amongst the readers of the second draft. This book would have been something quite a bit less and very different than it is without all his input.

The second reader was Goele Scheers who engaged with me in 2007 when working as the coordinator of monitoring and evaluation at the Global Platform for the Prevention of Armed Conflict (GPPAC), an international network based in The Hague. Together, we piloted the use of Outcome Harvesting for GPPAC, one of their first experiences of the Dutch government with the approach and which would bear fruit 10 years later. Subsequently, in 2011, she contracted me to lead a formative evaluation of GPPAC in the middle of which she left on maternity leave. After her baby was born, so too was her decision to become a consultant based in her native Ghent, Belgium, but working internationally. Today, Goele is one of the most accomplished Outcome Harvesting consultants in Europe, doing evaluations, training others, and writing about her experience. She, Paul Kosterink, who succeeded her at GPPAC, and myself wrote a chapter in *Developmental Evaluation Exemplars* on the GPPAC experience using Outcome Harvesting as a developmental evaluation inquiry framework—before any of us knew that was what we were doing. As I was writing the book, she and I began an Outcome Harvesting evaluation as co-evaluators. Her comments on the original draft of the book were instrumental in enabling me to better explain Outcome Harvesting as a useful tool for monitoring coupled with learning (M&E). She also helped me to be clearer about the approach's use for monitoring and evaluating foreseen outcomes along with the unforeseen. Goele contributed to the practical usefulness of the book.

My third reader was Wolfgang Richert, who is based in Amsterdam. He and I have worked together on three evaluation projects, the first in 2009 and two ongoing as I wrote the book. Wolfgang has done more than anyone else to influence the use of Outcome Harvesting in the Netherlands. After working with me on an evaluation of the global program of Oxfam Novib, he pioneered evaluating the outcomes of lobbying and advocacy of environmental issues, sustainable livelihoods, and economic justice in the Netherlands and Europe. He was one of the evaluators of the largest lobbying and advocacy evaluations ever done in the Netherlands, known as MFS-II, commissioned by the Dutch Ministry of Foreign Affairs, and the lead evaluator for two programs that were under evaluation. I consider his use of Outcome Harvesting was a key influence on the ministry's decision to design the PME-requirements for the next major round of subsidies in a complexity-aware manner, recommending "process oriented methodologies such as Outcome Harvesting." As this book goes to press, the majority of the 25 consortia of NGOs the ministry currently funds are introducing Outcome Harvesting as their system for the monitoring and ongoing evaluation of their work.

Wolfgang's comments on the book were especially helpful because he was able to make them with reference to our ongoing work together. This enabled me to see and understand faults that otherwise I fear I would not have been able to appreciate. He was especially incisive in pointing out what was unnecessary or superfluous.

I asked two more colleagues to only read the second draft in order to bring fresh eyes to the manuscript.

Barbara Klugman is a South African evaluator and strategy development consultant who supports civil society organizations, networks, and donors in strengthening their strategies and learning systems for promoting social change. In 2012 she and I were co-evaluators in a major evaluation of an international women's rights network. I remember when we first met she declared unabashedly that her interest was in learning the Outcome Harvesting methodology. She certainly did. Since then she has led teams evaluating a number of other programs, usually with a mixed method approach including Outcome Harvesting. One of those evaluations harvested the largest number of outcomes that I know of to date, which I refer to more than once in the book. Barbara read and commented on every chapter and helped persuade me to reorganize the book a second time.

The fifth beta reader is Richard Smith, who is based in the United Kingdom. Richard was the executive director of an international science for development network when he approached me in 2010 to lead an evaluation with two plant and ecology scientists as my co-evaluators. Richard became so involved in the methodological aspects of Outcome Harvesting that he led the customization of the approach to his network's special needs. Subsequently, he decided to become an evaluator himself and has been involved in supporting organizations, networks, and funding agencies to develop situation-specific approaches to evaluation using Outcome Harvesting and other approaches that encourage participation and innovation. As with Barbara, I asked Richard to only look at the second draft. His careful attention to conceptual detail was invaluable because in Outcome Harvesting so much rests on being crystal clear about meanings and nuances.

Editors

I was fortunate to have Jennifer Greene as my editor. Her work as an academic and evaluator focuses on the intersection of social science methodology and social policy and aspires to be both methodologically innovative and socially responsible. She has held leadership positions in the American Evaluation Association (AEA), including president and co-editor-in-chief of New Directions for Evaluation. Her own publication record includes a co-editorship of the *SAGE Handbook of Program Evaluation* and authorship of *Mixed Methods in Social Inquiry*. She applied this wealth of experience in assisting me to adapt the substance of the book to the needs and expectations of a readership that is unfamiliar with Outcome Harvesting, who hopefully will be the majority of the readers. In the degree to which I have made Outcome Harvesting intelligible to that audience, Jennifer deserves a large share of the credit.

Nikki Crutchley is based in New Zealand where, through her company Crucial Corrections, she served as my proofreader and copyeditor. She deserves much of the credit for the readability of this book.

The Influence of Michael Quinn Patton

Readers will find that the principal source for the evaluation theory that runs through Outcome Harvesting is Michael Quinn Patton, one of the founders of the profession in the United States and amongst the most influential evaluators worldwide. I believe you deserve an explanation up front of why Patton is the one person from whom I have learned the most about evaluation.

In the past (15–20 years ago), evaluators of nongovernmental international development were generally topic experts or managers but not evaluators. I realized with my very first evaluation that, one, I was uncomfortable with being considered an expert and two, the lack of expertise in evaluation per se would become untenable if I continued to do evaluations. I embarked on a steep learning curve. I spent a few years self-educating, learning as much from practice as from theory, which included developing a methodology[3] for evaluating international social change networks for which there was little written at the time.

On the way, I found that the work of Michael Quinn Patton consistently answered my questions and opened the way forward to evaluate projects and programs in a manner with which I was comfortable. His Utilization-Focused Evaluation simply made more sense than any other approach in the highly politicized evaluations I was contracted to carry out. Commissioners were development funding agencies and the international networks they funded. There was considerable tension around the expectations of results on the part of the funders and of imposition of donor agendas on the part of the network activists. The proposal that evaluation had to serve their needs as the primary intended users of the evaluation just made a whole lot of sense to everyone.

Furthermore, the approach I was developing, which was to become Outcome Harvesting, was based on qualitative data, and this was the other big area of Patton's contribution to the field. I was fascinated but also unsettled to apparently have found in one evaluator most of the expertise and guidance that I needed to become an evaluator.

In the summer of 2006, I took a 2-day course with Patton on qualitative evaluation under the auspices of the The Evaluator's Institute, that I had found through the AEA. I also took a 1-day course with him on managing your evaluation consultancy business. Among many pieces of advice I heard during those 3 days, Patton recommended that to be an evaluator you had to make a commitment to becoming part of the professional evaluation community.

The AEA is one of the first professional evaluation associations and is today, in my view, the leading professional evaluation association with over 7,000 members from all 50 U.S. states but also with 20% representing 60 countries. I took Patton's advice and became a member and since then I have attended every annual AEA conference except one. That is how serious I view the AEA. But I also participate actively in the biannual evaluators' conferences of the European Evaluation Society, the Latin American ReLAC, the African AfrEA, and the Brazilian RBMA. I recommend to anyone interested in using Outcome Harvesting for evaluation to become a member of your national or regional evaluation association.

I learned he practiced what he preached, having been, in 1988, the third president of the AEA. (The AEA presidents serve for 1 year overlapping with the previous president and then with their successor.) He attends every AEA annual conference. I also found out that he was generous with his knowledge, for example, giving courses at a fraction of his daily fee. He is also a founding member of ReLAC and AfrEA.

An integral part of my consultancy model was and is to devote one fourth of my time to learning and sharing. I was intrigued to know how much Patton's *Utilization-Focused Evaluation* and *Qualitative Research & Evaluation* (then in their third editions and today in their fourth) were used. I was not very successful with an internet search. (See these more recent hits on Google for "most popular evaluation textbooks": http://bit.ly/2sek6gl and http://bit.ly/2ryVltW.) The indexes in both his books were quite prolific, however, and so I decided I would assess them using three criteria. First, I compared the list of past AEA presidents against both indexes. I did the same with the winners of AEA's two annual awards for evaluation practice and theory.

In his two now classic textbooks on evaluation, Patton quotes over 1,600 authors with over 2,300 references. Amongst the authors whose work has influenced him 22 of the 31 are AEA presidents to date. Furthermore, he relies on the work of 15 winners of the 35 AEA Alva and Gunnar Myrdal Evaluation Practice award and 21 winners of the 33 Paul F. Lazarsfeld Evaluation Theory award. This list includes 10 of the AEA presidents who earned either award, including my editor Jennifer Greene and her co-editor Stewart Donaldson of the Evaluation and Society series of IAP, the publisher of this book. Michael Quinn Patton is only one of two past AEA presidents to have won awards for both evaluation practice and theory. David Fetterman is the other.

As I was developing as an evaluator, Patton co-authored *Getting to Maybe: How the World Is Changed* (Westley, Zimmerman, & Patton, 2006), which is one of the first books applying the insights of complexity theory to social change, a basic issue I was confronting in all my evaluations. By 2009, Patton and I had crossed paths professionally as consultants to a workshop on evaluation and complexity. That year he wrote *Developmental Evaluation* (Patton, 2011), which applies complexity concepts to enhance innovation and use. He asked me and three other people to read the manuscript and provide feedback as developmental evaluators: I did so through an international lens. By now Outcome Harvesting was emerging as an inquiry framework for this mode of assessing social change, and in 2014, Patton asked me to contribute a chapter to *Developmental Evaluation Exemplars*, a series of 12 cases of developmental evaluation principles in practice. With Paul Kosterink and Goele Scheers, I wrote "Outcome Harvesting: A Developmental Evaluation Inquiry Framework Supporting the Development of an International Social Change Network" (Patton, McKegg, & Wehipeihana, 2015). And our collegial collaboration continues. I contributed another chapter "Outcome Harvesting Evaluation: Practical Application of Essential Principles" to Patton's next book *Principles-Focused Evaluation: The Guide* (Patton, 2017). We have tag-teamed sessions at EES, AfrEA, and RelAC/IDEAS conferences. Patton was also the person who persuaded me to write this book.

Naturally, I am solely responsible for my use or misuse of Patton's thinking and that of the many evaluators who have also influenced my thinking through his work or independently.

Other Contributors

In addition to my five beta readers, Emilia Bretan, Mark Cabaj, Paul Kosterink, Lorina McAdam, Alix Tiernan, and Salome Tsereteli-Stephens also contributed to the book with their own innovative Outcome Harvesting experiences.

Without the contributions of almost 100 individuals with whom I have worked in developing Outcome Harvesting over 15 years, this book would never have been written. In a small or large way, all my primary users and co-evaluators contributed. I cite a number of them throughout the book. They are too numerous, however, to mention by name and contribution and so I simply dedicate this book to them.

The person who most contributed on a personal level was my *companheira* Erica Rodrigues. I took on the project of writing the book when we were in the middle of what turned out to be a 2-year hunt for a house in the foothills of the Mata Atlántica, 80 kilometers outside of Rio de Janeiro. She took over the task and we moved in as I finished writing the book. This was in the middle of her forced retirement due to health reasons, which made her support and understanding and solidarity all the more remarkable and precious.

How to Use This Book

The book is structured in the most logical order for someone who wants to learn about Outcome Harvesting. If you already have some knowledge of Outcome Harvesting, in this book you will find explanations rather than the description provided in most of what I have written previously—for example, the 27-page brief published in 2012 by the Ford Foundation, or the chapters in *Developmental Evaluation Exemplars* and Principles-Focused Evaluation: The GUIDE.

The first chapter presents an overview of Outcome Harvesting and its range of uses. These include monitoring the outcomes of an intervention and learning from them as an internal management function (i.e., monitoring and evaluation or M&E), serving as an inquiry framework in developmental evaluation or as a tool in an internal or external formative evaluation, or in a formal summative evaluation. I explain the essential concepts and conditionality ties of the approach and introduce the six steps you adapt when applying them to evaluate (or monitor and evaluate) the achievements of an intervention. I also introduce an exemplar that I use in the rest of the book. I present the nine underlying principles and a mechanism to alert you to their relative usefulness for each one of the six steps. I explain the special facilitator, coach, and mentor, as well as evaluator and roles of an Outcome Harvester. This initial chapter will give you a sound idea of what Outcome Harvesting is, what it is useful for and how you can apply it. It will also be clear when Outcome Harvesting is inappropriate.

Each of the six chapters that follow are devoted to one of the steps. Here I illustrate how to carry out an Outcome Harvest from beginning to end, including advice on what to customize, when, and with examples from my experience. As I begin each one of these chapters, I advise you how applicable I have found each principle for the step. These chapters are practical, down-to-earth, but nonetheless conceptually explanatory. Together they are designed to be a manual for adapting and customizing more than for instructing you what to do and what not do when you set out to commission or assume responsibility for an Outcome Harvest.

The last two chapters are devoted to the 9 principles that underlie the six steps. I present the guidance that I have found to be effective for customizing the six steps to different needs and contexts. The principles are important because Outcome Harvesting is not an approach to be taken off the shelf and applied the same way each time. You always have to adapt, and the principles will guide you in doing so.

The Glossary is a vital adjunct. Conceptual clarity is important in Outcome Harvesting because its use of terms will not necessarily be those of common usage. It could not be any other way since it is an alternative to usual approaches to monitoring and learning and evaluation. I define each term the first time I use it. But you may well jump around and miss a definition. If you have a glimmer of doubt about the meaning of a term I use, do consult the Glossary.

Lastly, please keep in mind that Outcome Harvesting is essentially experiential, derived from what Paulo Freire might call my "social praxis." I developed my knowledge and abilities as an evaluator in general, and in Outcome Harvesting in particular, through a very hands-on, inductive process in deep collaboration with colleagues who were generally thematic experts and not evaluators. Furthermore, I believe that whatever success I have had in my late-life career as an evaluator is due to being able to build on my prior experiences.

One of the things that became clear to me in writing this book was that my vocational experiences have been almost exclusively unconventional—selling encyclopedias door-to-door; serving as one of the first U.S. Peace Corps volunteers; graduating from the Universidad de Puerto Rio, at the time (at least) the only accredited U.S. university where the language of instruction was in Spanish; developing with the national university in Guatemala a pilot project in rural health using barefoot doctors; running the Latin American Program of Friends World College, an experientially-based Quaker institution offering an experientially-based university education; managing an alternative news agency during revolution and counter-revolution in Central America; serving as a senior manager with Greenpeace International; and creating development cooperation innovations for a major Dutch funding agency. While writing this book I have asked myself to what extent my propensity to do things differently may have been the driving force for me to develop Outcome Harvesting, rather than what I have always believed which is that I was only responding to circumstances and concretely to what the intended users of my evaluations demanded. Therefore, in my explanations throughout the book, every now and then I weave in my related life experiences to remind you that what you are reading are only my experiences. I believe that this experiential grounding may help you to sort out the roots of your own preferences to use, or not, the Outcome Harvesting principles and steps as I explain them, and as I experience them.

To emphasize that Outcome Harvesting is an organic, living approach enriched by the participation of a diversity of people and experiences, I have invited colleagues to share their innovations and adaptations with which I have not always had experience myself.

Notes

1. Over the years, my co-evaluators have been: Ahmad Alulayyan, Amrita Nandy, Ana Rubio Azevedo, Barbara Klugman, Bob Williams, Carmen Alaíde Wilson-Grau, Cate Broussard, Celena Green, Claudia Fontes, Elaine Van Melle, Fe Briones Garcia , Gabriela Sánchez, Genowefa Blundo Canto, Geoffrey Howard, Gina Solari, Goele Scheers, Grace Awantang, Jane Real, Jennifer Vincent, Jenny Gold, Joanna Durbin, Julie Lafreniere , Juliette Majot, Julie Muriuki, Kayla Boisvert, Kemly Camacho, Larry Gruppen, Lindsey Leslie, Marcie Mersky, Maria Möller, Martha Nuñez, Mike Jeger, Muhammed Lecky, Natalia Ortiz, Philip Marsden, Pinki Solanki, Sara Macfarlane, Sue Edwards, Wolfgang Richert, and Zainab Qassim Ali.
2. The primary users include: Alan Hall, Andrés Sánchez, Beris Gwynne, Chaitali Sinha, Charlotte Booth, Dale Chadwick, Daniel López, Dianna James, Elizabeth Silkes, Emma Holmberg, Erika Alfageme, Goele Shheers, Hannah Tsadik, Harrie Oppenoorth, Heloise Emdon, Jaana Kovalainen, Jacqueline Hart, Jenny Gold, John Mauremotoo, Karel Chambille, Konny Rassmann, Laurent Elder, Lisa Jordan, Lorina McAdam, Luis Guillermo Pérez, Manjima Bhattacharjya, Margo Mullinax, Mary Aileen D. Bacalso, Paul Kosterink, Paul van Paaschen, Richard Smith, Sharmila Mhatre, Stella Maris Cacace, Susana Rochna, Suzan van der Meij, Teyo van de Schoot, Tilly Gurman, Tricia Wind, Tycho Vandermaesen, Wenny Ho, and Yvonne Es.
3. "Evaluating International Social Change Networks: A Conceptual Framework for a Participatory Approach," with Martha Nuñez, *Development in Practice*, April 2007.

1

The Basics

The Essence

Outcome Harvesting is designed for grant makers, managers, and evaluators who commission, manage or evaluate projects, programs, or organizations that experience constant change and contend with unexpected and unforeseeable actors and factors in their programming environment. In this approach to monitoring and evaluation, harvesters identify, formulate, verify, analyze, and interpret "outcomes" of interventions in contexts where relations of cause and effect were not fully understood when planning or implementing. In the face of considerable *uncertainty*, unlike other monitoring and evaluation approaches, Outcome Harvesting does not necessarily measure progress towards predetermined objectives or outcomes, but rather, collects evidence of what has changed, and then, working backwards, determines whether and how an intervention contributed to these changes.

The core concept of Outcome Harvesting is that an *outcome is an observable change in the behavior* of individuals, groups, communities, organizations, or institutions. The demonstrated changes in behavior are understood broadly. They are actions, activities, relationships, agendas, policies,

Harvester: Person(s) responsible for carrying out the Outcome Harvest. Usually synonymous with "evaluator."

Outcome Harvest: The identification, formulation, analysis, and interpretation of outcomes to answer useful questions.

Outcome statement: The written formulation of *who* changed *what, when,* and *where,* and *how* it was influenced by an intervention. May include the outcome's significance, context, and history, amongst other dimensions.

Outcome: A change in the behavior, relationships, actions, activities, policies, or practices of an individual, group, community, organization, or institution.

Primary intended users: The people who require the findings of an Outcome Harvest to make decisions or take action. Synonymous with "harvest users."

Principal intended uses: The decisions and actions that the Outcome Harvesting process or findings or both will serve.

practices of one or more societal actors influenced by an intervention. That is, these are the actors the intervention influence to change their behavior, not the beneficiaries of that behavioral change.

For example, these are observable changes in societal actors targeted by policy advocacy interventions: a government minister publicly declares she will restrict untendered contracts to under 5% (an action); a civil society organization launches a campaign for governmental transparency (an activity); two political parties join forces to collaborate rather than compete in proposing transparency legislation (relationship); a senior government official for the first time acknowledges the need for off-grid, sustainable energy production in rural areas (agenda); a legislature passes a new anti-corruption law (policy); or a government implements norms and procedures for publishing all procurement records (practice). Thus, the definition of "outcome" in Outcome Harvesting contrasts with the definition of an outcome as observed changes in the intended program beneficiaries' wellbeing (learning, health, employment). Those changes would be the *impact* of these policy changes.

These behavioral changes, however, are only half an outcome. An outcome statement also describes how an intervention's activities and outputs plausibly influenced or contributed to each one of the changes. The outcome(s) can be positive or negative, intended or unintended, but you must identify a reasonable causal connection between the intervention and the outcome, however small or large, direct or indirect it may be.

Another essential part of Outcome Harvesting is that it must serve the *principal intended uses* of the *intended primary users* of the project, program, or organization (i.e., of the intervention) being evaluated, which may change throughout the process. These users are people who require the findings of an Outcome Harvest to make decisions or take action. The uses are the decisions and actions that the Outcome Harvesting process or findings or both will serve. Jenny Gold at the World Bank, after piloting Outcome Harvesting with 10 projects teams who together with her were the primary intended users explains:

> Outcome Harvesting is used to identify, monitor, and learn from changes in social actors, through harvesting bites of detailed outcome information with colleagues, partners, and stakeholders. The information describes what changed, for whom, when and where, why it matters to the development objective—the significance of the change—and how the program contributed to the change.
>
> Outcome Harvesting is useful for complex aspects of a program when the significance of particular milestones and outcomes may be unknown in advance. There is often a need for learning to understand how change happened.
>
> The harvesting process is stakeholder-centered and captures qualitative, tacit knowledge. It includes tools to substantiate and analyze this knowledge collaboratively and communicate progress toward impact to clients, management, and partners. The tools are flexible to adapt to a program's design and can provide useful details to inform the theory of change, implementation lessons, outcomes, and indicators. (World Bank, 2014, p. 5)

Since 2002 I have led Outcome Harvesting evaluative exercises involving almost 500 nongovernmental organizations, networks, government agencies, funding agencies, community-based organizations, research institutes, and university programs. In over 50 evaluative exercises, we have harvested outcomes on six continents through developmental, formative, and summative evaluations. These statistics do not include the evaluations that others have undertaken using Outcome Harvesting.

I have found the approach useful in evaluations of a great diversity of initiatives: human rights advocacy; political, economic, and environmental advocacy; arts and culture; health systems; information and communication technology; conflict and peace; water and sanitation, taxonomy for development; violence against women; rural development; organic agriculture; participatory democracy; waste management; public sector reform; good governance; eLearning; social accountability; and business competition; amongst others.

TABLE 1.1 Traditional Versus Outcome Harvesting Evaluations

Traditional	Outcome Harvesting
a) Assesses an intervention testing the predetermined activities, outputs, outcomes, and impact for efficiency and effectiveness.	a) Assesses what was achieved on the level of outcomes regardless of whether they were predetermined (i.e., intended) or not, and then how the intervention's activities and outputs contributed.
b) Evaluators are perceived as independent and objective.	b) Evaluators are perceived as facilitators in a common search with project implementers for the facts about what has been achieved and how.
c) Provides judgment on success or failure of an intervention.	c) Provides evidence of what outcomes were achieved, and how the intervention contributed, and answers questions about what the outcomes mean for the intervention.
d) Focuses on the fidelity of an intervention to a logic model or predefined plan.	d) Focuses on what actually happened, whether intended or not.
e) Accountability emphasis is external, especially to funders, and learning emphasis, if any, is for internal stakeholders.	e) Accountability centers on primary intended users' principal uses for the Outcome Harvesting process and results.

Source: Traditional characteristics adapted from Doucette, 2015

The approach has been used for simple monitoring: periodically and systematically collecting information on outcomes being achieved and on an intervention's activities and outputs that contribute to them. The approach is designed, however, to enable users to *learn* from the data collected. Since it goes beyond simple monitoring or tracking of results and supports learning about achievements, Outcome Harvesting is useful for monitoring *and* evaluation (M&E)—for timely decision-making to improve implementation or be accountable, or both. Nevertheless, Outcome Harvesting is distinct from other evaluation approaches. In Table 1.1, I present the added value of Outcome Harvesting compared to evaluation as commonly known.

Historically, Outcome Harvesting has proven itself as an effective evaluation approach in one or more of these situations:

- *The need is for evaluation.* Outcome Harvesting is used to register the changes in the behavior of societal actors influenced by an intervention in order to assess the merit or value of the intervention. The approach can be used for a broad range of evaluations, from ongoing M&E, developmental evaluating, or the piloting of an intervention, all the way to midterm formative and end-of-

term summative evaluations. You can use Outcome Harvesting alone or in a mixed methods mode, combining it with other evaluative approaches.
- *The focus of the evaluation is on outcomes.* I rush to add, the focus is on "outcomes" as defined in Outcome Harvesting. In the United States, for example, outcomes usually refer to changes in the conditions of people's health, education, income, and other indicators that demonstrate how they have benefited from an intervention. In Outcome Harvesting, however, while the purpose of the intervention is to improve the conditions of people's lives or the state of the environment, "outcomes" are the prior changes in *behaviors* of societal actors that are necessary in order that people or the environment benefit. You will also find the approach useful when what you need to learn is about what was achieved by the intervention and how; not everything about a project, program, or organization, and not information on goods or services delivered to beneficiaries. In sum, in Outcome Harvesting you focus on assessing effectiveness of an intervention rather than efficiency, performance, or the results in the wellbeing of beneficiaries.
- *The purpose of the intervention is social change.* Outcome Harvesting can serve you if you are evaluating whether an intervention influenced other societal actors to take the initiative to do something new and significantly different in any sphere of human endeavor—political, economic, social, cultural, environmental, amongst others. The approach is also a good fit when the aim is to understand the process of social change and how each outcome contributes to this change, instead of necessarily delving deeply into individual outcomes. Salient outcomes can be the focus of more in-depth study, of course, but the real value of the approach is enabling you to see and understand a pattern, or patterns, of social change.
- *The programming context is unpredic*table. Evaluation commonly compares planned results with what is actually achieved, and planned activities with what was actually done. In the uncertain, dynamic circumstances that characterize most social change, however, objectives and the paths to achieve them are largely unpredictable, and predefined objectives and theories of change must be modified over time to respond to changes in the context. Outcome Harvesting is particularly appropriate in these environments with many unintended outcomes, including negative ones.

- *The need for alternative monitoring and evaluation approaches is recognized.* While many organizations are obliged by the requirements of their funders to report on numbers of people who have benefited from an intervention, frequently these cannot be measured except by population-wide studies, which are not affordable or whose costs are disproportionate to the funds provided. And even if they were done, they could not show the specific contributions of a single initiative. The growing uptake of Outcome Harvesting by bilateral and multilateral governmental agencies shows the increased recognition that the types of outcomes that are meaningful for advocacy initiatives are not population-level outcomes.

For example, in a recent evaluation of an advocacy program addressing the root causes of early or forced child marriage (EFCM) in India, stakeholders beyond the primary intended users were having difficulty understanding the quantitative meaning of the Outcome Harvesting results for the intended beneficiaries. They understood that 488 outcomes do not mean 488 individuals have done something different. For example, consider these two outcomes:

> Between January 2016 and May 2017, for the first time, parents of 160 adolescent girls from 10 different villages in Rajasthan gave their daughters permission to attend a 3-day residential training camp on the adverse impacts of early and child marriage, gender discrimination and violence, the importance of education, self-defense and relevant laws on violence against women.

> From October 2016 and March 2017, six head teachers of high schools located in West Bengal took a proactive role to organize workshops in their premises on child marriage in which approximately 3,000 parents participated.

These stakeholders also knew the outcomes were not a sample in a statistical sense. But they were concerned that in light of their multimillion-dollar investment in the program over 3 years, 488 outcomes do not sound like many.

I explained that Outcome Harvesting is not a methodology for establishing the numbers of beneficiaries of an intervention. That would be an impact evaluation. But more importantly, if what people wanted to know was the numbers of girls who have benefited per dollar invested, is there not a misunderstanding about the nature of the intervention? Even if the purpose was to save as many girls as possible from marrying before the legal age of 18, how many of the 4.7 million Indian girls who marry each year before they are 18 could the intervention hope be saved by five dozen civil society organizations (CSOs), however effective they might be? It would be miniscule.

What Outcome Harvesting did do through collecting, analyzing, and interpreting 488 outcomes was demonstrate the progress those CSOs were making towards empowering people (girls, boys, women, and men) and their communities to challenge and change three of the root causes of EFCM: (a) patriarchal norms that discriminate against girls and women and undermine their agency; (b) the sexual politics of shame and honor that exercise control over female sexuality; and (c) the denial of equal opportunities for girls and women to obtain knowledge and skills, engage in income-generating activities, and achieve financial independence. Furthermore, in the process, the five dozen CSOs were exemplifying new, different, and effective ways to wage the struggle against EFCM that potentially will be of value to the other 645,000 Indian CSOs working in the area of community and/or social service and education, and who wish to join the effort to address the root causes of EFCM.

My colleague Barbara Klugman summarizes this added value of Outcome Harvesting very well:

> What is radical and groundbreaking about Outcome Harvesting is that it moves away from the fantasy world in which many funders are now colluding, and into reality. What has happened over time is that with the best intentions of supporting social change, government programs and donors have persuaded their sources—parliaments, wealthy individuals, corporate sponsors, the public—to provide money for ends that are lovely but are not real. To ask a small advocacy group you have given funding for one, two, three years, or even four or five, to present you with the numbers of people who have benefitted is ridiculous when the change they're aiming to influence is about policy or attitudes of the public at large. What is meaningful is to know if and how their advocacy has influenced concrete, observable change in the behavior—what they do, not what they receive—of individuals, communities and governments that represents progress towards development or social justice objectives. How have they influenced other organizations or key individuals to join in their efforts to influence change? Have they influenced debates among policy makers? Have they influenced how the media engages the issues? Have they influenced a change in an approach to service provision? Outcome Harvesting provides the answers. (Klugman, 2018)

In sum, Outcome Harvesting is a good choice for monitoring and evaluating projects, programs, and organizations that face situations in which the relationships between cause and effect, between what you will do and the results you will achieve, are ones of influence rather than control and are not fully understood, before or during the intervention. It is not as useful, however, for evaluating tried and proven interventions in which you are fairly certain of what the outcomes will be and when they will be achieved.

That is, Outcome Harvesting is particularly suitable to assess innovative and development work for which social change is the purpose or is a significant part of what is required for success.

The Outcome Harvesting Steps and Process

Over the years, commissioners, users, and especially co-evaluators and I have pinned down six generic steps for Outcome Harvesting (Figure 1.1).[1]

1. *Design the Outcome Harvest* based on the principal uses of the primary users. Come to agreement with the people who will use the results of the Outcome Harvest on priority Outcome Harvesting questions to guide the harvest. Users and harvesters should also agree on the process: what information is to be collected, how, from whom, when, and with what resources in order to credibly answer the questions.
2. *Review documentation* by identifying and formulating draft, potential outcome statements contained in secondary sources of information: reports, evaluations, press releases, and other documentation. These statements should comprise (a) changes in individuals, groups, communities, organizations, or institutions; and (b) how the intervention plausibly influenced them. They may contain other useful information such as the significance of each outcome.
3. *Engage with human sources.* The harvester facilitates conversations with the people who have the most knowledge about what the intervention has achieved and how. They usually are the authors of the documentation, the intervention's other field staff, allies, and others closest to the action. They review and fill gaps in the potential outcome statements extracted from documentation, identify and formulate additional ones, and together with the harvester agree on a set of robust outcome statements that are sufficiently precise to be verifiable.
4. *Substantiate with external sources* a select number of outcome statements. Substantiators are one or more persons knowledgeable about the change but independent from the organization to ensure accuracy, or deepen understanding, or both. For example, they may be the societal actors who changed their behavior or allies who collaborated in the intervention, unless of course they already served as a primary source in the third step. This fourth step ensures that the whole set of outcome statements is sufficiently credible for the intended uses. These outcome statements are the evidence used in the next step.

5. *Analyze and interpret* by first organizing outcome statements so they are manageable, for example, categorising them by evaluation question, and then using this to provide evidence-based answers to the prime evaluation questions, where the evidence is the information contained in the outcome statements generated in the previous three steps.
6. *Support use of findings* after the evaluation questions are answered so the users make better use of the process and findings.

The six steps are not wholly distinct. They may overlap and can be iterative. Feedback can spark decisions to redesign a next step or return to or modify an earlier step. That is, design decisions are necessarily made throughout the harvest and not just at the beginning. Users and uses may shift as outcomes are identified.

The harvest evolves and adapts as the process unfolds and information emerges in a downward spiral. Often emergent information requires a harvester to skip a step. For example, there may not be any written, audio, or visual documentation to review (Step 2), in which case you may need to go on to engage with your internal human sources (Step 3). New sources of outcomes may emerge. You may uncover outcomes that alert you to the likelihood of more recent outcomes not yet documented, or to other

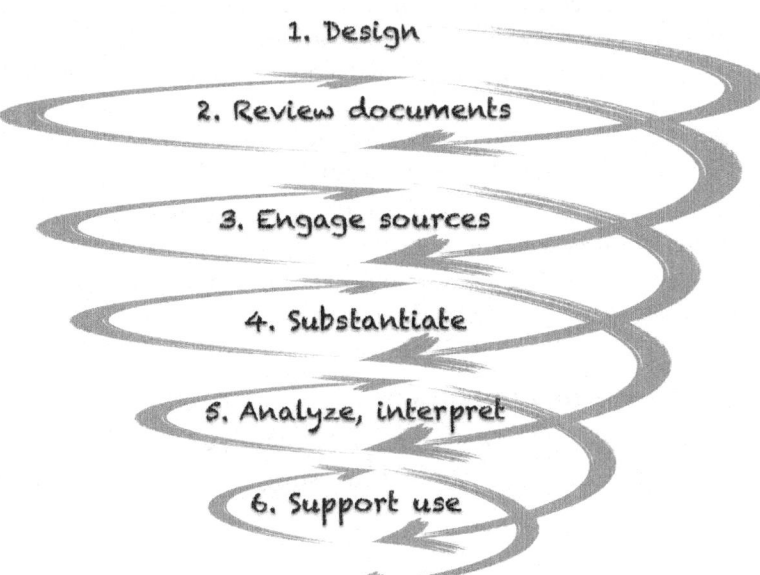

Figure 1.1 Outcome Harvesting process.

processes that have been key influencers and need investigation. The people to be engaged as sources of information (Step 3) will often depend on what is uncovered in the document review (Step 2). What outcomes should be substantiated (Step 4), by who and how—or if at all—is unknowable until both users and harvesters have the outcomes in hand. Depending on the original sources, approaching others to substantiate may not be necessary; in some contexts it may not be feasible; and in others the harvester and the users may decide it will not be useful.

Similarly, how to analyze outcomes may be further developed depending on what outcomes are harvested; how to interpret them to answer the prime questions may finally be clear only after you have seen them and the patterns they reveal (Step 5). How to support use of the process and findings (Step 6) usually is not evident right from the beginning. It may emerge as internal sources are engaged and come to appreciate the value of the Outcome Harvesting data, findings, and process. Only then may primary users decide, for instance, to use the findings to inform the design of an intervention or introduce Outcome Harvesting into their M&E system.

Depending on the time period covered and the number of outcomes involved, the approach can require a substantial time commitment from internal sources and users. The initial and ongoing time commitment of users in the harvest design can also be a surprise to some harvest commissioners. To reduce the time burden of harvesting, outcomes may be harvested monthly, quarterly, biannually, or annually. Findings may be substantiated, analyzed or interpreted less frequently. It should be noted that Outcome Harvesting can be done anytime during the life of an intervention, as well as after. The criterion of frequency is that it be as often as it is useful to understand what the intervention is achieving.

In sum, the six steps are to be taken more as guidelines rather than rigid formulae to follow. Nonetheless, the rigorous, conscious decision on using, or not, each one of the six steps is necessary for a sound and credible outcome harvest.

Outcome Harvesting Exemplar

The next six chapters focus on the Outcome Harvesting steps. In order to ground my explanation of Outcome Harvesting, I will use the exemplar of an organization operating in one unnamed country.

> A national rights-based organization is dedicated to women's empowerment in order to improve their lives through the achievement of equality of opportunities, the elimination of discrimination against women and girls, and participation in economic and political life. This organization sponsors an

intervention with three programs: service delivery, capacity-building, and advocacy. The intervention is implemented with community-based partner organizations through five provincial projects.

After seven years of operation, the organization has not had a formal evaluation. In two years, funding must be renewed or new funding found, and donor priorities are changing. Furthermore, there are internal tensions about who has achieved what, when, and where. The board decided to authorize the executive director to contract an evaluation during 2017 of the current five-year plan.

This is a composite drawn from several evaluations that I have done using Outcome Harvesting. Although the individual pieces are derived from real experiences, the aggregation was created by me.

In Figure 1.2, you have a partial product of the Exemplar Outcome Harvesting evaluation that over the next six chapters you will see unfold.

Overall, in 2017 the intervention was partially successful in terms of the breadth of the outcomes it influenced, but impressively successful in the depth of the change it influenced with *duty bearers*. First, on the weak side, the intervention was unsuccessful in influencing changes in women's and girls' exercise of power as rights-holders vis-à-vis primary or secondary education or health. No outcomes were registered in those areas because the intervention has not had sufficient time to influence change. Three outcomes were achieved in the area of income generation but they are initial steps. In one, two women's organizations changed their missions to emphasize right-based empowerment to demand income-generating support from municipal government and in the other two, the Ministry of Labor strengthened evaluation of its intern program for women entrepreneurs. The first outcome was influenced by the intervention through two open discussion forums it ran between November 2016 and February 2017 for the four leading women's rights organizations in the country, including these two. The program was designed to enhance their awareness and appreciation for the importance of a rights-based approach to gender discrimination. The second and third outcomes were influenced by the same contribution from the intervention. In January and April 2017, the intervention held press conferences on its experiences having internal/external evaluations of their capacity-building program for women's empowerment. This led to five articles in the print media, including the ministry of labor's in-house bulletin, and one TV interview with the intervention's program director.

In 2017 the intervention primarily influenced duty bearers in the executive branch of government to take action in the areas of income and rights-based policy for women and especially vocational education. The intervention contributed through a combination of vocational capacity-building and advocacy activities. The capacity building included a vocational awareness-raising initiative in classrooms and a vocational counseling service for secondary school students, both boys and girls. It also involved recognition in early 2017 that the intervention's vocational training program was undermining a similar program run by the Ministry of Labor

Figure 1.2 Exemplar—Summary of Outcome Harvesting evaluation report.

(continued)

with both offering the traditional sewing, hairdressing, receptionist and bookkeeping courses: this negative outcome was that women stopped enrolling in vocational training at the Ministry of Labor, which decreased 19% in the first half of the year. As soon as the intervention realized it was unwittingly competing with the government program, the intervention suspended its courses and enrollment at the Ministry bounced back by 5% in the second semester.

In spite of almost three times as many outcomes in vocational education, it was in policy that the intervention achieved its greatest success, beginning with influencing the minister of women's affairs to declare in January that women's empowerment would be the keystone of the Ministry's policies followed by the ministers of education, labor and women's affairs working together to submit the Empower All Women Through Crafts and Trade Education bill to the legislature on 1 June 2017. The intervention then shifted gears from the executive branch and focused on the legislature culminating in two major outcomes:

> On 13 December 2017, 9 members of the national legislature voiced their support before over 1,000 activists for the proposed Empower All Women Through Crafts and Trade Education bill to benefit lower income women.
>
> In the first session on 5 January 2018, the national legislature passed the Empower All Women Through Crafts and Trade Education bill.

Furthermore, the second outcome was also a vocational outcome. One more directly influenced the advocacy process that led to the legislative victory: On 15 April 2017, Science for Women, Act Now and Lean on Government—experienced in research, community mobilization and lobbying, respectively—signed a memorandum of understanding agreeing to join forces in our campaign for vocational training for women entrepreneurs.

In terms of changes in behavior in *rights holders*, the two outcomes in 2017 are not only limited to girls (and do not include women) but also are less important in terms of the nature of the change. At the beginning of the year over 500 girls voluntarily attended half-day workshops about the importance of encouraging girls to enter into vocational training after graduation. The intervention contributed by visiting in late 2016 each one of the eight schools in the lowest-income neighborhoods of the capital where these girls lived to request permission to hold half-day workshops, in the school building after class, about the importance of girls receiving vocational training after graduation. The second change in the behavior of rights holders was by the end of 2017, 125 school girls living in the five largest slums of the capital city had enrolled in the intervention's new post-secondary program for training in driving commercial motor vehicles and as plumbers and electricians. The intervention influenced this outcome through a complementary activity to the one for outcome #2: since January 2016 the intervention provided vocational counseling services for secondary school students in these five communities, both boys and girls, to support the adolescents to discover their occupational vocations regardless of gendered norms and practices. As beneficial as these outcomes potentially are for the school girls living in relative poverty, they do not address the intervention's goal of empowering girls to make claims and hold duty bearers accountable.

In conclusion, it is the advocacy and campaigning outcomes with the executive and legislative branches of government that the intervention registered its principal achievements in 2017.

Figure 1.2 (cont.) Exemplar—Summary of Outcome Harvesting evaluation report.

The Guiding Principles

Since conceptual clarity is so important in Outcome Harvesting, I begin by defining what I mean by "principle." It is a statement to guide you in successfully customizing Outcome Harvesting. A principle does not tell you exactly what to do, as would a rule, but requires that you interpret and adapt guidance to context. Rules would *control* what you must do and not do in applying the six Outcome Harvesting steps, whereas a principle *guides* you in your decisions about customizing the steps. For example, the utilization-focused evaluation principle applied to Outcome Harvesting is to facilitate usefulness throughout the harvest by involving users in decision-making from the beginning to the end. This principle does not specify how many uses or users should be involved or what each user should do and when during the evaluation process, which is what a rule would do. Nonetheless, an Outcome Harvesting principle is prescriptive to the extent to which it advises and guides you about what you should do so that your Outcome Harvest remains methodologically true to the approach.

I identify nine core principles that co-harvesters and I have used to maintain the fidelity of the approach when customizing the six steps to specific needs and different contexts (Figure 1.3). In 2015 I began a process

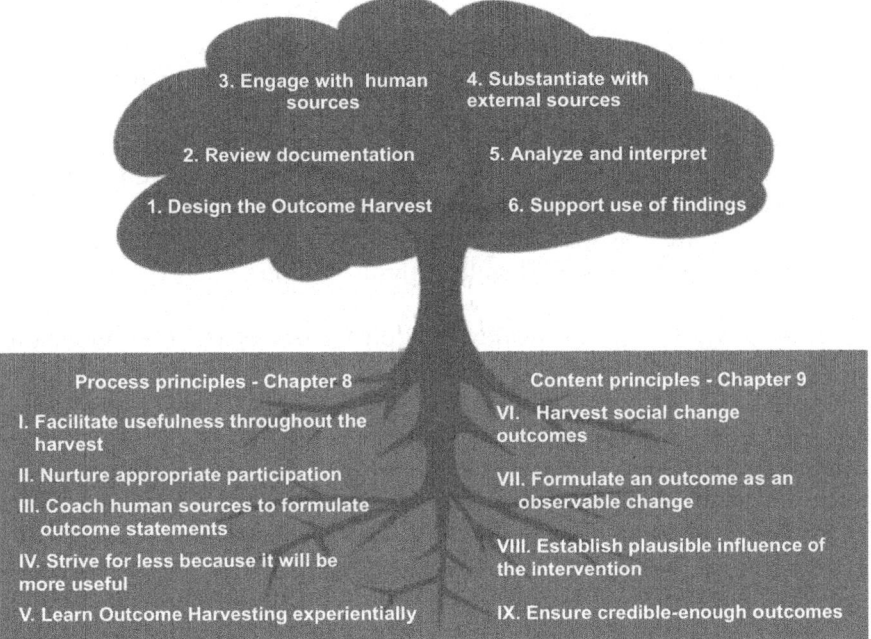

Figure 1.3 Outcome Harvesting steps and principles.

of making the implicit principles explicit, first for myself and co-harvesters and then for others. It was a moment of synchronicity with Michael Quinn Patton, who at the time was writing his book *Principles-Focused Evaluation: A GUIDE* (Patton, 2017). He offered me an opportunity to present Outcome Harvesting's effectiveness principles in Chapter 32 "Outcome Harvesting Evaluation—Practical Application of Essential Principles."

I find a useful way of ordering the principles is by those that provide guidance for process and those for content.

Process principles are those that in my view and experience guide *how* to apply the six Outcome Harvesting steps:

I. *Facilitate usefulness throughout the harvest.* Involve intended users in decision-making throughout the Outcome Harvest.
II. *Coach human sources to formulate outcome statements.* Provide hands-on support to primary sources of information to craft concrete, verifiable descriptions of what has been achieved and how.
III. *Nurture appropriate participation.* Whether the harvesting is internal or external, developmental, formative, or summative, the harvester works facilitates the contributions of users, human sources, and independent third parties. The harvester ensures they make decisions that contribute to the collection, analysis, and interpretation of data in ways that enhance the harvest's rigor and credibility.
IV. *Strive for less because it will be more useful.* Do only as much as necessary to achieve the desired result of answering usefully the prime harvesting questions.
V. *Learn Outcome Harvesting experientially.* Become competent in the steps and principles of Outcome Harvesting by actively applying them, reflecting on the results, modifying the application, and repeating the process, ideally with mentoring.

The *content principles* provide direction for *what* should be the results of the harvest.

VI. *Harvest social change outcomes.* Social change in Outcome Harvesting is defined as societal actors modifying the way they do things in new and significant ways (outcome) that the intervention plausibly influenced (contribution).
VII. *Formulate an outcome as an observable change.* To qualify as an outcome, an individual, group, community, organization, or institution must have demonstrably done something different. Also, new understanding or heightened awareness or sensitivity does not count as an outcome until evidenced in perceptible changes in behavior.

VIII. *Establish plausible influence of the intervention.* To qualify as the intervention's outcome, there has to be a reasonable relationship of cause–effect between the intervention's activities and outputs and the outcome. Activities of other social actors may also have had an influence.
IX. *Ensure credible-enough outcomes.* Apply thorough evaluative thinking to ensure that the quality of the data and of the Outcome Harvesting exercise are as trustworthy as necessary for the primary users' principal uses.

The principles for Outcome Harvesting are based on my experiences and those of some co-harvesters; they are far from revealed truths and are certainly open to revision based on the experiences of fellow practitioners. The nine principles have emerged as essential guidance, but always require interpretation and adaptation to the specific process and context.

Another caveat concerns whether the nine principles comprise interconnected and interdependent guidance. "To what extent do principles in a set (or on a list) constitute separate and autonomous principles versus an integrated whole?" (Patton, 2017, p. 87). That is, do all nine principles have to be applied for a harvest to be considered Outcome Harvesting? Or, is one or more of the principles independent from the others? And, should whether or not it applies be judged from harvest to harvest?

In my own experience, I have found that all nine principles are applicable to a greater or lesser degree to all six steps of the Outcome Harvesting process; every principle is indispensable for at least one of the six steps. That is, in an Outcome Harvest, all nine should be adhered to at one time or another, and some more than others. So I trust the reader will appreciate the inherent tension between principles providing prescriptive guidance but stopping short of being rules that prescribe precisely what to do and not do. The nine principles must be interpreted according to circumstances; they require situational analysis and judgment. I dare say that one major reason for the faulty application of Outcome Harvesting is harvesters misunderstanding, using wrongly, or simply not taking into account the principles.

Principles Applicability Rubrics

The last two chapters of the book explain the nine principles that underlie the six steps in the Outcome Harvesting approach. Therefore on the first page of each one of the six chapters on the steps, I highlight for you the relative importance I have found for the principles for that specific step in my own

> **Applicability of Key Principles to Step 1**
>
> **Process principles—Chapter 8**
> ***** I. Facilitate usefulness throughout the evaluation
> ***** III. Nurture appropriate participation
> ***** II. Coach primary sources to formulate outcome statements
> ***** IV. Strive for less because it will be more useful
> *** V. Learn Outcome Harvesting experientially
>
> **Content principles—Chapter 9**
> ***** VI. Harvest social change outcomes
> ***** VII. Formulate an outcome as an observable change
> ** VIII. Establish plausible influence of the intervention
> ***** IX. Ensure credible-enough outcomes
>
> **Legend of Ricardo's rubrics**
> ***** High: I always apply this principle; **** Considerable: I almost always apply it; *** Moderate: I usually apply it
> ** Occasional: I apply it sometimes but with quite a few exceptions; * Low: I rarely apply the principle in this step

Figure 1.4

practice. For example, in the next chapter on design, you will see Figure 1.4. Thus, right from the beginning of the chapter you are alerted to the principles that I have found most applicable to that step.

Nature of the Outcome Harvesting Data

In Outcome Harvesting, the manner of collecting outcome data can be counterintuitive to many seasoned managers and evaluators because program people are used to reporting data on the outcomes to which they have committed in advance, often called the intended outcomes. Many evaluations begin with the program theory, strategic plan, theory of change, logic model, logical framework (logframe), or other representation of what the intervention intended to do and achieve. In contrast, Outcome Harvesting does not necessarily measure progress towards predetermined activities and outcomes or objectives, but rather collects evidence of what has been achieved, and works backward to determine whether and how the intervention contributed to the change. This approach is analogous to how a detective, forensic scientist, medical doctor, archaeologist, or anthropologist works, beginning with the effect and discovering its probable cause. The reason for this approach is that the people responsible for an intervention ripe for Outcome Harvesting operate in uncertain and dynamic circumstances, where program implementation and outcomes are substantially unpredictable, even with a strong, evidence-based program design.

Outcome Harvesting generates both quantitative and qualitative data about outcomes—in the form of numbers and in the form of text. Strictly speaking, an outcome statement has only two essential parts: (a) the societal actor who changes his, her, or its behavior (the change per se), and (b) how the intervention contributed to the change. Increasingly, however, I include information about the significance of the outcome, from the perspectives of those who contributed to the change. This offers two advantages. One, you have to define what are relevant and irrelevant changes in the light of the prime harvesting questions. In doing so you bound the outcome by establishing criteria for which outcomes are in and which are out of your harvest. Second, you gather information on why the outcome is important. That said, in contrast to the description of the outcome and the contribution, which are about the facts of the matter as known by the source of information, the significance is an opinion about actual or potential importance.

I crystalize the essential criteria for the quantitative and qualitative data used in Outcome Harvesting with the mnemonic acronym SMART, elaborated in the table below. This acronym provides criteria to ensure the verifiability of outcomes *once they have been achieved* (Figure 1.5). Applying these criteria enable me to ground the formulation of outcome statements and ensure the necessary quantitative and qualitative information is contained in them.

In Outcome Harvesting these are the five criteria for verifiable outcome statements:

Specific: Each outcome statement is formulated in sufficient detail so that a reader without specialized subject or contextual knowledge will be able to understand and appreciate what is described. For example, for the outcome description:
- When—day, month and year that the change happened?
- Full name of who changed?
- What did he, she, or they do concretely that is significantly different?
- Where—located on a map?

Measurable: The descriptions provide objective, verifiable quantitative or qualitative information, independent of who is collecting data. How much? How many? When and where did the change happen?

Achieved: (by the intervention while not necessarily attributable to it): There is a plausible relationship, a logical link between the outcome and what the intervention did that contributed to it. Who did what that wholly, but probably partially, indirectly or indirectly, intentionally or unexpectedly, contributed to the change described in the outcome?

Relevant: The outcome represents a significant step towards the effect that the intervention seeks.

Timely: The outcome occurred within the time period being monitored or evaluated, although the intervention's contribution may have been months or even years before.

Figure 1.5 SMART criteria for achieved outcomes.

The Professional Parameters

Outcome Harvesting is inspired and informed by three methodological pillars. First is *Outcome Mapping* (Earl, Carden, & Smutylo, 2001) widely used by development and social change programs operating in uncertain and dynamic environments. This methodology, developed by the Canadian International Development Research Center (IDRC), provides a definition of "outcome" as behavioral change influenced by a project, program, or organization. It powerfully establishes the conceptual difference between the three types of results: outputs, outcomes, and impact. You control the products and services that your activities generate (outputs). You influence change in behavior of societal actors beyond your sphere of control (outcomes). And over time, your outcomes will contribute to changes in the conditions of people's lives and in the state of the environment (impact). Since Outcome Mapping bills itself as an approach to planning, monitoring, and evaluation, I am often asked why Outcome Harvesting does not take more from Outcome Mapping. I speak as a longtime member of the Outcome Mapping Learning Community (www.outcomemapping.ca), first chair of the board of stewards, and currently a member of their advisory board. First, seven of the 12 Outcome Mapping steps are used to plan an intervention. The four that are designed to monitor are, in my view and that of others, excessive, and only the twelfth step concerns evaluation and then only the evaluation plan. Thus, it is the core concepts of Outcome Mapping about an intervention's sphere of influence and the conceptual understanding of outcomes as the type of result that represents social change that have proven so useful for Outcome Harvesting.

Second, *Utilization-Focused Evaluation* (Patton, 2008, 2012) exerts an equally important methodological influence on Outcome Harvesting. This approach to evaluation focuses on the usefulness of the evaluation findings and process from beginning to end. The utilization focus means that the process and findings have to be useful and not just useable. It is especially appropriate for evaluations that necessarily have to involve key stakeholders in decision-making during the evaluation and who need the evaluation for programmatic improvement and learning as well as accountability. Interestingly, IDRC (2012), the originator of Outcome Mapping, has an established evaluation policy focused on usefulness: "At IDRC, evaluation should only be conducted if the primary intended user(s) and use(s) can be identified. Unused evaluation is a waste of human and financial resources" (p. 1).

Third, in addition to Outcome Mapping concepts and Utilization-Focused Evaluation processes, Outcome Harvesting stands on professional evaluation standards. To begin, an Outcome Harvest is guided by four broadly accepted professional criteria (Yarbrough, Shulha, Hopson, & Caruthers, 2011). The evaluators accept the responsibility to ensure that their evaluation complies with:

1. *Utility:* Serve the information needs of intended users and be owned by them.
2. *Feasibility:* Generate a process and findings that are realistic, prudent, diplomatic, and frugal.
3. *Propriety:* Are conducted legally, ethically, and with due regard for the welfare of those involved in the process, as well as those affected by its results.
4. *Accuracy:* Reveal and convey technically adequate information about the features that determine worth or merit of the program being evaluated.

The order of the standards is important as Dan Stufflebeam (2008), the chair of the original committee who produced them, explains the historic case for the sequencing:

> Originally, that sequencing was recommended by Lee Cronbach and his Stanford University colleagues. They argued that an evaluation's potential utility should be the first concern of evaluator and constituents, because evaluators should not waste time and money in designing, conducting, and reporting studies that would not be used. Once a study's potential utility is established, then it makes sense, in turn, to assure that the study is feasible to conduct in the particular setting, to subsequently make sure it can meet requirements for propriety, and ultimately to design it to produce accurate findings. The Joint Committee endorsed this rationale, particularly because it was a step toward assuring that scarce evaluation resources would be used to conduct sound evaluations that make a positive difference. Clearly, it makes no sense to engage in extensive technical planning of an evaluation before determining that the evaluation is worth doing. (para. 3)

In addition to the program evaluation standards, as an evaluator I strive to abide by the American Evaluation Association (AEA) Guiding Principles for Evaluators. The AEA cautions that "the principles were developed in the context of Western cultures, particularly the United States, and so may reflect the experiences of that context. The relevance of these principles may vary across other cultures, and across subcultures within the United States" ("American Evaluation Association," n.d., p. 2). Therefore, while I personally apply them in an outcome harvest, I do not propose that they necessarily guide all outcome harvesters. The principles are:

1. *Systematic Inquiry:* Evaluators conduct systematic, data-based inquiries about whatever is being evaluated.
2. *Competence:* Evaluators provide competent performance to stakeholders.
3. *Integrity/Honesty:* Evaluators ensure the honesty and integrity of the entire evaluation process.
4. *Respect for People:* Evaluators respect the security, dignity, and self-worth of the respondents, program participants, clients, and other stakeholders with whom they interact.
5. *Responsibilities for General and Public Welfare:* Evaluators articulate and take into account the diversity of interests and values that may be related to the general and public welfare.

The six Outcome Harvesting steps that stand on these three pillars have proven most useful for a wide diversity of interventions operating in dynamic contexts with considerable uncertainty about exactly what will be achieved until outcomes emerge. Consequently, applying Outcome Harvesting requires that you customize it each and every time. Expectedly, this has presented a major challenge for knowing when a harvest remains true to Outcome Harvesting. When do the changes made in applying Outcome Harvesting cross the line and the harvest stops being Outcome Harvesting?

The lines are not easy to draw. Outcome Harvesting turns the normal evaluation process on its head in many ways. For example, the customary pattern is for evaluation commissioners to consult internal stakeholders to agree on the terms of reference and their procurement or bidding regulations do not permit evaluators who wish to submit bids to dialogue with the commissioners. This clashes with the harvester's need to know, at least, who are the users, what are their intended uses and thus what do they need to know through the harvest in order to submit a proposal. Another common expectation of evaluation commissioners is to contract an evaluation and then stand back and wait for independent, external experts to collect data and render their judgments. This contrasts with the participation in decision-making and information collection that are at the core of Outcome Harvesting.

During the course of the harvest, similar obstacles emerge. I witness people falling into the trap of following the logic of looking at what was done in order to see what was achieved, and then missing unintended outcomes, both negative and positive. Similarly, the active participation of those being evaluated, which has proven to be a key to success in data collection, runs against the ethos of the external, independent evaluation norm. It is common for stakeholders to balk at staff participating and evaluators serving the role of facilitator and coach; instead they expect evaluators to go about collecting data as experts, wielding measuring sticks and making judgments about performance. That can be confusing and deadly for success. Right from the beginning of an Outcome Harvest, the users and harvesters alike are under pressure to adapt to circumstances. And the adaptation and customization continue throughout the harvest.

In sum, along with interesting innovations that continue to enrich the approach, I have been concerned, if not anguished, to find almost as many misuses and abuses of the Outcome Harvesting approach as creative advances in developing it further. I concluded that one of the fundamental reasons, and perhaps the principal one, was that I had not identified and much less explained the Outcome Harvesting principles that underlie the approach. That was a major motivation to write this book.

The Common Thread of Complexity-Awareness

Over the last 10 years or so, the term "complexity" has become a buzzword in social change and development to such an extent that I find it of little use in discussions with commissioners, primary users, intervention staff, substantiators, and colleague harvesters. What has proven extremely useful, however, is to make sure Outcome Harvesting is "complexity-aware," by which I mean being sensitive to three things:

1. *Uncertainty:* The relationships of cause and effect between what an intervention does and what it achieves are unknown until the achievements emerge. For example, this is commonly the case when an intervention is to be carried out in a new context.
2. *Dynamism:* The intervention faces unforeseeable changes amongst actors and factors in the environment in which it is implemented. Even if the intervention is in the same context, if it is dynamic, what worked last year will not necessarily work this year because the variables have changed.
3. *Unpredictability:* Consequently, the intervention cannot predefine what an intervention will achieve or detail what it will do beyond the short term. There are no tried and proven models; the intervention has to innovate and experiment to discover what will work and to understand why.

Thus, the first concern requiring sensitivity is that Outcome Harvesting is generally *not* useful for the monitoring and evaluation of an intervention that uses tried and proven models of change. For example, running the provision of social services, implementing an annual polio vaccination campaign, managing an adult literacy program, building a road, and constructing schools are *usually* interventions with prior knowledge about what to do and how to achieve the intended results. The context is stable enough for you to rely on past experience with considerable confidence. That is, logic models and results-based frameworks make a lot of sense. You can plan what resources you need in order to carry out the activities that will produce outputs to influence outcomes and eventually have the impact you wish to achieve. At the moment of monitoring or evaluating, you can assess the plan against performance in order to determine if you have been efficient, and you can assess the results against the plan to see if you have been effective in achieving what you wanted. Evaluating the original plan will provide you with the information you need to decide the merit, worth, or significance of the process and the results.

Second, I suggest you be sensitive to the special appropriateness of Outcome Harvesting when it is used for one or more of these four purposes:

1. Monitor the implementation and evaluate the outcomes of an innovative approach to an intractable challenge or to a new, emerging problem.
2. Provide evidence and insights on the outcomes achieved by a goal-oriented project, program, or organization that was launched without predefined objectives or even predetermined activities beyond the short-term.
3. Learn about the changes in societal actors' behaviors that an intervention influenced directly but also *indirectly*. For example, in my experience donors consider that what their grantees do with a grant is substantially under their control because of the contractual grant agreement. Therefore, the donors see their outcomes to be the changes influenced directly by their grantees in other societal actors but consequently only indirectly by the donor.
4. Evaluate an intervention that underwent so much change that it is not useful to assess what it did and achieved against what was originally planned, as is done in normal evaluations.

Each one of those purposes is laced through with the uncertainty about relationships of cause and effect and dynamism that characterize "complexity." They also tend to apply to most but certainly not all situations of development and social change. For example, in all the evaluations I have done, the commissioners agreed that their original plan (a) had been overtaken by changes in the environment in which they were being implemented, (b) was too general in defining expected results, or (c) simply did not exist in any evaluable form. This is understandable. When your intervention faces uncertainty, dynamism, and unpredictability, you have to innovate or create a new strategy to address the current challenge. In other situations, some planned activities will bear fruit, but others will have to be abandoned as the need for unplanned activities emerges. There will be unanticipated outputs and outcomes—and some activities will never have results at all. Thus, the greater the unpredictability when planning and implementing, the more you require a complexity-aware approach that will take into account unforeseeable developments and outcomes.

Lastly, Outcome Harvesting itself can be uncertain and unpredictable. There can be disagreement about who are the users or about what are the uses for the harvest process or findings. Similarly, there can be a lack of agreement about what will be most useful to know and where to obtain the answers. And there is uncertainty about what will be the outcomes you will find. Often, you cannot foresee with certainty what will happen during the next step in the harvesting process.

In sum, uncertainty, dynamism, and unpredictability pose special challenges to evaluating development and social change initiatives but they can be overcome. To identify and understand what has been achieved and how, implementers and harvesters can opt for goal-free methods. Outcome Harvesting is one that can serve for monitoring and learning from outcomes, and evaluating outcomes in piloting, ongoing developmental, midterm formative, and end-of-term summative evaluations. The approach may be used as a comprehensive evaluation approach or combined with other methods. Nonetheless, however you use Outcome Harvesting, the role of the harvester is not simply that of an M&E person or an evaluator—it is also that of a facilitator, and coach, and mentor.

Facilitator, Coach, and Mentor

When I assume the responsibility for carrying out an outcome harvest, I see my initial role as much more of a *facilitator* than as an evaluator. The first four steps of design and data collection require that the harvester ensures the effective participation of users and internal and external sources of information. Even in the fifth step of analyzing and interpreting the data, making judgments and drawing conclusions, when my role is principally that of an evaluator, I and my co-evaluators do not stand back from the users and their uses and what they need to know. We engage with them to make sure that we answer the evaluation questions in the ways that are going to be useful to them as well as rigorously evidence-based.

Not surprisingly, my colleague outcome harvesters and I are not alone realizing that facilitation is the essence of ensuring usefulness of a harvest. Utilization-focused evaluators have identified a few characteristics that have emerged over time as the way to most effectively ensure use as a facilitator. "Being active-reactive-interactive-adaptive is, in a nutshell, the facilitation style of utilization-focused evaluation" (Patton, 2012, p. 47). As a harvester you *actively* propose how to customize the six Outcome Harvesting steps to the users' needs and context, guarding against tendencies to treat the principles and steps as recipes. You are attentive to changes and *react* to what emerges in the harvesting process and to changes in users, uses, or what they are learning in order to identify new opportunities or risks to the harvest and potential solutions. You continuously *interact* with your users to discuss modifications to the harvest design and implementation. And in consultation with the users you *adapt* the harvest in the light of greater understanding of changes in the situation.[2]

Another key difference between your role as a harvester and the more conventional evaluator or M&E role is that when gathering data, you *coach* your sources in a co-learning mode rather than interrogate them as an external judge of the merit, worth or value of what they are doing and achieving. Your task is to ensure a solid evaluative process. In Outcome Harvesting Steps 1–5, you are responsible for gathering information on outcomes that are well-formulated, plausible, and verifiable and for following a credible process of data collection, analysis, and synthesis to enable you to draw useful conclusions from solid evidence. The evaluative judgments only come in the fifth step, once you have harvested solid, credible-enough outcomes to serve as your evidence with which to answer the prime harvest questions.

In that role, you are a coach because you support your sources of information to perform a particular task: Identify and formulate outcomes. That is, you support them to express in succinct written descriptions what they have achieved, why it is important, and how they contributed. I have found this is not easy, for two reasons. Firstly, people have been schooled in reporting on their activities—how many people they trained, how many events they held at a global forum. There is work to be done in identifying outcomes and frequently the information has not been gathered or is shared anecdotally but without the detail that makes it verifiable. Secondly, after performing this role with a wide diversity of sources running across just about every imaginable variable of diversity, I discovered that few people readily express themselves well in writing. This holds true regardless of gender, education, authority, status, language, culture, to mention a few variables.

On the positive side, you are coaching people short term and it is performance driven. As soon as you have mutual satisfaction with the form and content of an outcome, the job is completed. To get there, you need to be clear about your criteria and standards of success, and that means understanding the nature of the data you will need to obtain.

As colleagues and I were discovering the importance of the facilitator and coaching roles for Outcome Harvesting, Ricardo Ramírez and Dal Brodhead were discovering a third dimension when the harvester serves as a *mentor* to people learning Utilization-Focused Evaluation (U-FE), one of the two methodological legs of Outcome Harvesting. They were responsible for supporting evaluation professionals using U-FE for the first time with five Asian research projects in the field of information and communication technology for development. In their excellent *Utilization Focused Evaluation: A Primer for Evaluators* they share that what they found most effective was the "team approach where evaluation mentors coach and mentor project-based evaluators and project implementers—and everybody learns together" (Ramírez & Brodhead, 2013, p. xi).

This third role as mentor to M&E staff within interventions or to my co-evaluators new to Outcome Harvesting includes but is broader than coaching. As an Outcome Harvesting coach, you support someone to learn how to use the whole Outcome Harvesting methodology of six steps and to appreciate the underlying nine principles. Coaching focuses on the task of helping another person to learn how to identify and formulate outcomes. It requires an investment of hours of clock time over a few weeks, ping-ponging back and forth. It requires mutual respect and confidence, as does mentoring. But in contrast, mentoring is more intense and prolonged, it is characterized less by being focused on the tasks and more on developing the relationships and environment needed for applying the Outcome Harvesting approach in the mentees context. It requires a working relationship in which you both are investing considerably more time, usually days of clock time over months of calendar time.

In sum, facilitating, coaching, and mentoring all have a part in making someone proficient in Outcome Harvesting.

In Summary

Since 2003, the Outcome Harvesting tool had been used by grant makers, managers, and harvesters to monitor and evaluate the interventions of hundreds of diverse types of organizations, programs, and projects on six continents. It has been and continues to be developed through a basically empirical, experiential process of co-creation between harvesters and users: between those responsible for the customized design of the process, collection and verification of outcome data, using it to answer the harvesting questions and then supporting those people that need the process and findings of an Outcome Harvest.

The approach is especially useful when the purpose is evaluating a development or social change initiative with the purpose of learning as well as accountability. The six steps you follow in the process of harvesting outcomes are methodologically based on Utilization-Focused Evaluation and conceptually on Outcome Mapping. The process is always customized to the context of the primary users and their principal uses, which must include understanding the changes in behavior of other societal actors to which an intervention has contributed. One special characteristic of Outcome Harvesting is that it is complexity-aware, and therefore particularly useful in situations of uncertainty and dynamism in which the cause–effect relationships between what an intervention does and what it achieves only become evident after outcomes emerge.

Notes

1. The six steps were initially presented in the Outcome Harvesting brief Heather Britt and I wrote published by the Ford Foundation's Middle East and North Africa office (Wilson-Grau & Britt, 2012, revised November 2013) and subsequently as chapters in two books (Wilson-Grau, Scheers, & Kosterink, 2015; Wilson-Grau, 2017).
2. I explain in greater detail this active-reactive-interactive-adaptive mode of facilitation in *Principle I. Facilitate usefulness throughout the evaluation*, which you will find in Chapter 8.

References

American Evaluation Association Guiding Principles for Evaluators: Revisions Reflected Herein Ratified by the AEA Membership, July 2004. (n.d.). Retrieved from American Evaluation Association website: https://www.eval.org/p/cm/ld/fid=51

Earl, S., Carden, F., & Smutylo, T. (2001). *Outcome mapping: Building learning and reflection into development programs*. Ottawa, Canada: International Development Research Centre. Retrieved from https://bit.ly/2OIHKJW

International Development Research Center, (February, 2012). *Identifying the intended user(s) and use(s) of an evaluation*. Retrieved from https://bit.ly/2LQ2CkV.

Patton, M. Q. (2008). *Utilization-focused evaluation* (4th ed.). Thousand Oaks, CA: SAGE.

Patton, M. Q. (2012). *Essentials of utilization-focused evaluation.* Thousand Oaks, CA: SAGE.

Patton, M. Q. (2017). *Principles-focused evaluation: The guide.* New York, NY: Guilford.

Ramírez, R., & Brodhead, D. P. (2013). *Utilization focused evaluation: A primer for evaluators.* Penang, Malaysia: Southbound. Retrieved from http://bit.ly/2s8NWz4

Stufflebeam, D. L. (2008, September 10). Excerpt from letter to the Joint Committee on Standards for Educational Evaluation, posted by Michael Quinn Patton in honor and remembrance of Stufflebeam, who recently had died. American Evaluation Association Discussion List (EVALTALK@LISTSERV.UA.EDU), 2017, July 27.

Wilson-Grau, R. (2017). Outcome harvesting evaluation: Practical application of essential principles. In M. Q. Patton (Ed.), *Principles-focused evaluation—The guide.* New York, NY: Guilford.

Wilson-Grau, R., & Britt, H. (2012, revised November 2013). Outcome harvesting. Cairo, Egypt: Ford Foundation Middle East and North Africa Office. Retrieved from www.outcomemapping.ca/resource/resource.php?id=374

Wilson-Grau, R., Scheers, G., & Kosterink P. (2015). Outcome harvesting—A DE inquiry framework supporting the development of an international social change network. In M. Q. Patton, K. McKegg, & N. Wehipeihana (Eds.), *Developmental evaluation exemplars: Principles in practice.* New York, NY: Guilford.

World Bank. (2014). *Cases in outcome harvesting: Ten pilot experiences identify new learning from multi-stakeholder projects to improve results.* Washington, DC: World Bank. Retrieved from https://openknowledge.worldbank.org/handle/10986/20015

Yarbrough, D. B., Shulha, L. M., Hopson, R. K., & Caruthers, F. A. (2011). *The program evaluation standards: A guide for evaluators and evaluation users* (3rd ed.). Thousand Oaks, CA: SAGE.

2

Step 1—Design of an Outcome Harvest

The design process begins with agreement between the commissioners of the harvest and the harvester(s) on the terms of reference (TOR) for the Outcome Harvesting project. Commissioners are well-advised to involve the harvesters who will be responsible for an Outcome Harvest in

---

Applicability of Key Principles to Step 1

Process principles—Chapter 8
- ***** I. Facilitate usefulness throughout the evaluation
- ***** III. Nurture appropriate participation
- ***** II. Coach primary sources to formulate outcome statements
- ***** IV. Strive for less because it will be more useful
- *** V. Learn Outcome Harvesting experientially

Content principles—Chapter 9
- ***** VI. Harvest social change outcomes
- ***** VII. Formulate an outcome as an observable change
- ** VIII. Establish plausible influence of the intervention
- ***** IX. Ensure credible-enough outcomes

Legend of Ricardo's rubrics
***** High: I always apply this principle; **** Considerable: I almost always apply it; *** Moderate: I usually apply it
** Occasional: I apply it sometimes but with quite a few exceptions; * Low: I rarely apply the principle in this step

developing the TOR: a general statement of the background, objectives, and purpose of the evaluation.[1] Harvesters, too, must insist on being involved in developing the TOR, which I realize is often easier said than done. Since this advice, which is based on my Outcome Harvesting experience, runs against the procurement procedures of many organizations, in Appendix B (Developing Terms of Reference to Commission an Outcome Harvest), I explain how it can be done.

The purpose of the design (Figure 2.1) step is to agree on a harvest plan. Harvest users and harvesters apply an approach adapted from the first 12 steps in Michael Quinn Patton's Utilization-Focused Evaluation (U-FE), which is the principal methodological pillar on which Outcome Harvesting stands. U-FE is "a comprehensive approach for doing evaluations that are useful, practical, ethical, accurate and accountable" (Patton, 2015, p. 18). Harvesters and users reach agreement in principle on

1. the primary intended users who will use the Outcome Harvesting results,
2. the users' principal intended uses for the Outcome Harvest findings and process,
3. the prime Outcome Harvesting questions the harvest will answer,
4. what outcome information primary users need to answer the questions,
5. the secondary (documentation) and primary (internal people) sources and how the harvester will obtain information from them, and
6. the financial, human, and time resources required for the harvest.

Figure 2.1 Outcome Harvesting design process.

The harvest plan details the first three of the six Outcome Harvesting steps: design the Outcome Harvest, review documentation, and engage with human sources. Users and harvesters find it fruitful to discuss in principle the other three steps—substantiate with external sources, analyze and interpret, and support use of findings. I always caution, however, that they rarely can hope for more than preliminary, tentative agreements because of the uncertainty and dynamism that usually characterize the Outcome Harvesting process.

Who Will Use the Outcome Harvest?

Primary intended *users* are involved in the M&E or evaluation process from beginning to end. A user requires the outcome harvest to make decisions or take action. Since users need the harvest, the assumption is that they are willing to participate in it and will develop ownership of the process and the results.

There may be a lead user and a harvest team leader. The users and harvesters together clarify intended uses; identify prime Outcome Harvesting questions; agree with the methods to be used to collect, analyze, and interpret data; participate in methodological decisions made in the course of the harvest; review drafts of findings for accuracy and legibility; and carry out an appropriate dissemination strategy. This involvement typically results in increased use of the harvest. If these individuals or groups are not included, the harvest runs the risk of producing results that may never be used.

In their primer on U-FE, Ricardo Ramírez and Dal Brodhead conclude that identifying primary intended users "is part art, part strategy, and part intuition" (2013, p. 30). Indeed, in Outcome Harvesting the harvester's role is to identify and obtain the commitment of users of the harvest who are, "committed, dedicated, engaged, open to learning and dialogue, and keen to gain a new outlook on evaluation" (Ramírez & Brodhead, 2013, p. 30).

To sort out primary users from other stakeholders, primary users should respond with a resounding "yes" to these three questions:

1. Given the available resources and expected uses, is the harvest as we have designed it worth doing?
2. Are we individually and as a group ready to make the ongoing investment of time and effort needed to conduct this harvest?
3. Are we committed to using the results of the harvest?

Each one of these questions generally requires discussion. For example, the second question usually leads to a discussion along the lines of, "What do you mean? How much time is this going to take?"; and we go from there.

Distinguishing between users and other stakeholders is a challenge. I find it useful to distinguish primary from secondary users, as well as the users from the audience, by identifying an active versus passive relationship to the harvest process and findings:

- *Primary Users*: Those who need the findings in order to make decisions or take action and *must be involved in decisions* throughout the harvesting process.
- *Secondary Users*: Those who need the findings in order to make decisions or take action but are *not involved in decisions* throughout the harvesting process, although they may be consulted by the primary users.
- *Audience*: Other stakeholders who will be interested in knowing the findings.

These, too, are points that users and harvesters may initially only agree to in principle and will want to come back to when they have completed the design process.

The users (and their uses) are not set in stone. As the harvest proceeds and outcomes emerge, usefulness may change. Furthermore, too many primary users may be unwieldy for much of the decision-making that has to take place during the implementation of the outcome harvest. A mechanism I often use is forming a steering group with, in our exemplar (Table 2.1), the planning, monitoring, and evaluation (PME) coordinator serving as liaison to the members of the management team and one of the

TABLE 2.1 Exemplar of Primary Users and Principal Uses

Primary Intended Users	Principal Intended Uses	Secondary Users
National management team: Executive director; finance director; director of programs; coordinator of planning, monitoring and evaluation (PME)	1. Report to our stakeholders on our progress in fulfilling our mission. 2. Make decisions on our fundraising strategy, branding and profiling of the organization. 3. Provide the board of directors with evidence of our achievements and make projections for the coming 3 years. 4. Review the 5-year strategic plan.	Board of directors Donors Communication director
Three program coordinators	5. Improve the service delivery, capacity-building and advocacy programs for the last 3 years of the 2016–2020 strategic plan.	Field staff

three program coordinators assuming the same responsibility with her or his colleagues. They are the interface with the harvest team and they decide when and how they will consult their colleagues.

It is vitally important to understand that designing the harvest is a sociocultural and political challenge as well as a methodological one. Jérôme Leblanc is an evaluator with Avenir d'enfants, a Quebec government program that funds community coalitions working on early childhood development. He is using Outcome Harvesting for M&E, and underscores these key considerations when customizing Outcome Harvesting:

> One of our greatest challenges of Outcome Harvesting at Avenir d'enfants and the 140 community coalitions in early childhood we support in the province of Quebec, is to make the experience as useful as it can be for our board of directors, who want to know what are the outcomes of this 400 million dollars, 10 year project, and at the same time make it very useful for the coalitions to provide them the opportunity to make a summary/assessment of their own outcomes. Balancing the tools and the method the right way is therefore crucial, and participation of various stakeholders, from up-stream to down-stream in the process, is definitely vital. (LeBlanc, 2017, personal communication, October 5)

What Are the Principal Uses?

One of the most difficult decisions in M&E and evaluation is to decide what you will not monitor or evaluate. The same can be said of identifying users and their principal intended uses. During the design step, when virtual communication is not sufficient, I commonly facilitate a workshop with the potential primary intended users to review where we will draw the boundaries for who are users and who are not, and what their priority uses are and which are not. The mapping enables us to discuss the targeted uses for which Outcome Harvesting will generate evidence. For example, Outcome Harvesting does not provide you with data about financial performance, although it can inform that assessment. Thus, Outcome Harvesting will not be useful for checking cost/benefit or value for money, although it may present information that can inform a qualitative return on investment.

The main intended uses of both the process and findings must be clear.

Process uses are changes expected to result from the harvest activity itself. For example, field staff will learn how to identify and formulate outcomes and are likely to retain and apply this skill thereafter. Other examples:

- Build capacity to evaluate.
- Improve communication and foster common understanding—frequently it is only at the time of commissioning or participat-

ing in an evaluation that an organization or program really pins down its understanding of what it hopes its strategies are achieving. These conversations can be critical in building a common vision and commitment.
- Strengthen the assessment of the implementation of the intervention because what is measured tends to be what gets done.
- Increase participation and ownership over the evaluation findings.
- Foster a learning culture.

Findings refer to the information collected and the answers to the harvest questions. The findings of an Outcome Harvest will be used to support decision-making, further learning or changed thinking and behavior, or they might solely be used for accountability—but often it is a mix of both. Findings will enable the users, for example, to

- be accountable to donors for outcomes the intervention has influenced,
- inform stakeholders what was done and is being achieved by the intervention,
- take decisions to modify an intervention,
- plan future work,
- evaluate performance, and
- use the evidence when engaging allies or funders about future strategies.

Naturally, not all users will have the same uses for the process or findings. Thus, it is through facilitating a thorough discussion weighing the pros and cons of multiple options, that you arrive at a manageable and realistic set of primary intended users and principal intended uses. To arrive at them requires your facilitating, coaching, and mentoring in the active-reactive-interactive-adaptive mode I explain in Chapter 1.

What Do the Users Need to Know?

The *prime harvesting questions* in M&E and in the different modes of evaluation serve a purpose similar to that of a hypothesis in scientific research: they guide what you do. The questions are "prime" in two senses. First, they represent what the users need to know in the light of their intended uses of the information. Second, they guide the Outcome Harvesting process. So the questions should be as specific and detailed as necessary, enabling appropriate and targeted data collection. I see all the time requests for proposals in which dozens of evaluation questions are listed. That is simply unrealistic, as it would require more resources than are available. Too many evaluation questions also diffuse the focus and likely utility of the Outcome Harvesting process.

There are many tools and techniques you can use to facilitate users arriving at useful, actionable questions (Ramírez & Brodhead, 2013; Preskill & Jones, 2009). Since I work mainly internationally, most of my experience is working virtually with primary users to craft prime harvest questions. I also engaged in person when language or culture make it necessary. Either way, I have a discussion in the light of the primary intended users' principal uses for the Outcome Harvest. I ask the user: "*What* do you need to know and *why* will it be useful information?" I ask "what" and "why" at the same time in order to correct the tendency of wish listing. With that clarity, I draft prime harvest questions (Table 2.2).

When there are more than 2–5 prime harvesting questions, I always ask the user to reconsider the priority of what they need to know. In the "Why?" column, I use the five evaluation criteria common in international development (OECD-DAC, 2012) on purpose in order to explain that Outcome Harvesting is less appropriate or even inappropriate for meeting some information needs. For the findings to be useful, they must inform decisions or actions that need to be taken. Usually, and concretely in the case of our exemplar, Outcome Harvesting is less appropriate for addressing the impact, and especially the efficiency criteria, than it is for effectiveness, relevance, and sustainability. Therefore I customarily suggest that if answers to Questions I and II in Table 2.2 are necessary, then a different method than Outcome Harvesting would be more appropriate to generate data to answer them.

To write prime harvest questions is an art. I have found that the basic challenge is to arrive at questions that ask for both information and interpretation, for description and explanation. This is because rarely will information alone—a description of outcomes and the activities and outputs that contributed to them—be useful for making decisions or taking action. Thus, ensure each question clarifies *what* data have to be collected and asks for a judgment: *so what* do the data mean? My goal is to arrive at "so what" questions that incorporate the what, as exemplified in Figure 2.2.

Identifying the harvest questions can take time and considerable negotiation, but the questions should be as specific as possible because vague questions usually yield vague answers. The proof of usefulness is the extent to which the process and findings of an Outcome Harvest enable the primary intended users to decide *now what* to do on the basis of outcomes

What?	So what?
What are the policy and practice outcomes that the organization influenced since 2016? Which activities of the organization influenced those outcomes?	Are the policy and practice outcomes the organization achieved in line with its strategic plan? Which are the strengths and weaknesses of the intervention strategies that contributed to outcomes?

Figure 2.2 Exemplar of What? and So what? prime evaluation questions.

achieved. Working with them on their questions, I sensitize them to clock and calendar-time demands in Outcome Harvesting. Thus, I remind users that each question will require different or additional information and time, including their own time.

Lastly, I am often asked for examples of generic prime harvest questions that can be answered using Outcome Harvesting. I caution that you cannot divorce questions from uses and from users and their context. Furthermore, users with similar or even the same uses may have very different needs for what they need to know because one user's M&E system may be generating knowledge that another user's M&E system does not. (See Table 2.2 and Figure 2.2 for examples of Outcome Harvesting questions.)

In summary, to arrive at a manageable number of priority harvest questions, I have found utilization-focused criteria to be helpful.

1. *The primary intended users want the question answered.* I test this criterion by making sure users can indicate how they would use the answer to the question for future decision-making and action. I am surprised by users frequently posing harvest questions for which they already have the information or that pale dramatically in comparison with other questions. For example: "What has our program done to pursue our strategies?" In addition to not being information that Outcome Harvesting will provide, the answers to this question are already in reports or can be easily answered by managers asking implementers to report on their activities.
2. *Questions can be answered sufficiently well to inform understanding and support action.* A major challenge in Outcome Harvesting is to understand that data about outcomes, however rich it may be, is limited. The results focus of the approach can create enormous ex-

TABLE 2.2 Exemplar of Arriving at Useful Harvest Questions

What Do You Need to Know?	Why?	Potential Prime Harvest Questions
In the light of how you plan to use the findings, what information do you require that you do not already have?	*For what purpose do you need this information? Which use will it inform?* [Numbers refer to Uses in Table 2.1]	*What questions must the data you collect serve to answer?*
The outcomes we have achieved that potentially will lead (or actually have led) to changes in the conditions of women's lives.	To know the *impact* produced by our interventions because this, at the end of the day, is what our stakeholders consider to be most important. 1, 3, 4	I. How have the outcomes of our interventions contributed, directly or indirectly, intended or not, to a process of change that potentially will affect—or already has affected—positively or negatively, the rights-based empowerment of women in ways that would not have happened anyway?
The activities and outputs of our five provincial projects that contributed to the most and the best outcomes with the fewest resources.	Our funders expect us not only to achieve outcomes but to do so in the most cost/*efficient* manner possible. 2, 3	II. How do our activities and outputs that influenced outcomes compare quantitatively and qualitatively?
The most and the least significant outcomes being achieved by each of our three programs.	To understand the extent to which our programs are *effective* in achieving the objectives in our 2016–2020 strategic plan. 4, 5	III. In the light of rights-based empowerment of women, what is the relative importance of the outcomes we have influenced through our service delivery, capacity-building and advocacy programs?
After 7 years, the extent to which our goals and objectives are still relevant.	Our stakeholders rightfully question whether everything we do is *relevant* to our vision and mission. 3, 4	IV. How do the outcomes we achieve correspond to the goals of the three programs of the organization and how do they not?
Evidence that our achievements will continue once we cease our intervention.	Our board and donors are keen that we expand our work but only if its achievements are *sustainable*. 3, 4	V. What are the signs that the processes of change represented by the outcomes to which our three programs and five projects have contributed will endure without our intervention's support?

pectations for understanding all kinds of results, but Outcome Harvesting only collects, analyzes, and interprets evidence of outcomes achieved. This includes outputs but only those that have contributed to outcomes. And as I just explained, Outcome Harvesting does not assess impact although it can inform about the potential significance of outcomes to affect the conditions of people's lives or the state of the environment.
3. *Data can be brought to bear on the questions.* I broaden this criterion for Outcome Harvesting users to mean their questions require *outcome* data. This is not always clear cut. For example, in a project developing a methodology for evaluating interreligious peacebuilding, the religious peacebuilders considered the assessment of the presence of the supernatural in their work to be fundamental. At first glance, this would appear to be beyond the possibilities of evaluation, especially for this nontheist, a-religious and philosophical, materialist evaluator! With further exploration, however, it became clear that these religious peacebuilders did not expect to determine and much less measure the presence of the divine in their work, but they did need to understand the part that their *belief* in and experience with the supernatural played in their faith-based peacebuilding efforts. Assessing this with Outcome Harvesting is possible (Wilson-Grau & Steele, 2016).
4. *Questions can be answered in a timely manner and at reasonable cost.* Resources are the sixth design consideration I will address below, but it is never too early to have the feasibility of answering your questions in mind. Financial, human, and time resources often are the determining factor of which questions can realistically be answered.

Necessary Information

The fourth piece of an Outcome Harvesting design is the *information* you require to answer the harvest questions. This is the data you want to collect in the *outcome statement*. The essential information is always the *outcome* and the *contribution* of the intervention that influenced the change in behavior. In my own practice, a third component that is almost always incorporated in the outcome statement is the *significance* of the outcome. That is, why is the outcome noteworthy for the intervention's vision, mission, goals, objectives, theory of change, logic model, or other purpose for taking the outcome into account? The three components can be described in 1–2 sentences (Figure 2.3). When you take the description of the "when," "who," "what," and "where" of the outcome, the "how" of the contribution and the "why" of the significance, the outcome statement adds up to more than three

Step 1—Design of an Outcome Harvest ▪ 39

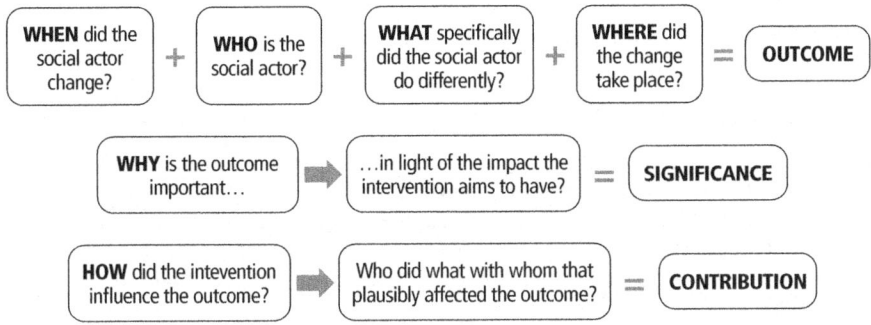

Figure 2.3 Three components of an outcome statement.

separate descriptions and becomes an explanation of the intervention's achievement. I urge you to make these decisions on the basis of real-life examples. *Simulate* for the primary intended users, what the *process* will be and what *results* can be expected (Patton, 2012, pp. 309–310). To produce the example, I ask the user for a recent annual or field report, minutes of evaluative meetings, presentations to the board and such in which there is information about their achievements and what they did to achieve them. I then formulate an outcome statement based on that documentation. If there is no document to review, or I could not find even one outcome in any document, I will interview someone who will have the information in order to be able to formulate one outcome that I can use as an example. I find that using a real example is more effective than a generic example.

Then, present the sample to the primary users (Figure 2.4). Ask them: "This is the data an Outcome Harvest can generate for you. Is this the information you need to know about each outcome?" Do not stop there. As a way to ensure they know what they are getting into, I exemplify for them the types of decisions they may face if the way they hope to use the harvest change is through process dynamics or emerging findings, or due to external factors.

In addition to helping you decide what in-depth detail is necessary, having examples of outcomes on the table will help users and you decide if it will be more useful to have *breadth* instead of *depth*. For example, leading up to the outcome of nine members of a national legislature voicing their support, there were preliminary or intermediate steps: one legislator took up the initiative with colleagues; another collaborated with the national action campaign to organize the launch; a third mobilized over 1,000 activists for the proposed International Violence Against Women Act (IVAWA). Harvesting these actions as outcomes will enable you to see the process of changes that

> **1. The *outcome*—*Who* changed *what*, *when*, and *where*?**
> On 13 December 2017, nine members of the national legislature voiced their support before over 1,000 activists for the proposed International Violence Against Women Act (IVAWA).
>
> **2. The *significance* of each outcome—*Why* is the outcome important for the rights-based empowerment of women?**
> With legislators speaking out, the campaign for passage of the IVAWA now stands a better chance of mobilizing thousands of supporters to sign petitions, speak out through social media and lobby the other legislators to pass this lifesaving legislation.
>
> **3. The intervention's *contribution*—*How* did the intervention influence the outcome: Who did what with whom that plausibly affected the outcome?**
> Since 2016, based on testimonials obtained through our service delivery projects in 29 rural communities in five provinces, we have been lobbying on the issue in the legislature. On 13 December 2017, we launched the national action campaign with three allies, calling on the government to help end violence against women and girls and stop hate crimes against LGBT people. The nine legislators we had invited to accompany the launch spoke in turn.

Figure 2.4 Exemplar of a sample outcome statement.

culminated in the nine legislators' public stand. Consequently, the number of outcomes in a harvest can be small or large depending on what will be most useful for answering the prime Outcome Harvesting questions. Thus, if the primary users need to know what *policy changes* their intervention has influenced, you would not count the actions of individual legislators given above as outcomes. Instead, you would be identifying instances where, for example, the ruling party declares it will support IVAWA; the Ministry of Women's Affairs proposes a bill to prohibit domestic violence against girls and women; or the national legislature passes the bill into law.

You can add any other information that will be useful for answering the prime Outcome Harvesting questions. Here, I exemplify the other components that have proven as useful to one or more primary intended users as are the description of the outcome, its significance, and the contribution. An example of each is in italics.

- *Sources*. Name of person or document who provided the information and date they did so. Sources can be specified for each category of information: outcome, contribution, significance. *Annual report 2017, page 21.*
- *Collaboration with other social actors in the activity*. With whom, how, and when the intervention worked to influence the outcome.

Three of our allies—the National Gender Network of Victims of Domestic Violence, the LGBT Coalition, and Police Officers Association—have been coordinating efforts in favor of IVAWA since January 2016.
- *Contribution of other actors to the outcome.* The how, what, and when by which the actions of other individuals, groups, communities, organizations, or institutions influenced the outcome. These criteria can be further refined to specify the other actors, for example: (a) allies, (b) donors, (c) government officials, (d) the people who are the subjects of the outcome, (e) the individuals, groups, or organizations who benefit directly or indirectly from the intervention. *Our ally, the governmental Office for Women's Affairs, in September 2017, produced a briefing paper on the draft IVAWA law in which they quoted our policy position.*
- *Contribution of other factors.* How, what, and when social, economic, political, cultural, environmental, or other variables affected the outcome. *The 2010–2015 economic recession forced many male heads of households to migrate in search of work leaving women as the sole providers for their families and opening up employment opportunities.*
- *History.* The sequence of past events relevant to the outcome, including the patterns of cause and effect that caused them. *Over the past 30 years, women's organizations became increasingly militant on the rights of girls to post-secondary education and created a backlash and a worsening of respect for women's rights.*
- *Context.* The conditions, objects, and circumstances that form the setting for the outcome in terms of which it can be fully understood and assessed. *Currently, however, the dip in the "J" curve has passed and there is more and more openness amongst men in this patriarchal society to rights-based measures for the empowerment of women, creating an enabling environment for political parties to draft laws with incentives for vocational or professional higher education.*
- *Impact.* The effect of the outcome on the conditions of people's lives or in the state of environment. *Over the past 2 years the government's funding of women-driven development initiatives increased 12% per year, almost double the increase in the previous 2 years.*
- *Classification.* Used if you want to know how the intervention would classify their contribution to each outcome, for instance in our exemplar (Chapter 1—Table 1.1 and Figures 1.1–1.2), by service delivery, capacity-building, or advocacy.

You have to take care, however, when including additional information. Make sure it is going to be useful to answer one or more of the prime harvest questions. In order to compare and contrast your outcome statements, you must have the same information for each one. Adding a component will involve adding more work to your harvest to identify and formulate those descriptions.

Once you have the different components of your outcome statement agreed, discuss with the user how much *description* is necessary in the light of their uses. Do not assume that more detail will be more useful. Even a small number of outcomes are less manageable if your descriptions run to 1–2 paragraphs rather than to 1–2 sentences. Furthermore, I strongly advise the outcome statements be consistent in the length of the text from description to description and outcome to outcome. Otherwise, the reader will either expect a similar amount of text in all descriptions or will skip over too detailed descriptions. Occasionally, however, *explanation* rather than straightforward descriptions of each component may be necessary. That is, you may require additional facts that clarify the *context* of the outcome, the *causality* of the contribution, and, if you use significance, the *consequences* of the outcome.

How much detail is right depends on usefulness—what do the primary users need to know in the light of their principal uses? To make this point, I use the sample described above. This enables users to decide if indeed explanation rather than description is the information they need, and what really is the level of detail required.

Primary and Secondary Sources and How to Engage Them

Logically, once you are clear what information you need to harvest, the next step is to identify the sources. There are two kinds of sources for an Outcome Harvest: (a) *primary sources* who are people usually internal to the intervention with direct knowledge of the outcomes and the motivation and time to share what they know, or (b) *secondary sources* or documentation produced by such people. Both sources must be accessible. More specifically, and in the order in which you normally consult the sources:

- *Documentary Sources*: I list the secondary sources first because this is where you start. The reason is practical. It is discourteous to go to a primary human source before you have reviewed the written and audiovisual materials and documents that he or she or they produced. You chose documentation that promises to be outcome rich such as, official publications, results of surveys, annual reports, minutes of meetings, emails, reports of field visits, recorded speeches, photographs and videos, and podcasts about the intervention and its results.

- *Human Sources—People Internal or Sometimes External:* The primary human sources you want to engage are those that have firsthand knowledge and experience of the outcome and how the intervention influenced it. The people responsible for the intervention's activities that aim to influence outcomes are generally the most knowledgeable about what changes have been achieved and how. In addition, they will have a vested interest—and thus are motivated—to share what they know and subject it to public scrutiny. Nonetheless, you go to anyone who meets the criteria of knowledge and availability.

Although usually in the course of a harvest some sources do not pan out and others emerge, in the design step you strive to identify the documentation and internal people you will use as secondary and primary sources. The reason is practical: to estimate the cost in time and human and financial resources of an Outcome Harvest, you need to know, tentatively at least, the sources for the data required to answer the harvest questions.

This discussion should also address any issues of *confidentiality* with the information you receive from primary and secondary sources. That is, to what extent is it necessary or desirable for the harvester to take measures to protect the identity of a source of information or actors and factors about which you obtain information. Furthermore, are there to be any restrictions on public use of the identities of certain sources or types of information? Or could there be negative consequences for a source if a particular substantiator is used to verify or deepen the understanding of an outcome? As explained in the first chapter, in Outcome Harvesting we accept a responsibility for propriety: we ensure that Outcome Harvesting is "conducted legally, ethically, and with due regard for the welfare of those involved in the process, as well as those affected by its results" (American Evaluation Association, n.d.). Commonly summarized as "do no harm" to human beings, propriety also applies to the projects, programs, and organizations involved. In highly politicized development and social change, there may be information that must be kept secret or private.[2] For example, in advocacy and campaigning work, making public the specific ways and means by which an intervention influenced individual outcomes could endanger or compromise future work, as well as people's lives. If that is the case with regard to documentation, you want to address the implications and agree how it will be managed. In principle, we want to support transparency, but when necessary we accommodate confidentiality realizing, in Bob Williams's words, "in evaluation you always will break some eggs because there will be winners and losers revealed by the findings" (Williams, personal communication, March 19, 2018).

Requirements of Time, Human, and Financial Resources

The last piece for designing an Outcome Harvest is to agree on the practicalities of the harvest plan. The timing of an Outcome Harvest depends on intended uses. For example, if the purpose is monitoring and learning from outcomes as in a developmental or a formative evaluation, the right moments to harvest outcomes will be when the findings are necessary to ensure the intervention is heading in the right direction. If the certainty is high that doing A will result in B, the harvest can be timed to coincide with when the first results are expected. Conversely, if much uncertainty exists about the results that the intervention will achieve, the harvest should be scheduled as soon as possible to determine the outcomes that are actually being achieved in as real time as possible.

I emphasize that this is a calculation of *estimated* resources, even for steps 1, 2, and 3, and certainly for the subsequent steps. The reason is that Outcome Harvesting is customized in an iterative process in which decisions are made and revisited as the process unfolds and results emerge. Naturally there is a wide range of efficiency and productivity amongst individual harvesters. Although my time estimates are based on working with over three dozen co-harvesters new to Outcome Harvesting, they should be used cautiously, always emphasizing they are estimates.

Step 1. Design the Outcome Harvest

Negotiating and forging a common understanding of the design elements in the harvest plan depends not solely on the number of users and the number of harvesters but their individual efficiency. Based on my experience, on average, working with one primary intended user will require on average 3 days to make design decisions and another 2–3 days of clock time to design and pilot the harvesting instruments.

If the user and I do not know each other personally, I arrange for us to meet face-to-face in this moment. Preparatory work can be done virtually but sitting together here is important. For example, we devote a morning to discussing a draft design. I spend the afternoon and the next morning producing examples. We meet the second day in the afternoon to agree on the harvest plan.

If there are more users and harvesters, however, the time will increase but not necessarily linearly: two harvesters and two users will require less than

TABLE 2.3 Step 1

Step 1. Design the Outcome Harvest	Number of Users	Time per User	Number of Harvesters	Estimated time per Harvester
Final decisions on harvest users, uses, questions, data, sources and resources	2	1 day	1	3 days
Harvest plan and format		0.5 day		2.5 days

twice as much time to agree on a harvest plan. In the case of our exemplar, there are two primary users: one representative of the management team and one of the program coordinators who work with me as the sole harvester. For example, if I and a co-harvester (who is new to Outcome Harvesting) work with four users, we will need an estimated 8–9 days to reach agreement on the plan, not 11. The calendar time naturally depends on time commitments, but a plan can be done in one go or stretch over weeks (see Table 2.3).

Step 2. Review Documentation and Draft Potential Outcome Statements

The purpose of this step is to review all existing secondary sources where outcome data may already be found. I ask my users to carefully select documents for their potential outcome data richness—typically, annual reports but not annual plans. When they do so, the average time my co-harvesters who are new to Outcome Harvesting and I require for reviewing, identifying, and extracting outcomes from documents is five pages per hour. This depends on their knowledge and experience with evaluation and on the quality of the documentation. In our exemplar, we have 200 pages of documentation to review and from which to extract outcomes. I am working alone and so my calculation is 200 pages/7 pages per hour/8 = 3.6 days. In addition, as in all the Outcome Harvesting steps, users will have to be consulted when decisions must be made such as about additional or different documentation; I estimate half a day (see Table 2.4).

This calculation of clock time required is intimately related to the next step.

TABLE 2.4 Step 2

Step 2. Review Documentation and Draft Potential Outcome Statements	Number of Pages	Time per User	Number of Pages per Day	Estimated time per Harvester
Desk work with 200 pages of documentation	200	0.5	56	3.5

Step 3. Engage With Human Sources

This step is basically one of the harvester facilitating communication and coaching the primary sources of information to generate outcome statements. As suggested above, a virtual harvest assumes that all the human sources of information have email access and are comfortable expressing themselves in writing. How much clock time does it take a primary source to review the potential outcomes and propose additional ones? This varies considerably from person to person. My rule of thumb is also 1 hour per outcome for each human source of information to answer questions about the potential outcomes, provide additional information on some, and identify and formulate additional outcomes. The calculation is based on outcome statements with 1–2 sentence descriptions of the outcome, its significance and the intervention's contribution. If you add more detail or more dimensions, naturally the time required increases. For example, often the information on outcomes achieved in a project is spread within a team. Then the human source needs to find a way to consult with his or her team to identify all outcomes.

Since, as a harvester, I work with each person to facilitate her or his crafting of the intervention's outcomes, I alert them that I will require several hours of their clock time over a calendar time of a couple of weeks, for us to go back and forth crafting their outcome statements.

If fewer outcomes are found in documents (Step 2) and more are identified by sources of information (Step 3), or vice-versa, the amount of days required for each step will vary but the total should remain more or less the same. Continuing with our exemplar, and assuming 24 internal sources and five outcomes average per source, we will have approximately 120 outcome statements (see Table 2.5).

In sum, success in Step 3 depends on two factors. One is that the people providing information are knowledgeable and motivated to share what they know and have time available to do so. The second is the harvesters' ability to supportively but rigorously craft outcomes with them.

TABLE 2.5 Step 3

Step 3. Engage With Internal Sources	Time Sources	Number	Estimated time per Evaluator
Email communication or interviews, excluding travel time	5 hours each	1	15 days

Step 4. Substantiation

In the fourth step, the harvester consults with knowledgeable, independent human sources about the veracity of the outcome statements. The goal of this step is to have a whole set of outcomes—in this case, an estimated 120 outcomes—that are credible enough findings to meet the users' needs. At the moment of design, I recommend you do not attempt to decide what will be done for substantiation because of the considerable uncertainty about what outcomes you will harvest. The decision is difficult, if not impossible, until you actually have the outcomes in hand. So, for this step, as for Steps 5 and 6, the estimated clock time at the moment of designing the harvest will be very tentative.

Nonetheless, at this design phase users understandably want to have an idea of the clock time and calendar time implications. The first challenge is deciding how many and which outcomes to substantiate. This requires that the users look at the outcomes and consider what substantiation is required to make them all credible enough for their uses. The evaluator supports them in making this decision. For our exemplar of a projected 120 outcomes, I would estimate 8 hours for users and evaluators alike. My rule of thumb is to estimate for the evaluator a half hour per outcome actually substantiated. In our exemplar, the users believe we should plan on substantiating 20% of the outcomes. Those 24 outcomes would require 12 hours of an evaluator's time.

Step 5. Analyze and Interpret the Outcomes

In this step, when there are more than 30–40 outcomes, I recommend you classify the outcome statements. This is in order to be able to group and cluster them, so they serve as manageable evidence as the harvester interprets them in answering the prime Outcome Harvesting questions. In this process, *classifying* outcomes is a function of the number of outcomes and the number of classifications. It takes one person 1 day (8 hours) to classify 140 outcomes with 10 classification categories. When there are two evaluators, time is not saved, and so it would take them the same time multiplied by two, of course.

Entry of outcome information into a database is based on 20 outcomes per hour. The number of evaluators does not matter because it is a one-person task. Estimating the time for interpreting the data to answer the harvest questions and *write a report* is more complicated because it depends on how many evaluators will write it, their ability and speed in writing, as well as number of questions, number of outcomes, and how much detail is required. The rule of thumb estimate I use is that one question requires on average 2 days for one evaluator to answer with 60 outcomes as evidence. Plus, general writing and preparation of the report on average takes an additional 2 days per evaluator.

It is not uncommon for the harvest questions to be renegotiated with the primary intended users after they have seen the outcomes. This may also involve them in agreeing the most useful classification categories. And I always ask them to read a draft to correct factual errors and identify unintelligible text. The amount of clock time to estimate at the design step is also, at best, an educated guess. This is serious business, however. On the one hand, you want the findings to be useful, and answering no longer relevant questions is not useful. On the other hand, users and harvesters have to be sensitive to the danger of moving the goalposts once the ball has been kicked. This issue is especially germane when Outcome Harvesting is used in independent evaluations.

Step 6. Support Use of Findings

The purpose of this step is for the harvester to accompany the users as they make decisions and take action based on the results of the Outcome Harvest. Calculating the clock and calendar times required is even more difficult for this support of use. In our exemplar I estimate use will be supported through a 4-hour workshop, which requires 2 hours of preparation for each hour of workshop. If the organization needs the evaluator to produce findings in more accessible formats, such as a PowerPoint or briefing document, this time also has to be calculated. Does it need a professional layout that requires hiring a graphic artist? Do the terms of reference include the evaluator writing blogs or doing presentations to secondary audiences? You must estimate the time to perform such additional tasks.

Estimating Resources Required

As you can see, the major resources required by an Outcome Harvest are people and time. The financial resources required flow from the estimates of the clock time required of the people involved and the calendar time that will be necessary to traverse the six steps. How they do the harvest will, of course, determine other financial resources required. In Table 2.6, I present a summary of the estimated clock time required for our exemplar.

TABLE 2.6 Exemplar of Estimated Clock Times at Design Step, in Days

Step	Users Time in Days	Evaluator's Time in Days
Step 1. Design of the Outcome Harvest, two primary intended users, one evaluator	1.5	5.5
Step 2. Draft potential outcome statements from 200 pages of secondary sources	0.5	3.0
Step 3. Engage with six internal sources to harvest final outcomes	0.5	15.0
Step 4. Substantiation of 20% of 120 outcomes	1.0	2.5
Step 5. Analyze and interpret the 120 outcomes to answer three harvest questions	1.0	7.0
Step 6. Support use of harvest findings for 2 + 5 primary users	0.5	1.5
Total Estimated Time	**5.0**	**34.5**

Design Summary

I have found that the key issues in Outcome Harvesting are not methodological but professional: at the end of the day, quality in evaluation depends on rigorous evaluative thinking and not on fidelity to a method. By "evaluative thinking" I mean:

> Evaluative thinking is critical thinking applied in the context of evaluation, motivated by an attitude of inquisitiveness and a belief in the value of evidence, that involves identifying assumptions, posing thoughtful questions, pursuing deeper understanding through reflection and perspective taking, and informing decisions in preparation for action. (Buckley, Archibald, Hargraves, & Trochim, 2015)

In fact, rigorous evaluative thinking is preferable to methodological rigor because it avoids rigor mortis: "Rigid designs rigidly implemented, then rigidly analyzed through standardized, rigidly prescribed operating procedures, and judged hierarchically by standardized, rigid criteria" (Patton, McKegg, & Wehipeihana, 2015, p. 297).

The rigorous evaluative thinking in Outcome Harvesting begins as you write the terms of reference and continues through this design step and on to the other five. Outcome Harvesting is fundamentally inductive: you develop the design by working with primary intended users to clarify their uses and their priority "need to knows" that the outcome harvest should give them. The agreement on information and sources will feedback into revising the users, their uses and the harvest questions. There will be similar adjustments as estimated clock and calendar time, human and financial resources become clear. This participation of primary intended users is indispensable for getting the design step right and setting up a viable M&E system or carrying out a developmental, formative, or summative evaluation.

Notes

1. Synonymous with scope of work, call for proposals or request for applications.
2. In Outcome Harvesting I have not had to follow standard "informed consent" procedures and approvals. In the few cases where the issue arose, the decision was that it was unnecessary because the human sources were not reporting about themselves but about what they know of the intervention's influence on third parties.

References

American Evaluation Association Guiding Principles for Evaluators: Revisions Reflected Herein Ratified by the AEA Membership, July 2004. Retrieved from American Evaluation Association website: https://www.eval.org/p/cm/ld/fid=51

Buckley, J., Archibald, T., Hargraves, M., & Trochim, W. M. (2015). Defining and teaching evaluative thinking: Insights from research on critical thinking. *American Journal of Evaluation, 36*(3), 375–388. Thousand Oaks, CA: SAGE. Retrieved from http://tinyurl.com/hxh8la6

Patton, M. Q. (2012). *Essentials of utilization-focused evaluation.* Thousand Oaks, CA: SAGE.

Patton, M. Q. (2015). *Qualitative research and evaluation methods* (4th ed.). Thousand Oaks, CA: SAGE.

Patton, M. Q., McKegg, K., & Wehipeihana, N. (Eds.). (2015). *Developmental evaluation exemplars: principles in practice.* New York, NY: Guilford.

Preskill, H., & Jones, N. (2009). *A practical guide for engaging stakeholders in developing evaluation questions.* Princeton, NJ: Robert Wood Johnson Foundation. Retrieved from http://rwjf.ws/2s1pLDk

Ramírez, R., & Brodhead, D. P. (2013). *Utilization focused evaluation: A primer for evaluators.* Penang, Malaysia: Southbound, pp. 43–53. Retrieved from http://bit.ly/2s8NWz4

Wilson-Grau, R., & Steele, D. (2016). *Belief in the supernatural and the evaluation of faith-based peacebuilding.* New York, NY: The Peacebuilding Evaluation Consortium. Retrieved from https://bit.ly/2MmzK46

3

Review Documentation and Draft Potential *Outcome Statements*

In this chapter I will explain how you prepare to collect data in Outcome Harvesting and then how to extract potential outcome statements from documentation. Please keep in mind that reviewing documentation is your

Applicability of Key Principles to Step 2	
Process principles—Chapter 8	**Content principles—Chapter 9**
** I. Facilitate usefulness throughout the evaluation	***** VI. Harvest social change outcomes
** III. Nurture appropriate participation	***** VII. Formulate an outcome as an observable change
** II. Coach primary sources to formulate outcome statements	*** VIII. Establish plausible influence of the intervention
*** IV. Strive for less because it will be more useful	**** IX. Ensure credible-enough outcomes
*** V. Learn Outcome Harvesting experientially	
Legend of Ricardo's rubrics	
***** High: I always apply this principle; **** Considerable: I almost always apply it; *** Moderate: I usually apply it ** Occasional: I apply it sometimes but with quite a few exceptions; * Low: I rarely apply the principle in this step	

initial data-gathering step and is intimately related to the next step, engaging with human sources, that I explain in the next chapter.

Organizing the Collection of Data

Once the design is agreed, the next task is to work with the primary intended users to discuss the instruments and sources needed to collect the targeted harvest data. In the design step, you laid the groundwork; you know what information you need and where you can obtain it. Before setting off to do so, however, you have to agree with your users on the Outcome Harvesting instrument you will use. An important piece of the process is clarifying the concepts in the prime evaluation questions, spelling out ambiguous terms, and making sure you understand their meaning for your users. You may have accomplished this during the design step. If not, you want to do it here. For instance, consider this evaluation question for our exemplar of a national rights-based organization dedicated to women's empowerment in order to improve their lives:

> **III:** *In the light of rights-based empowerment of women, what is the relative importance of the outcomes we have influenced?*

What is understood for "rights-based" and "women's empowerment"? The users and the evaluators must understand the same thing before that question can be used as a guide for collecting data with which to answer it. The two terms require definitions in order to be clear about what outcomes have to be harvested (and which not). The discussion goes something like this:

> I ask, "What is your understanding of 'rights-based empowerment of women'?"
>
> They reply, "Rights-based empowerment is about changing the power relations between human rights duty bearers and human rights holders."
>
> "OK," I say, "but what specifically do you mean by 'changing power relations' and concretely what power and between whom?"
>
> "We are referring to ensuring that women, as rights holders, are able to control their lives for their personal benefit as well as for their families, community, and society in order to become everything they dream of being at home and in the workplace. This requires that State institutions, as duty bearers, fulfill their obligation to create an environment in which women can exercise their human rights. Neither is currently the case."
>
> "I understand. But can you be more specific about what it is that you want women and State institutions to change?"

"We work to support women to build their capacity to make decisions and informed choices, hand in hand with holding State agencies responsible for fulfilling their duty to create an environment that provides women with equal access to quality educational and health services and income generating opportunities, all free from discrimination and violence."

I clarify, "I understand income generating opportunities, discrimination, and violence."

I go on to ask, however, "When you say 'educational and health services,' to what concretely are you referring?"

"For us, the human right to education means quality primary and secondary education for girls between six and 18 years of age. We also advocate for the right of adult women 18 years and older to vocational education and income generating activities, whether informal or formal employment. By 'health services' we refer to the means for girls and women to live a state of complete physical, mental, and social well-being and not merely the absence of disease or infirmity or just reproductive health."

I summarize, "Let me see if I understand correctly. By 'rights-based empowerment of women' you mean that girls will be able to freely access primary, secondary, and vocational education and women can access vocational education that enables them to engage in income generating activities, all in good health and free from discrimination. This will all be a result of State agencies fulfilling their obligations to ensure all women of any age have access to education, health care, and dignified work. Did I understand correctly?"

I conclude by explaining, "The reason why we need to have a common understanding is that the data we collect has to serve as verifiable evidence of the extent to which you have contributed to 'rights-based empowerment of women' as you, and now I, understand it."

Once there is clarity about what information is required to usefully answer the prime harvesting questions, you can construct the harvesting instrument. I have found that it is more effective to make the instrument self-explanatory than rely on separate instructions on how to use it. Also, for similarly practical reasons, I have found that an instrument in a Word table with rows and columns is handier than a narrative format in which one outcome statement follows another. A Word table has the additional advantage that you can more readily cut and paste into an Excel database (see Chapter 6, Step 5). In our exemplar, the instructions fit in less than one page (Figure 3.1) and the questionnaire on another (Figure 3.2).

> **Instructions**
>
> This form is for identifying and formulating outcomes initially from documentation and subsequently from knowledgeable people such as the intervention's field staff. We are aiming for an average of 8 outcomes from each one of the three projects per region or a total of 120 outcomes in the last fiscal year.
>
> We seek to identify the changes in societal actors to which the intervention has contributed in some way. Outcomes describe what girls and women as rights holders or state agencies as duty bearers did or are doing differently. The change can be *directly* or *indirectly* influenced by the intervention's activities and outputs. Outcomes thus are different than outputs:
>
> | OUTCOMES | OUTPUTS |
> |---|---|
> | Demonstrated changes in women's or state agencies' behaviors—relationships, activities, actions, policies or practices—to which the intervention has contributed. The intervention only *influences* outcomes through its activities and outputs. | Processes, goods or services produced by the intervention's service delivery, capacity-building and advocacy activities. The intervention *controls* its outputs and activities. |
>
> Only those changes that represent progress towards rights-based empowerment of women count as outcomes. By this we mean changes so that girls will be able to freely access primary, secondary and vocational education and women obtain vocational education and engage in income generating activities, both in good health and free from discrimination, as a result of State agencies fulfilling their obligations to ensure all women of any age have access to education, health care and dignified work.
>
> To count as an outcome, the change has to meet these three criteria:
>
>   a) Be a demonstrated, verifiable change in behavior.
>   b) Address issues related to rights-based empowerment of women.
>   c) Be influenced by the intervention's activities and outputs.
>
> Please note that there can also be negative outcomes that the intervention did not intend to influence. That is, if in spite of the intervention's best intentions, the intervention has influenced anyone to take action that undercuts, weakens, impairs or otherwise undermines rights-based empowerment of women, they should be formulated too.
>
> Page 1 of 2

Figure 3.1 Exemplar of instructions for an Outcome Harvesting instrument.

Extracting Outcome Data From Documentation

With an agreed harvesting instrument in hand, you are ready to begin collecting data.

You begin with secondary sources, assuming there are potentially outcome-rich documents to search through. I find it is really important not to skip this step. Outcome Harvesting is demanding, and if you go directly to your human sources (in Step 3) without obtaining information they have already made available in documents, you run the risk of undermining your

Review Documentation and Draft Potential Outcome Statements

Name of the person, position and project/region:
Date:

Positive Outcomes	Significance of the Outcomes	Contribution of the Outcomes	Sources
In 1–2 sentences please specify *when* did *who* do *what*, and *where*, that enhances rights-based empowerment of women.	In another 1–2 sentences, please describe *why* the outcome is important for the rights-based empowerment of women.	Again, briefly describe *how* and *when* your intervention influenced the outcome. What did you do that directly or indirectly, in a small to large way, intentionally or not contributed to the change?	Name of person or document who provided the information and date they did so.
1.			
2.			
3.			

<<ADD ROWS IF NECESSARY>>

Negative Outcomes	Significance of the Outcomes	Contribution of the Outcomes	Sources
In 1–2 sentences please specify *when* did *who* do *what*, and *where*, that undermines rights-based empowerment of women.	In another 1–2 sentences, please describe *why* the outcome undermines the rights-based empowerment of women.	Again, briefly describe *how* and *when* your intervention influenced the outcome. What did you do that directly or indirectly, in a small to large way, contributed to the change?	Name of person or document who provided the information and date they did so.
1.			
2.			
3.			

<<ADD ROWS IF NECESSARY>>

Page 2 of 2

Figure 3.2 Exemplar of an Outcome Harvesting instrument.

coaching relationship. Ask the people responsible for the intervention, who will generally be amongst the users, to select the documents, ideally electronic, they have on file that they believe will indicate changes in societal actors that they have influenced—monitoring data, evaluation reports, periodic field reports, minutes of meetings, and so forth. You have to make a judgment about which documents to tackle first; as a general rule, I start with those that are potentially richer in information about outcomes actually achieved. If these documents do not exist, then certainly skip this step.

I begin by identifying outcomes, followed by the sources, the contribution, and the significance (Figure 3.3), I also start in the outcome column because if you do not have outcomes, you cannot have contribution or significance. Cite the source for each outcome, including the page number, to be able to come back and look for information about the contribution and significance of the outcome. If I have monthly and annual reports to be reviewed, I begin with the annual report for the year. This will generally have the most important outcome data. When I have identified and extracted the available data from the whole annual report on potential outcomes, noting of course their sources, I will go back and complete the contribution and then the significance all before searching in the monthly reports for outcomes and additional necessary detail for those I gleaned from the annual report. For instance, often the annual report will not have specific dates but the monthly report will.

The most promising reports are chock-full of activities and outputs, which potentially have influenced outcomes. If the documents are electronic, obviously search first for *outcome* but also *output* and *impact* because these terms may be used differently than as defined in Outcome Harvesting. Consider also searching for surrogate and related words that may lead you to indications of the changes in societal actors. Outcomes come in many guises: the terms include achievement, after effect, aim, by-product, conclusion, *consequence, effect,* end, finding, goal, fruit, objective, *product,* purpose,

1	4	3	2
Outcome	Significance	Contribution	Sources

Figure 3.3 Order for formulating outcome statements.

ramification, repercussion, *result*, and target. (I highlight in italics the ones that have proven most useful to my co-evaluators and me as we search for outcomes as defined in Outcome Harvesting.)

Whatever it is called, an outcome is a behavioral change in a societal actor influenced by an intervention. In Outcome Harvesting there are three key characteristics of an outcome. *Behavioral change* can consist of individual actions or activities but also of changes in relationships, policies, or practices. Furthermore, behavioral change is an observable change.

Societal actors are human individuals and collectives (groups, communities), but also organizations (from civil society organizations to government agencies or businesses), and institutions such as the judicial system or the Roman Catholic Church. The change in a societal actor must be influenced by the intervention, however partial, indirect, or unintentional it may be.

Influence is understood broadly: beyond the span of control of an intervention—from inspiring and encouraging, to facilitating and supporting, to persuading or pressuring a societal actor to change. For example, the documentation you review may include results of allies, but these would not count as outcomes unless the intervention also influenced them. Another common mistake is to identify what the intervention did, especially when it is impressive, as an outcome. It certainly may be an important result, but just not an outcome. It is an activity or output that may or may not contribute to an outcome. A practical way to shift through the maze of results is to look first for the subject or the protagonist of the change. If it is the intervention, it is not an outcome. If it is somebody influenced by the intervention, it may be.

A neat trick when crafting outcomes is to write in the active voice with the protagonist as the subject of the sentence. This enables you, and eventually the reader, to immediately understand who changed their behavior. For example:

Passive: In July 2016, half of the 1,200 women applicants in the Northern District, received ration cards.
Active: In July 2016, the block development officer of the Northern District approved digital ration cards for half of the 1,200 single women applicants.

Once you have identified data in a document about what appears to you to be an outcome, I have a suggestion that comes from 10 years as a print journalist writing to meet deadlines: Draft the descriptions as if they are final descriptions; get it as close to SMART as you know how, the first

Outcome	Significance	Contribution	Sources
1. In 2016, girls in the slums increased their enrollment in post-secondary training programs in trades and crafts.			2016 annual report, page 19

Figure 3.4 Exemplar potential outcome and source.

time. Do not postpone until later, working through partial or vague text if you can avoid it. The formulation of the quantitative and qualitative aspects of outcomes (and of the activities and outputs that contributed to them), should be specific and concrete so that third parties without the contextual knowledge will be able to appreciate and eventually to verify what has been achieved. That is the ideal, but as you see exemplified in Figure 3.4, you will generally not find all the information in documentation.

After you draft each outcome, move over to the Sources column and fill it in. Naturally, you have agreed what data is required for your sources. At a minimum, you want to identify the document, its date and page number(s). But it may be that documentation for each outcome can serve to obviate the need for external verification. So as with each element of the harvesting instrument, agree with your user what information is required in this column. Do you need documentary evidence or just the name of the person who cited the document? Do you need all the human sources of information or only the one who cites the others? Only collect source information that is going to be useful.

Looking for actually achieved, albeit potential, outcomes without reference to predefined objectives or results or even to intended or actual activities in principle helps you avoid confirmation or expectation bias. You minimize consciously searching for outcome information that corresponds with what was planned or intended. Just as only looking for predefined outcomes will lead you to focus on them and miss unexpected outcomes, so too would beginning with what the intervention did to see who it has influenced to change may mislead you to focus on expected changes in targeted actors. The danger, and it is a big one, is that the greater the uncertainty the intervention faced or faces, the higher the probability that there will be unexpected outcomes, and so you risk not identifying unintended outcomes, negative outcomes and outcomes influenced by the interventions' other activities and outputs.

I say "helps avoid" and "minimizes" because this is not foolproof. You extract outcomes from outcome-rich documents that are generally reporting against planned objectives and activities. In addition, when you engage with program staff as primary sources in the next step, they will naturally think of what they have achieved through their planned and implemented activities. So your coaching role will be to help them to think outside of their preplanned boxes.

Continue with the contribution. Remember that the contribution has to describe how the intervention influenced the societal actor to change. Therefore you want to focus on describing specifically what the intervention did, and when and where that influenced the societal actor who is the subject of the outcome. This is not easy in reports from the field that understandably highlight, and often explain in considerable depth, what the intervention did. Only extract from the documentation descriptions the activities and outputs that you believe are related to how the intervention contributed to a specific change in another societal actor. This can be challenging. The subjects of outcomes can be societal actors that the intervention influenced directly or indirectly. Also, you are looking for evidence of a plausible relationship, the logical link between what the intervention did and the outcome it influenced. Give as much detail as necessary so the contribution is clear.

In sum, the contribution describes who in the intervention did what that wholly but probably partially, directly or indirectly, intentionally or unexpectedly contributed to the change in the societal actor. Now in Figure 3.5 you see exemplified even scantier information about the contribution. Intriguingly, I usually find copious data about activities and outputs in intervention reports but not often are they clearly linked to a specific outcome.

Significance is different from the other parts of an outcome statement. The outcome, contribution and source are about things that the sources of information *know*, or think they know, have happened; they are tangible. In contrast, the significance is about what the sources *believe* about the

Outcome	Significance	Contribution	Sources
1. In 2016, girls in the slums increased their enrollment in post-secondary training programs in trades and crafts.	Their initiative demonstrates that girls are not satisfied with dropping out of high school or aspiring to unskilled employment.	We provide vocational counseling services for youth.	2016 annual report, page 19

Figure 3.5 Exemplar of a complete *potential* outcome statement.

present or future. Nonetheless, just as the description of the contribution has to have a plausible cause–effect relationship with the outcome, the significance has to be believable. So strive to identify facts and evidence that support the opinions and points of view, avoiding speculation, guesses, and rumor. For example, any actual or projected indicators of the impact of the outcome in the conditions of people's lives or in the state of the environment, certainly belongs in the description of significance. Also note that the significance can lie in the process rather than in the direct change. For example, if a committee of a national parliament for the first time puts on its agenda an issue that you advocated for, the significance is that it is a process result. It is now higher on the agenda and follow-up interventions can be planned. Lastly, significance is in the eyes of the beholder and requires that you weigh and value the authority of the source.

Practical Considerations

Rarely will you find data for complete outcome formulations, but you should be able to identify partial information for what are potential outcomes—potential because you will have to check with the internal informants whether what you identified as outcomes is correct. In addition, sometimes in the documentation review your sources will be incomplete and sometimes may not contain any potential outcomes. You are aiming at the very least to come up with one potential, as-SMART-as-possible (Chapter 1, Figure 1.5) outcome that can serve as a real-life example for the next step of engaging primary sources of information.

Incidentally, if there is no documentation to review, or I cannot find even one outcome in a document, I will engage with a primary source and formulate one outcome that I then use as an example. I insert it in a row before the blank rows of outcomes in the Outcome Harvesting Instrument (Figure 3.2). I find that using a real example is more effective than a generic example that is not recognizable to my primary sources. Producing a few samples in the design step (previous chapter) is also a good exercise to introduce you to the challenges of crafting outcome statements.

Lastly, here are five practical tips for identifying and formulating potential outcomes:

1. When you have to read between the lines to draft the pieces, write your descriptions to the extent possible using the terminology of the source and not your own. You are facilitating a search for the source of information's knowledge about what happened and how.

2. Quantify size (large or small) and amounts (a lot or a little) as much as possible: cite numbers of actors, events, occurrences, or ranges of numbers. Consider the difference between "a number of people voted for the first time" and "5–10 people voted for the first time." The latter is preferable because it is more specific. Also use what is called "quasi-quantification." When numbers are not available, use measures such as *all, some, frequently, few, rarely, often, many*: "a few people voted for the first time."
3. Be as specific as possible about dates—days and months, as well as the years. This holds for when the outcome occurred and when the activities and outputs that influenced the outcome took place, which logically must *predate* the outcome. It may sound obvious, but reports sometimes explain what the intervention did as a consequence of outcomes and not how it contributed.
4. Outcome Harvesting does not seek to attribute outcomes to the intervention's actions because rarely, if ever, does a social change or development outcome have a sole cause. The task is to describe a plausible relationship, a logical link between what the intervention did and the outcome, hence a contribution rather than an attribution.
5. Spell out acronyms the first time they occur *in each cell* (i.e., outcome, significance, contribution). The reason is that once the outcomes are in a database, when filtered according to different classifications, they will be separated from each other but also broken up as, for example, when outcomes or contributions are clustered together.

In Summary

In Outcome Harvesting the person who collects data from secondary sources in Step 2 and from primary sources in Step 3 is fulfilling a hands-on facilitation role. In other M&E or evaluation approaches, the organization of the data collection would be the lonely task of the evaluator. As a harvester, you engage and facilitate understanding between users, between co-harvesters if you have them, and yourself even as you do the work of identifying and formulating outcomes in documentation. You must be crystal clear that you are managing a rigorous process of flushing out outcomes that the representatives of the intervention will affirm they have achieved and how. The outcomes are theirs, not yours.

Similarly, when you apply the instrument to extract outcome data from documentation, you must resist falling into the evaluator mindset in which you make judgments about the data in the secondary sources you are working with in regard to merit, worth, or significance of what the intervention did or did not do, or did or did not achieve. Those judgments will come when you make sense of the outcomes to answer the prime evaluation questions in Step 5—analysis and interpretation. In this second step you also are not making judgments about the quality of the reporting or the intervention's management of information. Instead, you are actively facilitating a search for accurate information about what the intervention considers it achieved and how. In the next step, you engage directly with human sources of information, confident you have harvested all you can from what they have already reported.

4

Engage With Human Sources to Formulate Outcome Statements

As a harvester you now have potential outcome statements from your Step 2 extraction of outcome data from documentation using the Outcome Harvesting format (first and second rows in Figure 4.1). In our

Applicability of Key Principles to Step 3

Process principles—Chapter 8
- *** I. Facilitate usefulness throughout the evaluation
- ***** III. Nurture appropriate participation
- ***** II. Coach primary sources to formulate outcome statements
- ***** IV. Strive for less because it will be more useful
- ***** V. Learn Outcome Harvesting experientially

Content principles—Chapter 9
- ***** VI. Harvest social change outcomes
- ***** VII. Formulate an outcome as an observable change
- ***** VIII. Establish plausible influence of the intervention
- ***** IX. Ensure credible-enough outcomes

Legend of Ricardo's rubrics
***** High: I always apply this principle;   **** Considerable: I almost always apply it;   *** Moderate: I usually apply it
** Occasional: I apply it sometimes but with quite a few exceptions;   * Low: I rarely apply the principle in this step

exemplar, the outcome statements describe the available information you found about the outcomes, their significance, the contribution of the intervention, and the sources of this information (row three in Figure 4.1). As you can see, the data found in the documentation rarely is complete. That is, the outcome statement is still not sufficiently SMART to be verifiable. Therefore, in this third Outcome Harvesting step, your first task is to fill in the information gaps and make a decision when and if it is acceptably specific and measurable. The second task is to identify any additional notable outcomes that the intervention influenced and describe them in the same outcome statement format.

You accomplish both tasks by going to human sources with knowledge about what has been achieved and how. These may be the authors of reports that you reviewed in the previous step, or their substitutes, colleagues, allies, or participants in the intervention. The key criteria is that your human sources must have the knowledge and motivation to share what they know. In my experience this tends to be the participants in the intervention closest to the action—the field workers rather than managers; grantees rather than grantmakers.

The guidance in Chapter 1 on facilitation, coaching, and mentoring will help you as a harvester to engage with human sources of information to review the potential outcome statements that you formulated based on documentation. Equally important, however, in this step you also coach them to

Positive Outcomes	Significance of the Outcomes	Contribution of the Outcomes	Sources
In 1–2 sentences please specify *when* did *who* do *what*, and *where*, that enhances rights-based empowerment of women.	In another 1–2 sentences, please describe *why* the outcome is important for the rights-based empowerment of women.	Again, briefly describe *how* and *when* your intervention influenced the outcome. What did you do that directly or indirectly, in a small to large way, intentionally or not contributed to the change?	Name of person or document who provided the information and date they did so.
1. In 2016, girls in the slums increased their enrollment in post-secondary training programs in trades and crafts.	Their initiative demonstrates that girls are not satisfied with dropping out of high school or aspiring to unskilled employment.	We provide vocational counseling services for youth.	2016 annual report, page 19

Figure 4.1 Exemplar Outcome Harvesting instrument and one potential outcome statement.

identify and formulate additional outcomes. These primary sources should be knowledgeable about what the intervention has achieved and how, motivated to share what they know, and have the time available to do so. They may consult with others who are knowledgeable about outcomes to which the intervention has contributed but they "own" the outcome statements.

In the design step (Chapter 2) you will have tentatively identified these people. Nonetheless, based on the results of your documentation review, you may require more or different people. For example, the authors of the documentation in which you found outcome data and for which you require additional information may not have been on your original list or may no longer be available. Or, they may be available but not close enough to the action to identify additional outcomes. The decision who to consult is made with your primary users and this underlines the participatory imperative of Outcome Harvesting.

I will now explain the "ping-pong" process of iteratively engaging with these select human sources to arrive at final outcome statements. Next, I will advise you on how to prepare the scenario for a productive ping-pong exercise. Then, I will take you through the process ping by ping.

Gentle, Rigorous Ping-Ponging

You now facilitate and coach your human sources in filling out the outcome statements in the harvesting form. You pose questions to obtain necessary information for SMART formulations: *specific, measurable* outcomes that have been plausibly *achieved* by the intervention and that are *relevant* to the intervention's goals and occurred in the *time* period covered by the harvest (see Chapter 1, Figure 1.5). This may seem quite straightforward. It is not. On the one hand, you have to cope with cultural differences, political sensitivities, a variety of personal strengths and weaknesses in written communication, and different degrees of willingness to cooperate, all of which can lead to misunderstanding and confusion and frustration, complicated by personal idiosyncrasies. How do you avoid your sources of information becoming angry and uncooperative? You coach them by going back and forth in what I have come to term "gentle but rigorous ping-ponging" to arrive at your source's affirmation, or negation, of their outcome statements in as SMART a formulation as possible.

The purpose is to go back and forth to arrive as fast as possible at mutually agreed outcome statements. Thus, you use the most efficient and effective means—email, telephone, in person interviews. Goele Scheers, a very experienced Belgian Outcome Harvesting consultant and one of the beta readers of this book, emphasizes that this "ping-ponging" is an absolute necessity:

> I have seen quite a few examples where this step was left out. The harvesters send out a questionnaire via Survey Monkey and work with whatever they get back. These are never SMART outcomes. This is an aspect, however, of Outcome Harvesting that takes up the most time but represents a unique added value of the method. It will take some practice and is best done with somebody more experienced the first time. (Scheers, personal correspondence, April 8, 2018)

You are supporting your sources of information in a task that usually is new to them. In the development and policy and social change milieu where Outcome Harvesting has proven to be most useful, people are impassioned about what they do. They are self-directed individuals driven by values; ultimately their allegiance is to a cause and not to an organization that provides them with work and an income. Some do not have the temperament to focus their attention on the micro-details that must be captured in order for the outcome to be verifiable.

To get there you first effectively support your sources in identifying and formulating *their* SMART outcomes. You persuade your sources, through example, that you are *facilitating* a participatory process employing different methodological checks and balances to help them generate solid outcomes. If they and you are successful, they will understand and be committed to the harvest findings. To achieve this, you must set aside your personal opinions and be neutral, for now, about the merit, worth, or significance of the data.

Barbara Klugman, another experienced core Outcome Harvesting practitioner and beta reader exemplifies the coaching role:

> All too often sources will say "this garnered substantial media coverage." Take the initiative to find the media coverage online. If you cannot find it, ask the source to consult people who were there to ask if they can remember which media covered the issue. Your sources may see no value in this exercise, although I find that once they see the power of naming actual news coverage in order to influence their specific audiences, they do see the value.
>
> When you ask "What do you mean by 'we made a big impact at the regional consultation'?", they may not understand your question. You may have to specify: "Do you mean that decision-makers you were hoping to engage with attended your side meeting? Or that they quoted you or from your briefing documents when they spoke in plenary? Or that many other civil society groups joined your protest outside?" Human sources may feel frustrated that they have to make evident what is quite obvious to them. But here too,

the experience will hopefully strengthen the quality of their reporting in future. (Klugman, personal correspondence, April 10, 2018)

You do bring a methodological structure to the engagement: the harvesting tool (see Figures 3.1 and 3.2 in the previous chapter, and Figure 4.1). As you help them fill it in, creating outcome statements, you will have to challenge assumptions about what is and is not an outcome, raise difficult issues about the distinction between results that they control (outputs) and results that they influence (outcomes), and challenge them when what they say they did does not seem to you a plausible contribution to an outcome, or the significance is too vague, or one or another piece of information is not acceptably SMART.

At the same time, you have to be open to what they are trying to say because the outcomes are theirs and they know what is and is not their truth. They may not be able to express themselves adequately in writing, but the outcomes have to be in writing.[1] You have to acknowledge your limitations and be flexible. Donna Mertens summarizes quite nicely that evaluators who facilitate must suspend judgment and listen deeply, have the fortitude to listen to attacks calmly and the courage to challenge the status quo (Catsambas, 2016, p. 26).

There are usually 2–4 pings and pongs to craft the final outcome statements so they are mutually acceptable, depending on primary source's and your ability to communicate: rarely is there more back and forth because the sources tire or have to prioritize other work. So you have to concentrate on the coaching.

Setting Up the Ping-Pong Table So Everyone Wins

How do you start? Users often assume that the process of approaching the human sources begins with a workshop. That may be necessary but only if it will be useful to them and to the ping-ponging. For instance, a kickoff workshop usually will be appropriate if in the design you agreed a process use would be building the capacity of the sources to learn the Outcome Harvesting methodology. This is perhaps the most frequent process use for an Outcome Harvest—to develop the capacity of staff to identify and formulate outcomes, which is common when the organization wants to learn how to monitor outcomes. In fact, the potential to use Outcome Harvesting in M&E, developmental, formative, or summative evaluation as a step towards building capacity to use it in an ongoing M&E system has led some organizations to partially pay for the harvest out of their training budget.

Most of my experience has been international and interregional rather than national or provincial—leading evaluative exercises with primary users, and co-harvesters and primary, human sources of information based in different continents. Nonetheless, I have been involved with a diversity of national evaluations too: in Bangladesh, Belgium, Bosnia, Brazil, Burundi, China, Colombia, Costa Rica, Ethiopia, Ghana, Honduras, India, Iraq, Kenya, Mozambique, Nigeria, Peru, the Philippines, Tanzania, Uganda, Uruguay, the United States, and Zambia. Although our medium of choice has fairly consistently been email and voice-over-internet-protocols (VOIPs) such as Skype (but also other technologies including ZOOM and GoToMeeting), my co-harvesters and I have used in-person interviews, focus groups, and meetings to harvest outcomes. This has been when the sources of information are uncomfortable with the Internet or telephony, which can be the case in many rural communities, or when the language of communication is the person's second or third or fourth language. Grassroots organizations in India, local public health workers in Nigeria, creative artists in Central America, and Arabic-speaking government officials in Iraq all required different communication modalities. Consequently, I am confident in recommending that you consider first person-to-person virtual technologies such as email and VOIP for national as well as regional or international evaluations. It is more efficient and effective for both the people who provide information and for you as a harvester. Of course, there are exceptions.

At the end of the day, what is required from your human sources of information is twofold. First, you want to help them answer questions about what you have extracted from documentation (assuming there is documentation and you found potential outcomes). Second, you coach them in identifying and writing up additional outcomes. You need three things to do this successfully:

1. Management commitment and support communicated to the internal sources, ideally by one or more managers who are amongst the intended users of the harvest.
2. An outcome statement format with clear, straightforward instructions as in Figure 3.1 and Figure 3.2 in the previous chapter.
3. Straight-to-the-point instructions for the harvesting exercise you will coach them through. In Figure 4.2, I present instructions when the mode of communication is by email with an internal source of information.

You will note I recommend you also broach here the issue of *confidentiality*. When engaging with your sources you ask them to go "on the record" with what they know. They must understand that the information will be

> Dear [Name],
>
> I am following up on the communication from [manager] concerning your participation in the evaluation of the outcomes of [name of intervention].
>
> First, I want to emphasize that this is not an evaluation of your performance but of the changes [name of intervention] influenced in the period [dates]. We need your collaboration because you are one of the people most knowledgeable about what has actually been achieved simply because you are the closest to the action.
>
> Second, I have reviewed all the available documentation and identified the intervention's potential outcomes since [date]. The attached instrument contains the results. You can see that before being able to accept the outcomes as final, I need additional information, which I have posed to you in the Word Comment balloons.
>
> Third, I now wish to engage directly with you to obtain a) your answers to the questions I have about the potential outcomes I found in the documentation and b) your draft formulations of additional outcomes during the same period.
>
> Specifically, these are the tasks for which I need your collaboration:
>
> 1) Please answer the questions that are in the Word Comment balloons. If you wish, you can add the information directly into the text using the Word Track Changes tool, which is active.
> 2) As you do so, please correct the descriptions. I tried to use the text I found in the documentation but I may have misunderstood. What I need are your outcomes described as you understand them. You can edit following the instructions that are in the head of each column.
> 3) Equally important, in the additional rows please identify and formulate additional outcomes that I may not have picked up in the documents or that have taken place since your last reports were written. Do not worry if they are not perfect. My role is to work with you to make sure they are understandable to third parties while true to what you know. I will also help you make the descriptions specific and measurable enough so that the data they contain is verifiable. I know you are knowledgeable about [name of intervention]. Nonetheless, if there are other sources you wish to consult, please do so.
>
> The information you provide will be 'on the record' and subject to scrutiny by different stakeholders. If publicly sharing your information is not possible, please let me know and we will find an acceptable way to keep it confidential.
>
> I need your answers within [reasonable deadline] but if that is unreasonable, please let me know. Also, if you have questions, do not hesitate to call or write me.
>
> I will be most grateful for your cooperation and I look forward to ensuring we harvest your most important outcomes.
>
> Sincerely yours,
>
> Ricardo Wilson-Grau

Figure 4.2 Model cover first email to a human source of information internal to the intervention.

subjected to more or less public scrutiny. Therefore, as with documentary evidence, you must clarify right from the beginning if there are any reasons for confidentiality and how secret or private information will be managed.

Nevertheless, as I explained in Chapter 2, a harvester has a responsibility for *propriety*. Outcome Harvesting should be designed and conducted to respect and protect the rights and welfare of human subjects. In your interactions, you respect the human dignity and worth of your sources and indeed of all persons associated with a harvest, so that no one is threatened or hurt. For example, in one evaluation the source was concerned that if they gave the detail required to be SMART they would endanger the safety of a human rights defender they had influenced. In this situation, as harvester, you have to document the outcome without that information, noting it as confidential.

Treat confidentiality judiciously. Take care not to scare your informants into withholding information unnecessarily and undermining the accuracy of the information they provide. Explain that a large portion of the value of outcome statements is the learning that takes place amongst people who will use the information to make decisions or take action. Carefully explore any hesitation or desire for secrecy. There may indeed be, for example, ongoing, politically delicate situations in which the source does not want to reveal the strategy, or even the involvement, of the project, program, or organization. For example, in one evaluation for a major funder that targeted institutions representing powerful vested interests, some of the grantees did not want to reveal publicly their strategy for influencing changes in behavior of individuals in those institutions. Therefore, there was a confidential internal full version of our evaluation report and a public version that did not describe how the grantees' different interventions influenced the outcomes. Nonetheless, I have found that with few exceptions, most sources are glad to have others learn about their work. See Figure 4.3 for wording that we used in an Oxfam Novib evaluation—as a result, less than 2% of the outcomes had to have restricted access.

> As you may know, Oxfam Novib's policy is to make all reports of program evaluations available on their website. They do not have 'internal' and 'external' versions of evaluation reports, which some other agencies have. So the Global Program evaluation will be on their webpage. There can be exceptions to this rule (to be decided by Oxfam Novib directors), but up until now this has not happened.
>
> That said, my co-evaluators and I recognize that because of the advocacy nature of GloPro counterparts' work, in some cases making public the specific ways and means by which counterparts influenced individual outcomes could jeopardize ongoing and future work. Therefore, if for any reason you do not want one or more of your outcomes to be on the public record, please let us know so that we can make the appropriate provisions.
>
> —Wilson-Grau, 2009, p. 6

Figure 4.3 Oxfam Novib GloPro evaluation confidentiality statement.

First Ping—Facilitator Coach as Colleague

The style as well as the content of your first engagement with your sources of information establishes your role of facilitator coach. In his foreword to Ricardo Ramírez's and Dal Brodhead's *Utilization Focused Evaluation: A Primer for Evaluators*, Michael Quinn Patton summarizes the coaching role as:

> ... *walking the talk*. The *talk* (theory, if you will) is all about genuine collaboration, mutual understanding, shared ownership, and engaged learning. The *walk* (practice) is about engaging in evaluation processes to achieve the desired outcome of intended use by intended users. Walking the talk requires knowing the theory and putting it into action through reflective practice. (Ramírez & Brodhead, 2013, p. v, emphasis in original)

In Outcome Harvesting, this requires quite a bit of walking, and so you want to do it as sure-footedly as possible. I begin by first establishing my role as facilitator. Before you send the email, fill in the outcome statement form with the potential outcomes you have been able to extract from documentation (as explained in the previous chapter). The message you want to convey is that you have exhausted the information that you can gather by yourself and now require their assistance. Equally important, you want to demonstrate that you will work with them in a very hands-on way, as a colleague and co-learner whose role is to provide them with methodological support in identifying and formulating their achievements. Give succinct, clear instructions as close as possible to the spot where you expect text to be written.

For example, in the harvesting tool (see previous chapter, Figure 3.2), I place the specific instructions at the head of each column on page 2, rather than on page 1 or in an accompanying email. Similarly, insert the comment balloon at the precise point where you want to make an observation or ask a question. In Figure 4.4, I exemplify how to pose pertinent questions for your sources of information. Craft these questions with care because they are your first interaction with your human sources of information. These are some other lessons I have learned as a facilitator coach to add to the four practical tips in the previous chapter.

My colleagues and I have learned for the *first ping* there are a number of common issues that are reflected in the seven comment balloons.

1. Do not forget that just because instructions are well written, does not mean they will be read. If they are read, you have no assurance that the instructions will be understood. If they are understood does not guarantee the instructions will be followed. This really is

Positive Outcomes	Significance of the Outcomes	Contribution to the Outcomes	Sources
In 1–2 sentences please specify when did who do what, and where, that enhances rights-based empowerment of women.	In another 1–2 sentences, please describe why the outcome is the outcome important for the rights-based empowerment of women?	Again briefly, describe how and when your intervention influenced the outcome. What did you do that directly or indirectly, in a small to large way, intentionally or not contributed to the change?	Name of person or document who provided the information and date they did so.
1. In 2016, girls in the slums increased their enrollment in post-secondary training programs in trades and crafts.	Their initiative demonstrates that girls are not satisfied with dropping out of high school or aspiring to unskilled employment.	We provide vocational counselling services for youth.	2016 annual report, page 19

#1 RW-G, Thursday
Can you please characterize the "girls"? How many? What is their age range? Are they students, workers or what?

#2 RW-G, Thursday
Which slums?

#3 RW-G, Thursday
Can you name the types of vocational training? What is the range?

#4 RW-G, Thursday
Why does their vocational aspirations promise to empower these girls?

#5 RW-G, Thursday
Can you give the day if possible but at least the month and year when this happened?"

#6 RW-G, Thursday
Please describe what these services are intended to accomplish? What is their content?

#7 RW-G, Thursday
Specifically for who do you provide counseling? Where?

Figure 4.4 Exemplar harvesting tool with potential outcome.

the crux of your role as a facilitator coach—helping people identify and formulate outcomes as understood in Outcome Harvesting.

2. Use the comment tool in Word. It is tempting to insert questions or explanations within the text. Even if you distinguish them in some way—in brackets, italics, or with a different font or highlighting, I have found that your sources of information will often not see or answer them. Questions in comment balloons jump out. And you will speed up the process of agreeing on the text.
3. Use questions. Even if you are giving instructions, doing so in the form of questions engages your source in a different way than if you order them to do something. Remember, you are trying to help them clarify what they achieved and how and why it is important to them.
4. Make one observation or comment at a time. It is tempting to ask all your questions in one balloon. The danger is that they will not "see" all the questions, requiring that you go back and ask again.
5. Ask directly and specifically for additional information. You want to avoid your primary source coming back to you to ask, "What do you mean? I do not understand what you want to know?"

The harvester's primary, human sources must be the people who have the knowledge about the intervention, the motivation to share what they know and the time to do so. How you reach out to them depends on what will be most efficient and effective—email, Skype, personal interviews, group discussions, an outcomes writeshop.

Second Ping—Facilitator Coach as Expert

The core task of Outcome Harvesting *coaching* is to support people to identify and formulate rigorously what they consider the intervention achieved in terms of outcomes, why they are significant and how the intervention contributed. Your role is to make sure that the formulations of *their* outcomes are SMART.

Unless you are very lucky, your primary source's "pong" back will still require more information. You may want to go back and look at the answers to your questions and additional outcomes in the light of the five lessons learned with which I ended my explanation of the first ping. You will most likely want to suggest modifications of wording, at least for the additional outcomes.

Getting Clear on What Constitutes an Outcome

One of the biggest and most common challenges is that sources tend to report outputs instead of outcomes. The immediate results of development and social change activities are the products and services they generate. Understandably, people confuse these results that they control through the quality of their work with changes in the behaviors of others they have influenced. In our exemplar (Table 4.1), the intervention's activities are mistakenly suggested as an outcome. In 1a, the reason is that when thinking of their outcomes, people usually think of what they did rather than of what changes those activities influenced in others. The way to address this common error is to invert the process: first, identify the changes in another societal actor's behavior that an intervention influenced and then second, seek to understand what the intervention did that influenced the change. In 1b, you see the correct formulation of the outcome for which 1a is the contribution to the intervention.

The second case, 2a, exemplifies another common error: being aware is not an outcome; what the minister did differently that demonstrated her awareness would be the outcome, as exemplified in 2b.

In the third case, continuing to do something as described in 3a is usually not a change in behavior; the outcome would be a first-time action described in 3b. I rush to add, however, that context matters as demonstrated in the fourth case. The Ministry of Labor continuing to invite student assessments, 4a, becomes an outcome when it is understood that the Ministry of Education was moving in the opposite direction, 4b, and was convinced not to do so by, among others, the intervention.

TABLE 4.1 Exemplars of Mistaken and Potential Outcomes

Mistaken	Potential
1a) In January 2016, for all staff involved in our advocacy for vocational training for women entrepreneurs, we began training in the Centre for Evaluation Innovation's Advocacy Strategy Framework.	1b) On 15 April 2016 three allied civil society organizations—each one experienced in advocacy research, community mobilization or lobbying—signed a memorandum of understanding agreeing to join forces in our campaign for vocational training for women entrepreneurs, beginning with training in the advocacy strategy framework.
2a) The minister of women's affairs was aware that empowering women economically was better than providing them with food stamps.	2b) The minister of women's affairs announced that from now on women's empowerment would be the keystone of the Ministry's policies.
3a) In 2016, for the third year in a row, the Ministry of Labor's intern program for women entrepreneurs invested 15% of its budget in marketing the program.	3b) In 2017, compared to 2016, the Ministry of Labor doubled its budget for marketing its intern program for women entrepreneurs.
4a) In 2017 the Ministry of Labor's intern program for women entrepreneurs continued to invite students to anonymously evaluate the program at the end of each cohort's experience.	4b) In 2017, as the Ministry of Education completed the elimination of student assessments, the Ministry of Labor's intern program for women entrepreneurs continued to invite students to anonymously evaluate the program at the end of each cohort's experience.
4a) In 2017 the Ministry of Labor's intern program for women entrepreneurs increased its enrollment for the third year in a row.	4b) In 2017, after 3 years of declining enrollment, the Ministry of Labor's intern program grew 5%.

How to Formulate Outcomes Correctly

The task in this second ping progresses from facilitating the identification of outcomes in the first ping, to coaching how to formulate them correctly. The sources are clarifying or completing the content of the outcome statements and you help them in crafting the text so that methodologically it is sound. Thus, you need to strike a balance between having them describe the known facts of what they achieved and how, and why they think it is noteworthy, with your responsibility to have SMARTly described outcomes. In Figure 4.5, the first outcome is an example of a potential outcome extracted from documentation. Whether your source provided the information in the bold text or as a separate comment, you edit so that each outcome is SMART. (Note that new text I suggest, or text that I moved, is in **bold**; the ~~deleted~~ text is shown thus.) The outcome statement formulation

Engage With Human Sources to Formulate Outcome Statements ▪ 75

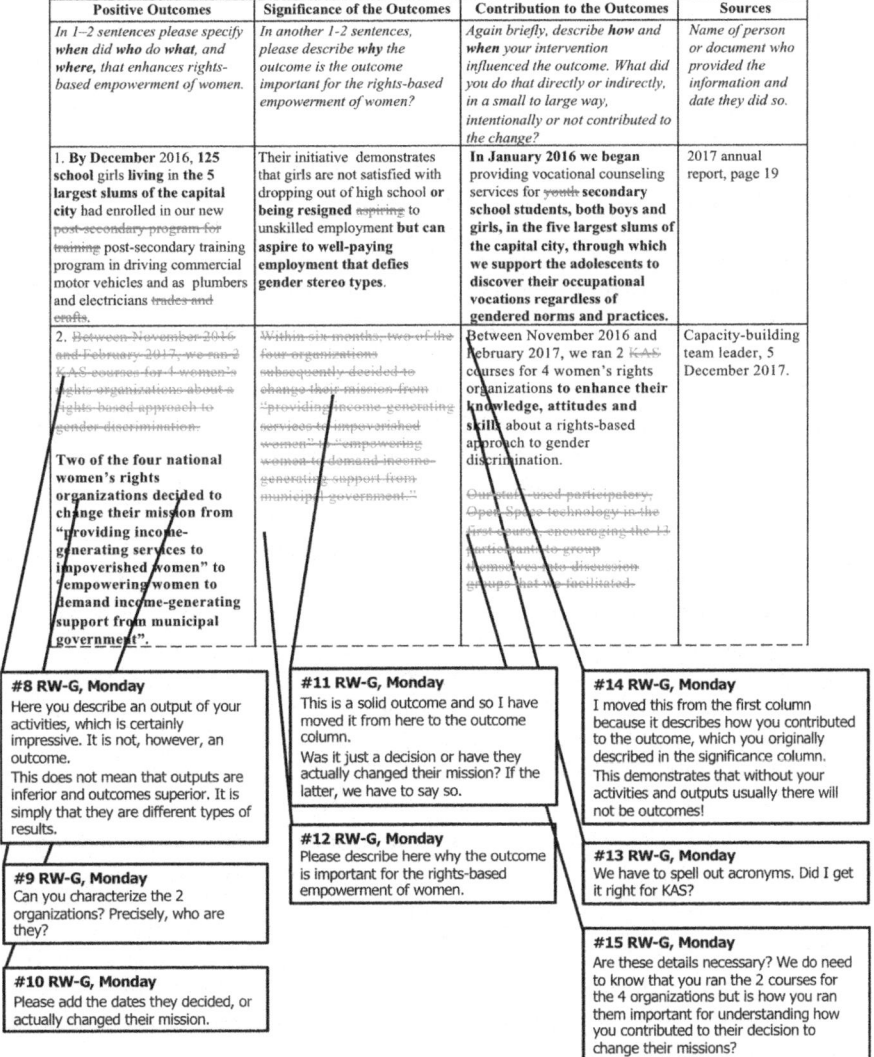

Figure 4.5 Exemplar—Harvesting tool with revised and additional outcome.

is now as SMART as I believe is necessary to serve as evidence for answering one or more of the prime harvest questions.

The second outcome is an example of an additional outcome that raises some other common challenges. I raise the issues both in suggested text (in **bold**) and in comment balloons. Read through them. They are self-explanatory.

Here are additional, more practical lessons that I have learned from serving in the coach-as-expert function in the pinging:

1. Use the Track Changes tool in Word (along with the Comment tool). This will enable your user to see clearly what you are suggesting be changed and what you added. Remember, the outcomes are theirs and they must agree with how they are described.
2. The descriptions must be intelligible to third parties without contextual or thematic expertise. They must be written so they stand alone—they should be self-explanatory.
3. Use the internet to fill in missing information. Often what is obvious to your source—abbreviations or initials, for example—will not be obvious to you. See the example for KAS in the contribution of the second exemplar outcome (Figure 4.5). A formal evaluator might challenge or order the source to "spell out all acronyms." A facilitator coach collaborates by filling in whatever information can be found in order to lessen the burden of time on the source.
4. Suggest clarifying wording in the text. This has to be done diplomatically—one of the skills of coaching. You do not want your sources to feel you are criticizing them for doing a poor job, which can be especially acute if the harvest is not in their mother language. When the source of information reviews the outcome, if you got it right, they will be grateful. Otherwise, they can correct you.

Engaging with primary sources to harvest outcomes should be done in the most useful manner possible. Goele Scheers, a Belgian colleague who is one of the core Outcome Harvesting practitioners working internationally, has substantial experience in facilitating harvesting workshops, which she finds are a potent tool. She illustrates in Figure 4.6.

In the end, it is the source, not you, who affirms the content of what was achieved in terms of outcomes, why it is significant and how the intervention contributed. The bottom line for you as a coach is that the formulation of outcome statements have to be SMART.

In this second ping, I always remind myself to practice *self-reflexivity*, to be attentive to, and conscious of, the cultural, political, social, linguistic, and economic origins and purposes of the information with which I work. It requires you be mindful of your own perspective but also that of your sources of information and of the eventual users of data you are collecting. The idea is to be aware that what they and you do and say about changes they have influenced, how and why, is affected by the differing life

In the majority of my projects I harvest outcomes in workshops. The basic modality is to convene the internal sources for 2-4 days, in which I introduce Outcome Harvesting and the harvesting instrument, and then have them identify and formulate their outcomes in a combination of plenary sessions and small group work. The exact sequence of activities depends on the uses of the harvest, how many people participate and their knowledge and group dynamics. Though the goal is to have SMART, verifiable outcome statements by the end of the workshop, follow-up work might be needed to obtain information from documentation or to check data with colleagues who are not present. In those cases, I use an online tool such as Google Docs to collaborate on finalizing the statements. The last part of the workshop is usually spent on analyzing and interpreting the data because most of my use of Outcome Harvesting is for monitoring and learning (M&E), developmental or formative evaluations. Nonetheless, even in evaluations where my role is as an external, independent evaluator, I find it useful to have the perspective of the internal sources even though they know, in the end, that I and not they must answer the evaluation questions. Substantiating the outcome statements before starting the collective analysis is not always possible, in which case of course the analysis and interpretation are tentative.

I find harvesting outcomes collectively has significant advantages over individual harvesting. First of all, harvesting workshops build Outcome Harvesting capacity amongst people who subsequently will be able to report outcomes with much less coaching. Secondly, they also obtain a good understanding about the Outcome Harvesting process and are therefore able to better relate to the findings. Thirdly, collectively discussing and reflecting on outcomes enhances common understanding and helps reduce barriers within and between organizations and projects. Fourth, people working together generate lot of energy and by seeing each other's results, people feel connected to each other and the intervention. More than once, I have seen this lead to organizations, projects or network members collaborating with each other, whereas previously they did not. Fifth, as a facilitator and coach working with a group, I am able to explain the approach and answer questions one time rather than multiple times and provide immediate feedback, which saves time in the harvesting process. Finally, internal sources tend to value the workshop because they do not only have to provide information, but they own their outcomes and can use them for their own purposes.

Do keep in mind, however, that a harvesting workshop does require hard work from all involved; they must be at their peak performance for several days in a row. Furthermore, these workshops have to be led by at least one facilitator with substantial experience in harvesting outcomes who can coach and give advice on the spot. Prior to the workshop, the OH facilitator and the primary users should think carefully about who to invite (and who not), who to assign to each small group and the number of facilitators needed. Without enough guidance at the workshop, the outcomes will not be finalized and more work will be needed after the workshop. All in all, harvesting workshops are a proven option for harvesting outcomes.

Goele Scheers, 2018

Figure 4.6 Harvesting Outcomes in workshops.

experiences and world views with which you all view the facts of the matter. As you craft the outcomes with your sources of information, keep in mind that you are in a relationship between people (not documents or organizations or methodologies).

Last Ping—Facilitator Coach as Decision Maker

Whether your source provides all the data you require with the second pong or requires a third or even fourth exchange, the goal of your last ping and their last pong will be the same: agreement on the formulation of their outcomes. If you have been successful so far as a facilitator coach, you both will have learned from each other. Your sources will understand the methodological reasons for separating the different dimensions of the outcome into succinct descriptions. You will understand what they report the intervention having achieved, how and why. The ping step is to decide, outcome by outcome, whether each one is SMART enough to be used as evidence to answer the harvest questions. In my experience, at this stage, problems with the formulations will usually be disagreement about too little or too much detail.

First, consider whether you are inadvertently disagreeing with the content rather than with the SMARTness. For example, in the second additional outcome in our exemplar, if my source objects to my comment about unnecessary specificity in the description of its contribution (#15 RWG in Figure 4.5) because they consider the use of Open Space Technology was a key to persuading one or both organizations to change their missions, then I must accept that detail.

Second, if it is methodological disagreement, I insist that the source has to defer to me just as I defer to the source on issues of content. Sometimes managing this decision is not easy precisely because of the collegial relationship you have as a coach. Nonetheless, if you are inconsistent in applying the SMART criteria, you will undermine the whole set of outcomes. These are some further lessons learned on how to communicate the decisions. The key element is to explain your decision:

1. If information is lacking, explain why it is unacceptable:
    - "I cannot accept this outcome without a date because without knowing when it happened, it is not specific enough to be verifiable."
    - "I need to know at least more or less how many women took this action. I understand that you do not know the exact number, but an estimate or approximation is necessary: Was

it 2–3, 20–30, 200–300 women? I trust you can understand that without this detail we cannot appreciate the significance of this outcome in comparison to others."
   - "I need to know the day or at least the month this outcome happened because otherwise we cannot see its place in the chronological process of change with the other outcomes."
2. To address the tension between a source's desire for more descriptive detail and yours for outcome statements that are crisp and comparable, explain along either or both of these lines:
   - "I have whittled down the detail here so that it is comparable with the detail in your other outcomes. You can appreciate that we want to avoid someone skipping over the outcome with lengthy detail or disqualifying the succinct ones."
   - "I have used the information you provided to suggest formulations that can be compared and contrasted with your other outcomes, and with the outcomes that other sources will give me. Naturally we have on file the additional information you have provided in case we need to refer to it."

Sometimes, you may decide to produce one or a few case studies of the role of the organization in influencing one or a group of outcomes. In those instances that additional information may prove useful.

The ping-pong product will be SMART outcome statements in which your questions have been answered and together with the source you have crafted final outcome statements. The ping-ponging is an iterative process—as you receive more information on individual outcomes you will often go back and edit earlier outcomes.

In Figure 4.7 you see the final versions of the framing of each outcome in its totality.

These are the most salient final lessons learned about less obvious pitfalls in facilitating and coaching the identification and formulation of outcome statements:

1. If the societal actor had decided to change its behavior before the intervention occurred, then it is not an outcome. In the exemplar outcome #1, if one or more of the 125 girls had already decided in 2015 to pursue vocational training as a commercial vehicle driver, plumber, or electrician, or if in outcome #2 the two women's organizations had gone to the open discussion forums to obtain information about rights-based approaches to gender discrimination because they had already made the decision to pivot their mission

Name of the person, position, and project/region: Advocacy and capacity-building team leaders
Date: 12 January 2018

Outcomes	Significance of the Outcomes	Contribution to the Outcomes	Sources
1. By December 2016, 125 school girls living in the five largest slums of the capital city had voluntarily enrolled in our new postsecondary program for training in driving commercial motor vehicles and as plumbers and electricians.	Their initiative demonstrates that girls are not satisfied with dropping out of high school or being resigned to unskilled employment but can aspire to well-paying employment that defies gender stereotypes.	In January 2016, we began providing vocational counseling services for secondary school students, both boys and girls, in the five largest slums of the capital city, through which we support the adolescents to discover their occupational vocations regardless of gendered norms and practices.	2017 annual report, p. 19
2. In March and April 2017, Employment Now and the Alliance of Tradeswomen, two of the four national women's employment rights organizations, changed their missions from "providing income-generating services to impoverished women" to "empowering women to demand income-generating support from municipal government."	Employment Now and the Alliance of Tradeswomen, will be able to mobilize between them over 3,000 women, to whom they provide services, to influence local government to move from its traditional paternalistic to rights-based programs in support of women. They can seize a unique opportunity because the current municipal government of the capital city increased in 2017 the tax on alcoholic beverages with the declared purpose of using this income to support poor, single mothers.	Between November 2016 and February 2017, we ran two open discussion forums for the four leading women's rights organizations to enhance their awareness and appreciation for the importance of a rights-based approach to gender discrimination.	Advocacy team leader, 5 January 2018
3. On 15 April 2017, Science for Women, Act Now, and Lean on Government—experienced in research, community mobilization and lobbying, respectively—signed a memorandum of understanding agreeing to join forces in our campaign for vocational training for women entrepreneurs.	These three allies—Science for Women, Act Now, and Lean on Government—will ensure that the vocational training campaign will be an integral advocacy approach.	In January 2017, for all staff involved in our advocacy for vocational training for women entrepreneurs, we began training them in the Centre for Evaluation Innovation's Advocacy Strategy Framework. This opportunity attracted the interest of Science for Women, Act Now, and Lean on Government to ally with us.	Advocacy team leader, 5 January 2018
4. On 13 December 2017, before over 1,000 activists demonstrating in front of the national legislature, nine members of the national legislature voiced for the first time their support for the proposed Empower All Women Through Crafts and Trade Education bill to benefit lower income women.	Five of these nine members sit on the legislature's appropriations committee and the other four are women legislators representing all parties in the legislature. If the bill is passed by the legislature, the key to success will be popular support for its implementation.	In August–November 2017, we lobbied 17 key legislators, including these nine, to support the Empower All Women Through Crafts and Trade Education bill. We collaborated with our allies Lean on Government and Act Now and the national women's rights organizations Employment Now and the Alliance of Tradeswomen, to organize this mass rally.	Advocacy team leader, 5 January 2018

Figure 4.7 Exemplar of 4 SMART outcomes.

to empowerment, then these would not be outcomes of the intervention. This can often be clarified, as in outcome #4, by stating that the nine members of the national legislature, speaking before over 1,000 activists, voiced *for the first time* their support for the proposed Empower All Women Through Crafts and Trade Education bill to benefit lower income women.
2. Another common challenge is to be sure that the intervention did not exercise control over what the societal actor began to do differently. If in outcome #1 the intervention paid the girls to go to their vocational training program, it would probably be an output of the intervention rather than an outcome. I say probably because if the social context is one in which the girls would suffer discrimination or worse—for example, violent repression from family, peers, or the broader community—then their daring to accept a scholarship for vocational training would be an outcome. From the significance, we see this is not the case. But, by clarifying the outcome description with "voluntarily" you resolve the question about control.
3. Similar to the mistake of listing outputs as outcomes, watch out for the tendency to describe the significance of the contribution rather than of the outcome. For instance, if in outcome statement #3 the significance was described as: *Our vocational training ensured that these three allies—Science for Women, Act Now, and Lean on Government—will bring an integral advocacy approach to our campaign*, this would be erroneous because it refers to the intervention's contribution and not to the change in behavior of the three societal actors. The correct description is: *These three allies—Science for Women, Act Now, and Lean on Government—will ensure that the vocational training campaign will be an integral advocacy approach*. This formulation correctly describes the importance of the outcome.

Facilitator Coach as Innovator

Ping-ponging exemplifies the active-reactive-interactive-adaptive facilitation mode that I have found so useful in Outcome Harvesting (see the section Facilitator, Coach, and Mentor in Chapter 1). Integral to that practice is, of course, learning and innovating. I will exemplify with the experience of Mark Cabaj, a well-known evaluation innovator in Canada, who discovered Outcome Harvesting as a result of one of his 2016 New Year's resolutions to "re-sharpen his saw" of innovative evaluation techniques. Mark and I have corresponded for the last couple of years as we found ourselves sharing an interest in the implications of complexity for evaluation and especially for developmental evaluation. He is president of the consulting company *From Here to There* and an associate of Tamarack—an institute for community engagement. Mark has firsthand knowledge of using evaluation as a policy maker, philanthropist, and activist, and has played a big role in promoting the merging practice of developmental evaluation in Canada. In Box 4.1, he shares an idea that I believe exemplifies how Outcome Harvesting practitioners will never stop innovating and improving the approach.

> **BOX 4.1 POTENTIAL OF CONTRIBUTION ANALYSIS FOR OUTCOME HARVESTING**
>
> I became immediately enamored with Outcome Harvesting (OH) when I learned about it in 2016 for a simple reason: it offered a more structured and rigorous way to capture the outcomes and contributions of social innovators than we had managed to do in the early days of Vibrant Communities (VC). The VC initiative, which ran from 2001 to 2011, included leaders of the 15 city-wide collaboratives in Canada who were keen to understand the extent to which their efforts—rather than other factors—were responsible for the scores of new policies, program innovations, and actions that improved the lives of vulnerable residents.
>
> Without knowing it, we devised a simple two-step approach that had elements of the OH methodology that we know today. The first was to prepare a 6–8 page "performance story" describing the challenge social innovators were trying to address, their strategy for addressing it, the roles and actions of each of the various actors involved, and the outcomes and learning that emerged from their efforts. Next, once each of the social innovators agreed that the story was accurate, we then asked them to "rate" each other's contribution to the eventual outcomes on a seven-point scale.
>
>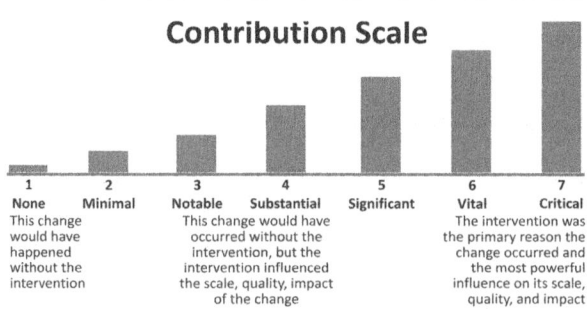
>
> Here are two typical examples of its use:
> - A "Leadership Roundtable" of community leaders generated a cluster of outcomes when they pulled together a group of trade unions, municipal governments, and real estate owners to assist

a nonprofit organization develop a large housing facility for people leaving violent family situations. After their collective efforts were described in a performance story, they asked a dozen people most involved from all the participating institutions to rate each other's contribution on the scale.

The average rating for each individual stakeholder was relatively high: for example, the stakeholders rated the $1 million in free labor offered by the local trade union for the plumbing and electrical work in the building as a 5 out of 7. The unexpected result was that the group rated the contribution of the activities of the Leadership Roundtable who brokered the relationships that made the entire enterprise possible as a 6.5 out of 7. This was a pleasant surprise to the Roundtable members who were sure that others would have forgotten their behind-the-scenes work.

- A coalition of advocates identified the decision of a government agency to adopt their recommendations for strengthening a popular income support program for persons with disabilities as an outcome they had influenced. The "evidence" their contribution made a difference was that the government agency had adopted, word for word, much of the language they had used in their official recommendations for policy change. When a researcher asked five senior civil servants in the government to rate the coalition's contribution to the upgraded program, however, she discovered that civil servants had already settled on the very same changes well before the lobbying efforts. Nonetheless, the external people consulted decided to rate the advocates' contribution as a 2 out of 7 because the adoption of the advocates' wording added extra legitimacy to the changes in the eyes of policy stakeholders.

The approach was immediately popular amongst VC network members. It (a) provided them with a better grasp of their contributions to changes in communities, (b) made it possible to acknowledge the contributions of multiple actors, and (c) was relatively easy to implement. They particularly liked the fact it was possible to go beyond simply describing the contributions made by different actors and include the opportunity to rate the value of that contribution from different perspectives.

It was, however, an imperfect approach. VC participants identified two technological and methodological limitations that the current OH methodology addresses nicely. First, while the comprehensive performance story offered a fulsome account of a group's activities and outcomes, it also required considerable time, resources, and expertise as well, and often required organizations to hire an outside consultant. The OH practice of developing smaller-scale outcome statements is more manageable and yet still able to describe outcomes in sufficient detail to provide helpful feedback.

Next, the VC approach to developing outcome statements encouraged social innovators to "zoom in" on their contributions to outcomes, but did not provide a structured way for them to "zoom out" to identify and weigh other possible contributing factors. This fed the natural tendency of people closest to a project to overstate the role of their efforts and impacts, and leave invisible other elements of the outcome story. For example, we learned later the social innovators that worked so well together to launch the housing facility described earlier somehow missed the role that a large housing grant from the Federal government played in getting the project off the ground. The "substantiation" step in OH, where third parties who are aware of the outcome but not part of the social innovation team that had a part in creating it, are asked to verify contribution claims goes a very long way to addressing innovators' bias and helps paint a more complete and accurate picture of outcomes and contributions.

I have since fully embraced the OH approach. Not only does it correct some of the shortcomings of the imperfect prototype we used in VC, but it's perhaps the most elegant, efficient and, if done well, rigorous way to capture the outcomes and contributions that emerge in complex change initiatives we have in the field today.

Mark Cabaj, 2018

In Summary

As with all metaphors, the ping-ponging has its limitations to explain the process of engaging with human sources of information to review potential outcomes and identify and formulate additional ones. To begin, there is not a winner and a loser; success is when both the source and you win. Also, the role of facilitator coach is not one of competing but cooperating. Nonetheless, in my experience, ping-ponging as a metaphor for the process of both coaching sources and collaboratively producing the best thinking you together can do is appreciated. However you prefer to describe the process, in this third step of Outcome Harvesting, as the harvester you co-learn with your sources how to identify and formulate the information you require to answer the prime harvesting questions. This requires that you collaborate in a mode through which you provide methodological guidance and expertise and your sources provide their knowledge. The end result must be their SMART outcome statements, not yours.

In the next chapter we will explore how to triangulate your sources of information so that the information you will use to answer the prime questions is as credible as necessary for the intended uses of your findings.

Note

1. Although I have not had the experience, conceivably outcome data could be collected through non-written audiovisual means. Nonetheless, to be manageable and serve as evidence for a harvest report, the audiovisual would eventually have to be transcribed one way or another into writing.

References

Catsambas, T. T. (2016). Facilitating evaluation to lead meaningful change. *New Directions for Evaluation, Spring, 149,* 19–29.

Ramírez, R., & Brodhead, D. P. (2013). *Utilization focused evaluation: A primer for evaluators.* Penang, Malaysia: Southbound. Retrieved from http://bit.ly/2s8NWz4

5

Step 4

Substantiate the Outcome Statements

Once all the SMART (Chapter 1, Figure 1.5) outcome statements are agreed upon between the primary intended users and the harvesters, the next step in the Outcome Harvesting process is to ensure that the

Applicability of Key Principles to Step 4

Process principles—Chapter 8
- *** I. Facilitate usefulness throughout the evaluation
- *** III. Nurture appropriate participation
- ** II. Coach primary sources to formulate outcome statements
- *** IV. Strive for less because it will be more useful
- *** V. Learn Outcome Harvesting experientially

Content principles—Chapter 9
- *** VI. Harvest social change outcomes
- ** VII. Formulate an outcome as an observable change
- ** VIII. Establish plausible influence of the intervention
- ***** IX. Ensure credible-enough outcomes

Legend of Ricardo's rubrics
***** High: I always apply this principle; **** Considerable: I almost always apply it; *** Moderate: I usually apply it
** Occasional: I apply it sometimes but with quite a few exceptions; * Low: I rarely apply the principle in this step

whole set of outcomes will constitute credible-enough evidence with which to answer the Prime Outcome Harvesting Questions. Said another way, the outcomes must be acceptable to the primary users in the light of their principal intended uses. Credibility is the quality of being believed or accepted as true. "Credible enough" means that the people who use the data in the outcome statements will trust that the data is solid evidence of what the intervention has achieved and how, and why the outcome data is important. This is a sociocultural and political decision as well as a technical one because different users will have different vested interests. Their decisions on what is credible-enough accuracy, deep-enough and broad-enough perspectives on the outcomes, and the legitimacy of the whole set of outcomes will all have consequences for other stakeholders.

For instance, if one of the intended uses of the evaluation results is accountability to a donor, the user and harvester must be sure that they know and take into account the different stakeholders and their stakes within the donor organization. In one evaluation, my primary user and I had the painful experience of first coming to agreement on how we would substantiate the evaluation results with the donor's program officer based in the Middle East. But then when we presented the findings in a high-level meeting at donor headquarters in the United States, there was a major blow up because the evaluation unit disagreed with their program officer.

It is important to ask, is substantiation always necessary? No. There can be solid reasons in favor of the trustworthiness and expertise of the primary and secondary sources that ensure the veracity of the outcome data you have collected through Steps 2 and 3 (see Chapters 3 and 4). These reasons include the following:

1. After due consultation, the users agreed with you on what primary and secondary sources they considered reliable.
2. The primary sources are the people who are the most knowledgeable about the changes their work is influencing.
3. The human sources formally and publicly went on record with their views. They knew that the veracity of the information they provided would be subject to scrutiny by others.
4. In your role as facilitator/coach you rigorously ensured that the outcomes are SMART.

In addition, other factors that may enhance the claim of credibility include:

5. The documentation from which you extracted potential outcomes in Step 2 was written by someone different from the primary source(s) with whom you engaged to review and add outcomes.

6. The primary sources were two or more people—a team or representatives of different organizations, for example—who discussed and agreed on the outcomes selected and thus presented collective rather than individual knowledge.

In sum, the Outcome Harvesting process itself generates highly reliable data about actual changes in behavior that took place, and how an intervention contributed. The harvester insists on specificity and measurability about the when, who did what, and where; why it was important; how the intervention contributed. This rigor leads to information that is often harder to achieve through other qualitative methods.

All to say that the Outcome Harvesting process may well generate credible-enough data with which to answer the prime harvesting questions and substantiation is not needed. Or it may not. Your task as a harvester is first to facilitate discussion and decisions about whether substantiation is necessary for the outcome statements to be credible enough for the intended uses.

All that said, identifying and formulating outcomes has a strong element of subjectivity. The sources provide information based on their knowledge and perspectives; they have told or confirmed the truth as they see it. But, all knowledge is fuzzy; there are only degrees of truth. Other knowledgeable people may very well have different knowledge and views about what happened—different mental models of the same reality. Do the uses for the harvest require independent verification that the outcome statements describe accurately enough the reality? If yes, then substantiation is a solution.

The Substantiation Options

Substantiation must be timely. In formative and summative evaluations, the right time to substantiate is right after you have harvested all the outcomes. In monitoring and evaluation (M&E) and developmental evaluations, however, when you harvest outcomes periodically, it is sensible to wait until you have gathered a sufficient number of outcomes to make decisions about their relative importance before making substantiation decisions. Thus, make sure you substantiate at the right time.

Substantiation offers two things to enhance credibility: verify the *accuracy* of the data in the outcome and contribution descriptions, and deepen and broaden *understanding* of the outcome, how the intervention contributed, and especially the significance of the outcome. You obtain third party opinions or other evidence to confirm that there are no factual errors or to correct them when there are, and to provide additional perspectives on what was achieved on the level of outcomes, why it is important and how the intervention plausibly influenced the outcome. In my experience, the first purpose has been most important for my primary intended users.

Obtaining third-party views is not a panacea for sceptics, however. To begin, it requires an investment of your and their time and so you only want to substantiate as many outcomes as is necessary for your purposes. The more important the use and the more controversial the outcomes are, the more effort should be placed on substantiating them, either for accuracy, to deepen and broaden understanding, or both. So should 0% or 50% or 100% of the outcomes be substantiated because they are controversial, dubious, interesting, or important? How do you decide which to substantiate? All the outcomes of one type and none of another, or all or some of the outcomes of one project or program rather than another? Those outcomes that are most vulnerable to contestation?

You can substantiate no outcomes or all outcomes or a sample to ensure the outcome statements are sufficiently accurate, that is, valid. I will illustrate with three cases of major, indeed mainstream, international donors.

First Case—No Outcomes Substantiated

A colleague and I did a major evaluation of an international advocacy program. Two dozen grantees served as the sources of information on their outcomes. We harvested several hundred outcomes. Then we consulted the primary user—the program officer who commissioned the evaluation—about substantiation. After reviewing the outcomes, she was very clear that substantiation was unnecessary; the outcomes were solid enough for her uses, which were learning and not accountability.

We proceeded to draft our report, which we presented to an international meeting of over half her grantees. The first morning we discussed the findings, illustrating with numerous outcomes. Over lunch my co-evaluator and I were pulled aside to hear a couple of grantees confide in us that some of the outcomes were inaccurate—they said another grantee had not contributed to one or more of their reported outcomes. After sharing notes and quite alarmed, my co-evaluator and I went to our primary user, and with grave concern we shared what her grantees had said. We suggested we revisit the substantiation issue.

She replied with the same conviction as before, that it was unnecessary. Frankly somewhat incredulous, we asked why. She explained, "My principal use for this evaluation is to know which international actors my grantees believe they are influencing and how. Your methodology assures me that what we have is accurate to the best of their individual knowledge. Now I will be able to find new grantees to fill the voids in my program so that together all my grantees are targeting the major players."

My colleague and I naturally asked, "But some of your grantees say others are lying." She replied,

> No doubt some may be exaggerating the importance of the outcome or their role in influencing it, but you two have been rigorous. You have obtained specific, measurable information about what each one of my grantees considers they know about the changes they have influenced. For each one, you have made sure they pinned down plausible cause-effect relations. They all know that the information they gave could be verified with independent sources. That is good enough for me. Listen, my program is highly political and intentionally diverse. I purposely have grantees with a variety of visions and missions who are targeting actors in different ways. Consequently, each one believes that what they are doing is the best way to effect change. I expect them to dispute what each other are doing and achieving when it is different than their strategy Frankly, I am glad when they disagree.

That is, the outcomes were accurate enough. What was contested was the relative contribution of ideologically, politically, and strategically diverse grantees. Thus, obtaining additional perspectives on this would not enhance her understanding in any useful way.

In addition to this rather dramatic case, I have done a number of evaluations in which substantiation was less of a priority for credibility because of the independence of the original sources. For example, I have completed evaluations in which government officials, who had worked alongside the internal sources of the intervention, served as primary sources. Although allies, they were considered sufficiently independent of the intervention for their information to be accepted as accurate for the veracity of the outcome formulations. They also added sufficient additional perspectives for a well-rounded-enough comprehension of the whole set of outcomes.

Second Case—All Outcome Statements Substantiated

On the other end of the spectrum, I did an evaluation of an international program whose principal use for the evaluation was accountability to its back donor. Thus, my users consulted with their donor program officer. She decided that she did not require triangulation with the opinions of other knowledgeable people, nor did she need to know what other people knew about the outcome statements. Instead, she required documentation from an external source for each outcome and an external or internal source for each contribution. That is, this was 100% × 2 verification. This was a realistic expectation because of the nature of the intervention and the small number of the outcomes. The program aimed to influence policy and practice changes within government agencies that would, as a matter of course, be documented. The total number of outcomes was 39. Thus, we went to external sources for the documentation. For the three outcomes for which there was no external documentation available, we interviewed directly by email or in person the subjects of the outcomes and the interview report served as documentation.

I caution you that when faced with the options of substantiating none, some, or all outcomes, or one or more projects or programs, there may be a tendency to minimize risk and verify the accuracy of each and every outcome, as in this case. Generally, however, this is too costly in terms of time, and human, and financial resources to be useful. But, even if the magnitude of the harvest and the availability of resources allows you to substantiate each and every outcome for accuracy or interpretation, be aware that you can never be 100% sure of their accuracy. Usually, if substantiation is required, something short of 100% substantiation will be useful. Furthermore, evaluations are not intended to provide proof or 100% certainty but only sufficiently accurate information with the depth and breadth necessary for the intended uses. In sum, in Outcome Harvesting, you only need to generate a level of confidence in the credibility of the data that will be useful for making decisions and taking action based on the findings of the harvest.

Third Case—Percentage of Outcomes Substantiated

Another major international donor decided we should verify the accuracy of 20% of 260 outcomes. When I questioned why not 10% or 30%, the program officer explained that the main audience for the findings were people in other departments of the same organization. For that audience, 20% was the right number; if 52 outcomes checked out for accuracy, the whole set of outcomes would be trustworthy. She did insist, however, that I as the external evaluator choose the 52 outcomes I considered to be the most important to verify, either because the accuracy or plausibility were questionable or the outcome was especially significant. Also, we had to verify with two categories of substantiators, one external and the other internal to the organization but external to her department. This required approaching on average three substantiators per outcome since not all the outside people responded.

How to Substantiate for Maximum, Useful Credibility

Once you have decided which outcomes have to be substantiated, then you must decide on the standards for substantiation. I find that amongst many of my clients in the world of development and social change, there is a popular belief that *random probability sampling* is the most accurate way to verify outcomes. We do not use this option in Outcome Harvesting because it is neither practical or useful. The average harvest size in my experience is 97 outcomes. If these outcomes were to be sampled through random probability, for the customary confidence level of 95% and a margin of error of ±3%, you would have to sample over half (51). In short, with an average number of 97 outcomes per harvest, Outcome Harvesting operates in a situation, in the words of William M. K. Trochim, professor in the Department of Policy Analysis and Management at Cornell University and 2008 president of American Evaluation Association (AEA), in which "it is not feasible, practical or theoretically sensible to do random sampling" (Trochim, 2017, para. 1).

Levels of confidence and margins of errors are important considerations. Understandably, I am often asked if random probability sampling is not used, what is the scientific basis for the substantiation process we use in Outcome Harvesting. The method used in Outcome Harvesting is known as *non-probability, purposive, expert sampling*. It is a non-probability sample because primary intended users and harvesters select the outcomes through a process that does not give all outcomes equal chances of being selected. It is purposive because they select the outcomes to be substantiated based on their judgments about the outcome's individual importance in the light of the prime harvesting questions, derived from the intended uses, and about its degree of credibility. And it is an expert sampling because the harvester decides who has sufficient expertise to be consulted about the veracity of each outcome. Trochim, explains the advantages of this sampling mode: "You are not out on your own trying to defend your decisions—you have some acknowledged experts to back you. The disadvantage is that even the experts can be, and often are, wrong" (Trochim, 2017, para. 5).

With the decisions made about which outcomes are to be substantiated, you next need to identify the substantiators. Two obvious candidates to be substantiators include (a) the person the intervention claims to have influenced, and (b) allies the intervention claims to have collaborated with in influencing that social actor. I usually do this by going straight back to the human sources of each outcome selected for substantiation. They will know who else knows about what happened, including proxies, for example, when the subject of the outcome is a high-level government official. I ask my sources for the name, position, organizational affiliation, email, and telephone of potential substantiators for each outcome. The individuals they recommend, of course, must fulfill the criteria of being are independent of the outcome and the contribution but also knowledgeable about them. And they should be people who will speak with authority and on the record. That is your judgment as harvester.

These are not simple checklist considerations. You must be confident that the people selected are not biased in favor or against the intervention. This can be an ethical issue—is there any reason to believe the proposed substantiators are untrustworthy? But it is also political—proposed substantiators may have vested interests in the outcome. For example, a common pool of potential substantiators are the staff of allied organizations with whom the intervention collaborates. Others are the societal actor who is the subject of the outcome, or if it is a community, organization, or institution, one or more of their representatives. As the person responsible for the integrity of the harvest, you the harvester must make the judgment that the people who substantiate are appropriate to do so. Therefore study the list of substantiator candidates carefully in the light of the outcomes they would substantiate, and do not accept any about whom you have doubts of their qualifications.

Sometimes a knowledgeable individual is difficult to access, and thus not highly motivated to share what they know, as is the case with presidents and CEOs, board members and elected officials, and senior civil servants. In those cases, someone close to these preferred substantiators is a better choice: a manager or a staff member. Sometimes, of course, potential substantiators can be too close to the intervention or its primary promoters, as is the case with allies who also contributed to the outcome or a societal actor with whom the intervention staff are actively collaborating. These evaluative judgments underscore the politics of many Outcome Harvesting decisions.

And there can be more practical challenges. Potentially ideal substantiators may not be able to give information via email for personal, political, or organizational reasons and require phone interviews.

Applying these criteria leads to other issues. Here are the most common questions, with my answers.

1. *Will one person per outcome suffice?* In my experience you can expect that six to seven out of 10 people you approach to substantiate, will agree to do so. So I approach a minimum of two substantiators per outcome in order to get at least one response.
2. *Are there any special qualities required of the substantiators beyond being knowledgeable, authoritative, independent, and accessible?* Literacy, language, and culture are sometimes complicating factors that I address by adapting. For example, in one evaluation in a heavily

patriarchal society, grassroots substantiators had to be interviewed in their language by one of my colleagues of the same sex.
3. *How many third parties—one, two perhaps, three, or more—confirming the outcome statements will give the whole set of outcomes sufficient credibility?* This question goes to the heart of substantiation: What is credible enough for the intended uses. It all depends case by case.
4. *Also, can one substantiator verify the accuracy of more than one outcome? If yes, how many?* Yes, is the short answer. In my experience it is more of a practical issue of how many outcomes they are willing to substantiate. Generally, I aim for one outcome per substantiator because I have found that guarantees the highest rate of return.

And to further complicate the decision, a big issue:

5. *What percentage of the select outcomes must be confirmed for you to be confident that the whole set of outcomes will be trustworthy?* The one statistical criteria I use is that at least 90% of the outcomes selected for substantiation must be validated by their respective substantiators to consider that the whole set of outcomes is credible enough for the intended uses. By "valid" I mean the description of the change in the behavior of a societal actor (outcome) *and* how an intervention contributed (contribution) are both considered accurate. If there are additional dimensions to an outcome statement—the significance of the outcome, for example—the description must also be considered accurate for the whole statement to be accepted as valid.

Why 90% and not 95% or 80%? After doing a number of substantiations, a pattern emerged of less than 10% of the substantiators finding that a description in the outcome statements was erroneous. That is, either the change in the societal actor or the contribution of the intervention had not happened as described. The users in each instance found that more than 90% accuracy made the whole set of outcomes credible enough. Importantly, the outcomes that a substantiator declares are wrong—did not happen as described or the intervention did not contribute—are excluded from the outcome data and will not be used as evidence to answer the prime harvesting questions in Step 5 (Chapter 6).

The Substantiation Process

Whatever the number of outcomes and of independent, knowledgeable, authoritative people to be consulted, and however they are to be engaged (by email, telephone, in person, individually, or even collectively), the nature of the verification is similar. In Figure 5.1, I exemplify the content of

Dear [name of substantiator],

I am writing at the suggestion of [name of primary source] to request your cooperation in assessing the accuracy about an outcome with which you are familiar. What I ask is for you to answer three multiple-choice questions about only one outcome, with the opportunity to comment if you wish to do so. It should not take more than 5-10 minutes of your time.

With [name of primary source], and she in consultation with colleagues, we identified and formulated this outcome and believe your opinion will provide us with valuable insight from the perspective of someone independent but with a working knowledge of this achievement. Below the description of the outcome, there is a short multiple-choice questionnaire. Please indicate to what extent you agree with the description of the outcome, its significance and [name of organization]'s contribution to the outcome. Please note that the organization is not attributing the change to itself. To the contrary, we describe how [name of organization] contributed in however a small, indirect or unintentional way it may have been.

Outcome: 1. Between January-March 2017, the ministers of education, labor and women's affairs committed themselves to working together to lobby the national cabinet to submit a motion to support a vocational education bill to benefit lower income women to the legislature.

Significance: The recently created ministry of women's affairs does not have enough political clout in the legislature because it is led by a member by the minority party in power. The other two ministers come from the majority partner in government.

Contribution: Since 2016, our advocacy program lobbied the three ministries to work together for a vocational education bill to benefit lower income women.

Following are my three questions to you about this outcome. Please mark with an X in the brackets [ ] next to your answer. If you wish to make a comment about your opinion, we would be delighted. Nevertheless, it is not necessary to comment.

1. We would like to know about the **outcome**: To what degree are you in agreement with how we describe the action of the three ministers?
[X] Fully agree
[ ] Partially agree
[ ] Disagree
[ ] No opinion
Comments if you like:
When the ministers are committed, the bill will move forward.

2- Regarding the **significance**: How much do you agree with our description of the importance of the three ministers' decision to work together in lobbying the national cabinet?
[ ] Fully agree
[X] Partially agree
[ ] Disagree
[ ] No opinion
Comment?
While the commitment of all three ministers will get the vocational education bill a hearing in cabinet, the three ministers have the opportunity to engage in more collaboration in order to convince the cabinet that this is not politics as usual with ministers exchanging favors.

3. To what extent do you consider accurate the description of how [name of organization] influenced the ministers' decision?
[ ] Fully agree
[X] Partially agree
[ ] Disagree
[ ] No opinion
Comment, which again is fully optional:
The intervention's lobbying certainly was incisive. I believe, however, this more because of the power of the research they had done rather than a result of all their oral arguments and cajoling.

And that is it!

The information you provide will be "on the record" and subject to scrutiny by different stakeholders. If publicly sharing your information is not possible, please let me know and we will find an acceptable way to keep it confidential.

I want to thank you beforehand for your collaboration with this evaluation. If you are able to answer my three questions by return email, I would be most grateful. At the latest we would appreciate your response within one week from today. If you wish to receive the full evaluation report, we will gladly make sure that you receive it.

Cordially yours,

Ricardo Wilson-Grau

Figure 5.1 Exemplar — The results of engaging with a substantiator.

the consultation, which can be printed, inserted into an email, or used as an interview format. I also include sample answers to help illustrate. As with the Outcome Harvesting Instrument, you are well advised to pilot the substantiation format with two substantiators.

When substantiating outcomes, as when extracting outcomes from documentation and engaging with human sources of information, the issue of *confidentiality* is always present. I suggest in Figure 5.1 that you address the issue of discretion and secrecy head-on, as I recommend you do regarding documentary sources and human sources of information explained in the previous two chapters. In fact, you will note I use the same wording about confidentiality with substantiators as I do with internal primary sources of information. Nonetheless, be aware that offering confidentiality is difficult. Even if information is registered anonymously, and the list of substantiators is published separately, it is not difficult for someone who knows the substantiators to figure out who said what if that someone knows who was asked to comment on which outcome.

Sometimes you may decide to consult a group of people together—for example, a panel of two or more experts. This *peer review* has additional value and a collective position on one or more outcomes naturally carries additional weight. And there may be other advantages. In one case in Peru, for example, an action-research project brought together representatives of different government agencies to substantiate a set of outcomes that represented changes in their individual agencies. In this case, we considered each one's response as individual verification of that outcome. The purpose of consulting them together, however, went beyond verification. We wanted to deepen our understanding. Thus, we decided only to show them the description of the change the action-researchers had perceived in their behavior and ask them: Do we adequately describe the change in your "behavior"? If yes, then we asked: Why was the change significant from their point of view and how did they consider the project influenced the change? We then compared and contrasted what the action-research team had described as the significance and their contribution with what the civil servants said. An added bonus was that the rich dialogue between the team and the government representatives led to the identification of 50% more outcomes. It is a common experience in Outcome Harvesting that substantiators provide valuable additional information.

If the substantiator simply checks off "fully agree," you are done, unless he or she says something contradictory in the comment. In our exemplar, the substantiator says she fully agrees that:

> "Between January–March 2017, the ministers of education, labor and women's affairs committed themselves to working together to lobby the national cabinet to submit a motion to support a vocational education bill to benefit lower income women to the legislature." But then in a comment adds, "When the ministers are committed, the bill will move forward."

Is she saying she does not, in fact, agree that they committed themselves? Or, as often happens, is she suggesting the significance of the outcome? I would write or phone and ask her directly:

> I want to be sure I understand your score and comment on the outcome description. Are you saying that you fully agree that the three ministers are committed to working together on the national vocational education bill and you comment to emphasize that you are hopeful they will be successful because of that commitment?

"Partially agree" or "Disagree" may mean that the substantiator disagrees with one or more of the facts in the outcome or contribution descriptions, or with the opinion described in the significance, which would mean the outcome is not validated. It may also mean, however, that he or she agrees with the facts but has more details to add, which would not disqualify the outcome; in fact, additional details can enrich it. Naturally, there is always the possibility that the substantiator misunderstood the description(s).

When in doubt, you ask the person to clarify:

> Regarding the significance, do I understand correctly that you agree the ministry for women's affairs alone does not have sufficient political gravitas, but that in addition, you consider that now they should seize the opportunity to collaborate on other issues to emphasize that they are seriously working together?

Similarly, with the contribution, I would seek clarity:

> I want to be sure that I understand you do not disagree that the intervention's lobbying contributed to the three ministries making their joint commitment to the new law. Nonetheless, you suggest that within their lobbying, the research they brought in was more important than their negotiations. Did I understand correctly?

For busy people, as many people in positions of authority tend to be, you want to avoid imposing a burden on their time. Therefore when I say to the substantiators that it will only take 5–10 minutes of their time, the calculation is serious. In fact, as I was writing this chapter, the fastest response from a substantiator that I have ever received came from Jessye Saavedra Conrado, who works in the Dirección de Innovación Empresarial, Consejo Nicaragüense de Ciencia y Tecnología (CONICYT). She responded within 13 minutes of my emailing a substantiation request to her—and her reply included comments.

Ensuring Rigor in Substantiating Accuracy

As you can imagine from my comments in Chapter 2 about rigor mortis, there is no rigid methodological procedure in substantiation to verify the facts of an outcome statement. The key to success is applying hard, critical evaluative thinking as you as the harvester now take on more the role of an independent evaluator.

What do you do if less than 90% of your outcomes are confirmed as accurate? In response, I will offer another example of the need for rigorous evaluative thinking in substantiation to ensure usefulness. The example involved an experience in piloting the use of Outcome Harvesting for M&E in a large multinational program. In this pilot, another Outcome Harvesting expert and I were supporting eight people nominated as "harvester coordinators" to learn how to facilitate and coach 36 of their colleagues who were serving as internal sources of information. We harvested 70 outcomes and agreed that we would substantiate the accuracy of 30% or 21 outcomes. If more than two of the 21 did not validate (that is more than 10%), not only would they be deleted from the 70, but we would then substantiate all remaining 49 outcomes to determine, one by one, which ones will be accepted as verified.

We applied my rule of thumb that not validated (or unsubstantiated) means that one independent, knowledgeable, and authoritative person considers the content of the description of the outcome *or* of the contribution to be inaccurate. That is, the outcome did not happen as described, or the intervention did not contribute to it as described. Then, that outcome is not validated. The substantiation revealed that three of the outcomes were not validated. More importantly, however, for a relatively large number of outcomes, while the substantiators did not disagree with the facts in each description, they had considerably more salient information to add to numerous descriptions. Conclusion: overall the outcomes were of poor quality, which was considered by the primary users as more relevant than three outcomes not passing the substantiation test.

Therefore the users, my colleague, and I decided that rather than substantiate the other 49 outcomes, what would be most useful for the program would be for the two of us to assess the outcomes one by one for SMARTness. Few outcomes met full SMARTness criteria in our review. We concluded that the harvester coordinators must pay much more attention to the instructions that outcome statements be *specific* and *measurable*, and we, as their coaches, shared a responsibility in their sloppiness. We all attributed the errors to the sharp learning curve in developing this client's customised use of Outcome Harvesting and to the multiple additional priorities in the program. But this case also illustrates the potential overlap between the two purposes of substantiation—verifying accuracy and deepening and broadening understanding—as well the need to customize the harvest process as it unfolds.

Rigorous Substantiation to Broaden and Deepen Understanding

The customary use of substantiation is to verify the accuracy of outcomes. The second, complementary use of substantiation is to obtain the perspectives of others in order to enrich understanding of the outcomes. This can serve additional concrete purposes:

1. Collect quotable comments that can be used in communicating the intervention's achievements to make them more intelligible and credible.
2. Suggest one or more case studies with interrelated outcomes that can be so important for the primary intended users that they can constitute a separate exercise.
3. Obtain the views of allies, beneficiaries, and other stakeholders, in addition to external experts, in order to make better sense of the context, relevance, and other dimensions of the outcomes and how they were achieved.

My most common use of substantiation to deepen understanding of what has been achieved and how, has been to explore the "value added" of the intervention. This is the other side of the contribution coin—accepting that a contribution can be partial, indirect, and unintentional raises the question of its relative importance. That is, you use substantiation in particular to obtain the perspectives of others on the significance of the outcome or contribution. For example, there is the case of a regional human rights network operating in Latin America, a part of the world where innumerable human rights organizations were supported by European donors. The four development agencies funding the network identified amongst the network's outcomes those that they were especially keen to have their regional human rights consultants review—not for accuracy but for significance. In this case, the task was big enough to offer payment to those consultants to comment on what was the relative importance that the outcomes represented in the struggle for human rights in the region.

The Cost of Substantiation

With or without substantiation, there will always be fuzziness, or a margin of error, in the outcome data. Just as the point of departure has to be accepting that you will never have 100% certainty, there are also practical limitations in time, money, and human resources. Substantiating also involves reputational risk with your internal sources of information, who usually are the intervention's own staff. So what are the limits to the resources that it will be worthwhile to invest in substantiation? Your internal sources will know who to recommend as substantiators because they know best who is knowledgeable and independent, but also authoritative and motivated, to respond to a substantiation request. So you must calculate the clock time for them to identify one, two, three, or more substantiators. Then there is the clock time and honoraria cost for the harvesters to engage with the substantiators. If done by email, it is minimal time—we require 10–15 minutes of each substantiator's time and about 2–3 times that of the harvester's time. If face-to-face communication and travel is involved, it can be considerably more. You also have to calculate calendar time; if done by email or telephone, I generally budget 3 weeks of calendar time: 1 week to obtain the recommendations for substantiators and 2 weeks to reach out to them and obtain their responses. It can take more time.

In Summary

When primary intended users see the product of the intense process of the harvester engaging their staff to formulate together SMART outcomes, understandably they are often so impressed that they do not see the need for substantiation. And there may not be a need, but you must ensure it is a conscious decision. The harvester facilitates users considering the pros and cons of the two purposes of substantiation: verifying the accuracy or deepening and broadening the understanding, or both, of the information contained in the outcome statements. The verification of the accuracy of the data you harvest may or may not be useful. Similarly, consulting third parties to deepen understanding about harvested outcomes is also an option that will not always be worth the investment of resources. The decision to substantiate or not is based on what will make the whole set of outcomes credible enough for the intended principal uses.

If the decision is to substantiate, the same criteria are used for deciding for what purpose, which outcomes, and how to substantiate. Since these are not simply technical decisions, and involve sociocultural and political considerations, there are no simple rules to be applied. Hard evaluative thinking and thoughtful judgments are required to make sure you do what will truly be credible enough. It often requires users consulting with other stakeholders; as harvesters you must pilot any formats you are going to use to substantiate accuracy or understanding. Once you have substantiated, as a harvester you shift into an evaluative role to make the judgments about which outcomes are accepted as validated and which are not. You will continue more in the evaluator mode as you take the fifth step in the Outcome Harvesting process that I explain in the next chapter.

References

Trochim, W. M. K. (2017). *Research methods knowledge base* (web-based textbook). Retrieved from https://www.socialresearchmethods.net/kb/sampnon.php

6

Step 5

Analyze and Interpret the Outcome Data

Scientists usually assume that no theory is 100 percent correct.
Consequently, truth is a poor test for knowledge. The real test is utility.
A theory that enables us to do new things constitutes knowledge.
—Harari, 2015, p. 259

Applicability of Key Principles to Step 5

Process principles—Chapter 8
- *** I. Facilitate usefulness throughout the evaluation
- **** III. Nurture appropriate participation
- *** II. Coach primary sources to formulate outcome statements
- ***** IV. Strive for less because it will be more useful
- **** V. Learn Outcome Harvesting experientially

Content principles—Chapter 9
- ***** VI. Harvest social change outcomes
- ** VII. Formulate an outcome as an observable change
- **** VIII. Establish plausible influence of the intervention
- *** IX. Ensure credible-enough outcomes

Legend of Ricardo's rubrics
***** High: I always apply this principle; **** Considerable: I almost always apply it; *** Moderate: I usually apply it
** Occasional: I apply it sometimes but with quite a few exceptions; * Low: I rarely apply the principle in this step

From Mainly Facilitator to Primarily Evaluator

Up until now you have been facilitating and coaching a process of data collection and verification. You have a credible-enough set of outcome statements to serve as empirical evidence with which to answer the key evaluation questions. In this fifth Outcome Harvesting step you will move from describing the findings to explaining what the findings mean. Thus, you will play more of an evaluative than a facilitative role. Concretely, you do two things. First, you undertake qualitative data analysis. You organize the raw data to make it more intelligible. Second, you interpret the data to produce evidence-based answers to the prime harvesting questions.

Analysis—Usefully Organizing the Mass of Outcome Data

In Outcome Harvesting, "analysis" is understood in its strict definition: the process of separating something into its constituent elements in order to clarify the meaning of the whole. The "something" in Outcome Harvesting is the raw set of individual outcome statements that you organize into related clusters. You will discuss and agree with the primary users the categories[1] with which to classify and then filter the data to cluster it in manageable chunks of information. The purpose is to break up the mass of information contained in the outcome statements so that it is manageable evidence with which to answer the prime evaluation questions.

That said, you do not always need to enter outcome statements into a database and then categorize them in order to group them into manageable clusters. If you have a small number of outcome statements, you can organize the data manually—on a table top or on a computer screen. The data can readily be transformed into an electronic visual using PowerPoint. For example, in Figure 6.1 you see the analysis of outcome descriptions done by one of the World Bank teams who piloted Outcome Harvesting with a solid waste management project in Bosnia (World Bank, 2014, p. 24). Under the dateline you can see that the World Bank does have two categories of outcomes, the first with three sub-categories:

1. *Institutional changes*—Outcomes related to societal, policy, and organizational changes:
    - political commitment, social norms, and citizen demand for service improvements;
    - policy improvement for utilities; and
    - operational efficiency/responsiveness/financial viability of utility.

2. *Learning/capacity changes*—Other outcomes related to awareness, knowledge or skills, collaborative action, or the use of knowledge or innovative solutions.

They cluster the outcomes visually using the solid red, broken green, and wavy purple lines. Furthermore, they show the chronological order of the outcomes and establish which outcomes contributed to other outcomes, thus showing a process of change. How many outcomes you can manageably organize this way depends on the size of the descriptions. Obviously, you will be able to manage more one-sentence descriptions, as in this World Bank example, than descriptions that are one or two paragraphs, or one or two pages.

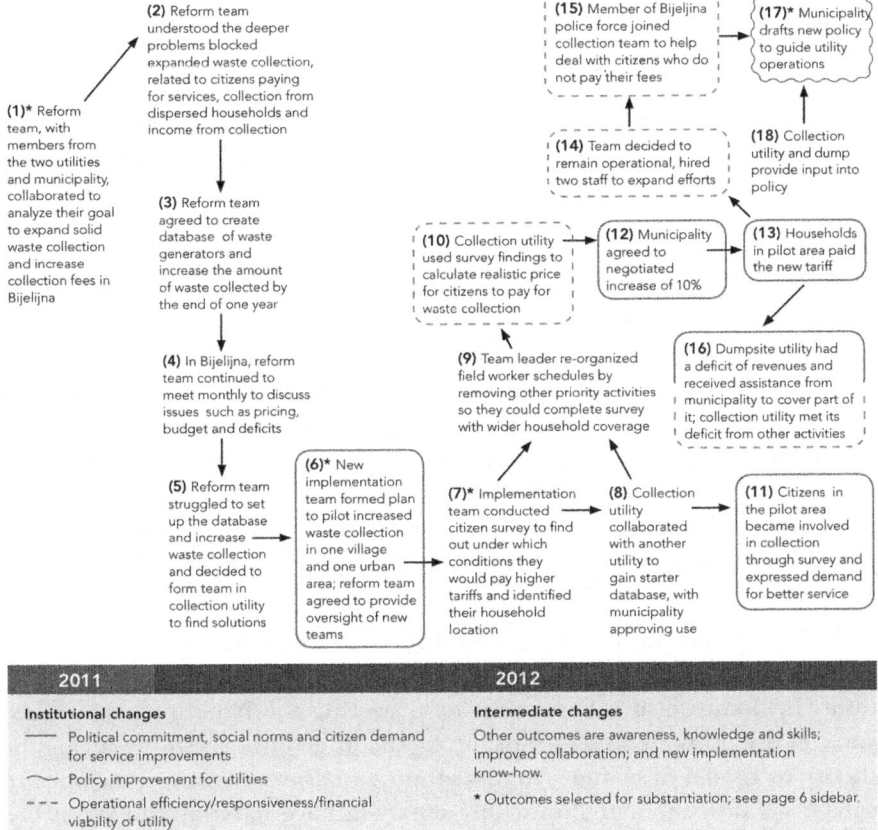

Figure 6.1 Portrayal of World Bank Institute outcomes in solid waste management in Bosnia, 2011–2012.

For more than a few dozen outcome statements, or if you wish to classify them in more than half a dozen ways—not just by year and four types of outcomes, as in the World Bank example—you should consider uploading the outcome statements into a database and classifying them there. I use Excel as a matter of course because of the many filtering and graphic possibilities. I have also used Access and my clients' own databases. There is no dearth of databases you can use to work with qualitative data such as the outcome statements.

For example, since 2013 Paul Kosterink, the monitoring, evaluation, and learning coordinator at the Global Platform to Prevent Armed Conflict (GPPAC), has been using the Drupal database. With this internet-based tool, GPPAC centralises outcome information so that the two dozen people who are identifying and formulating outcomes from 15 Regional GPPAC Networks and five global GPPAC programs can easily find their own information in the database and access each other's data. In addition, they store the outcome information with other information, such as press clippings, meeting reports, publications, PDF of an email, and other information, which serves as evidence and supports the credibility of the outcome statement.

Establishing Classification Categories

The development of categories is a deductive and inductive methodological challenge. Sometimes the categories will have been determined before you get to the analysis step. You will remember in Chapter 3, when agreeing upon the harvesting instrument, we unpacked an evaluation question to arrive at clarity about what "rights-based empowerment of women" means for the intervention. We realized that the user was using "women" as a synonym for "females." Thus, we agreed that we would use the category of "girls" for females between six and 17 years of age and "women" for females 18 years and older.

Whether you derive categories directly from the prime questions or not, they should serve to organize the data so you can answer those questions. In doing so, if it is relevant to answering the harvesting questions, you can use other prisms—for example, the intervention's strategic plan or theory or model of change. Across all potential processes, you try out the categories with the actual outcome data you have harvested to see if the classification will work—if the category fits the data. You do this in the spirit of grounded theory[2] because sometimes the actual harvested outcomes, and especially the unexpected ones, will suggest other categories.

I use these four criteria for generating categories for the descriptions of the different dimensions—in our exemplar, the outcome, its significance and the intervention's contribution—of an outcome statement:

- *Distinct:* A description may correspond to two or more categories, but each category should be conceptually differentiated from other categories. That is, outcome statements may overlap categories, but categories should not overlap each other. One outcome, however, can be categorized into two different categories.
- *Defined:* Each category must be concisely spelled out to the satisfaction of primary users and harvesters. Take care to describe in as few words as possible what you understand for the category.
- *Meaningful:* The definition of the category has to make sense to both the primary users and to the harvesters.
- *Useful:* The categories must be applicable to one or more final prime harvest questions, which may have changed as the harvest unfolded. It makes no sense to classify outcomes with categories that will be irrelevant to you in answering a harvest question.

Establishing categories can be done by users or by harvesters, always in consultation with each other. Often, users may be able to classify more accurately the outcomes because they know what the categories mean. This of course will add to the sense of ownership of those who classify. Either way, you as the harvester test the definitions to make sure they meet the four criteria. For example, in Figure 6.2, I present the categories you would use to classify the outcome descriptions in order to answer the exemplar evaluation question I referred to above. This requires facilitation in the active-reactive-interactive-adaptive mode described in Chapter 3. I actively seek to learn how the primary users understand the key terms—"rights holders" for instance. Then I react to ensure that I understand what they mean but I do this in an interactive manner.

They may say, "Right holders are people who do not have power but have a right to demand it."

I respond, "You mean specifically women and girls, correct?"

They add, "And civil society organizations too as organizations of rights holders."

I then ask, "Can you be more specific about what rights you mean?"

We continue in this manner specifying the categories until it is no longer useful. And the usefulness depends on whether the categories can be

> **Evaluation question: In the light of rights-based empowerment of women and girls, what is the relative importance of the outcomes we have influenced?**
>
> **Categories of the subjects of the outcome—WHO changed**
> 1. Rights holders: People who have the inalienable power to make claims and hold duty bearers to account for upholding their rights to education, income, health and non-discrimination:
>   1.1 Women (females 18 years of age and older)
>   1.2 Girls (females between six and 17 years of age)
>   1.3 Civil society organizations
> 2. Duty bearers: State actors who have a particular obligation or responsibility to respect, protect and fulfil human rights and to abstain from human rights violations. State institutions and their representatives in the:
>   2.1 Legislature
>   2.2 Executive
>   2.3 Judiciary
>
> **Categories of areas of change—WHAT changed**
> 3. Primary education: Right of women and girls to enroll in public school grades 1–8.
> 4. Secondary education: Right of women and girls to enroll in public school grades 9–12.
> 5. Vocational education: Right of women and girls to enroll in 1–2 year training culminating in certification to practice a trade or craft.
> 6. Engage in income generating activities: Right of women and girls to self-employment or wage labor.
> 7. Enjoy good health: Right of women and girls to physical, mental and social well-being, not merely the absence of disease or infirmity.
> 8. Free from discrimination: Right of women and girls not to be treated unfairly or differently because of their race, age, sex, politics, sexual orientation, gender identity, or religion.
> 9. Rights-based policies for women and girls: Modifications of the formal or informal, written or unwritten norms and perspectives that guide the actions of State actors who have a particular obligation or responsibility to respect, protect and fulfil human rights and to abstain from human rights violations.

Figure 6.2 Exemplar—Categories and their definitions for classifying outcome descriptions.

used to classify the outcome data in a manner that will help you answer the prime harvest questions.

When primary users see the outcome statements there is the danger they will become entranced with their richness. In one evaluation my users spent a month arriving at 125 categories with which to classify the outcome statements but their time ran out before they could check to make sure the categories were applicable to the outcome data we had harvested. The evaluation team then compared and contrasted those categories with the actual outcome data and ended up with half that number of categories. Thus, you have to adapt what may appear to be a conceptually sound classification when you actually apply it to classifying the outcome statements. For example, in our exemplar, breaking down "girls" into babies (under 1 year of age), pre-school, primary, secondary, and postsecondary ages would be too specific to be useful. But it is not a mechanical, quantitative exercise. It is about whether the category will be meaningful in helping answer the harvest questions. On the other hand, if you find you have only a handful of Judiciary outcomes [2.3] or policy changes [9] that does not mean you want to do away with those categories because the nature of the change is so important.

Nonetheless, not infrequently, I have found that in spite of intense efforts to establish and define the categories through a consensual process, doubts linger about how the definitions are understood and interpreted. Jennifer Greene suggests that it is helpful to understand a set of categories as not a list but a portrait of the whole set of outcomes, their significance or the contribution of the intervention. Rather than continue a conceptual discussion, it can be more expedient to simply begin to classify and refine the categories as you go along. Naturally, you want the people who are in disagreement to classify together and work out their differences. It can be tedious, of course, but I have found that agreeing on categories, and agreeing on their meaning, is well worth the investment of time and energy.

Classifying Your Outcome Statements

Either user or harvester can apply the categories to classify the outcome statements in the database. When the users classify the outcome statements in consultation with you, there is the added benefit of coming to a common understanding of the meaning of the categories. Your role as facilitator employing rigorous evaluative thinking is critical because there will be subjectivities, biases, and hidden agendas when the intervention staff classify. You have to guard against your own subjectivity as well, of course.

I exemplify in Table 6.1 the classification of the 13 exemplar *outcome descriptions*, four of which were originally presented in Chapter 4, Figure 4.5. (Note that the one negative outcome is in italics.) I have classified the outcomes according to what and who changed because that is what I need to know to answer the harvesting question (see Figure 6.2). Keep in mind, too, that you also develop categories for classifying the descriptions of the significance of the outcome and the intervention's contribution and any other dimension of the outcome statement. The procedure is essentially the same, and so I will only illustrate with the exemplar outcomes. There are two common issues illustrated by the classification of the 13 outcome descriptions.

First, there is the *error of too many categories*. In the light of Outcomes 2 and 3, you could be tempted to add for rights holders the subcategories of "low income women" and "low income girls." Or, you could consider "ministers" as a subcategory of executive duty bearers. The judgment you make is about usefulness. I did not create these or other subcategories simply

110 ■ *Outcome Harvesting*

TABLE 6.1 Exemplar—Classifying 13 Outcome Descriptions

	WHO changed						WHAT changed						
OUTCOMES (negative outcome in italics)	1.1 Girls	1.2 Women	1.3 Women organization	2.1 Legislature	2.2 Executive	2.3 Judiciary	3. Primary education	4. Secondary education	5. Vocational education	6. Income generation	7. Good health	8. Non-discrimination	9. Policy
In January 2017, the minister of women's affairs declared that women's empowerment would be the keystone of the Ministry's policies. [1]	X				X								X
In January–February 2017, 513 girls in eight secondary schools in the lowest-income neighborhoods of the capital voluntarily attended half-day workshops about the importance of encouraging girls to enter into vocational training after graduation. [2]	X								X				
Between January–March 2017, the ministers of education, labor and women's affairs committed themselves to working together to lobby the national cabinet to submit to the legislature a motion to support a vocational education bill to benefit lower income women. [3]					X				X				
In March and April 2017, Employment Now and the Alliance of Tradeswomen, two of the four national women's employment rights organizations, changed their missions from "providing income-generating services to impoverished women" to "empowering women to demand income-generating support from municipal government." [4]			X							X			
On 15 April 2017, Science for Women, Act Now and Lean on Government—experienced in research, community mobilization and lobbying, respectively—signed a memorandum of understanding agreeing to join forces in our campaign for vocational training for women entrepreneurs. [5]			X						X				
On 1 June 2017, the ministers of education, labor and women's affairs submitted the Empower All Women Through Crafts and Trade Education bill to the legislature. [6]					X								X

(continued)

TABLE 6.1 Exemplar—Classifying 13 Outcome Descriptions (continued)

	WHO changed						WHAT changed						
OUTCOMES (negative outcome in italics)	1.1 Girls	1.2 Women	1.3 Women organization	2.1 Legislature	2.2 Executive	2.3 Judiciary	3. Primary education	4. Secondary education	5. Vocational education	6. Income generation	7. Good health	8. Non-discrimination	9. Policy
In June 2017, the Ministry of Labor's intern program for women entrepreneurs began commissioning external evaluations of each cohort's experience. [7]					X					X			
In the first half of 2017, the number of women enrolled in the Ministry of Labor's vocational training courses in the capital decreased 7% in the first quarter and 12% in the second. [8]					X				X				
In the last quarter of 2017, the Ministry of Labor's vocational training courses for women entrepreneurs in the capital increased its enrollment 5%. [9]					X				X				
By December 2017, 125 school girls living in the five largest slums of the capital city had enrolled in our new post-secondary program for training in driving commercial motor vehicles and as plumbers and electricians. [10]	X								X				
On 13 December 2017, before over 1,000 activists demonstrating in front of the national legislature, nine members of the national legislature voiced for the first time their support for the proposed Empower All Women Through Crafts and Trade Education bill to benefit lower income women. [11]				X									
Throughout 2017, in the midst of the elimination of student assessment by the Ministry of Education, the Ministry of Labor's intern program for women entrepreneurs did not stop inviting students to anonymously evaluate the program at the end of each cohort's experience. [12]					X					X			
In the first session on 5 January 2018, the national legislature passed the Empower All Women Through Crafts and Trade Education bill. [13]				X					X				X
Totals	2	0	2	2	7	0	0	0	8	3	0	0	3

because so much categorization would not be helpful to organize the 13 outcomes into manageable clusters.

Second, there is the *temptation to connect everything to everything else*. This is a different dimension of the same challenge of deciding how many categories will be useful. The purpose of classifying will be defeated if you do not draw boundaries. I am inclined to be conservative, suggesting that each outcome be classified according to the one category to which it primarily corresponds. For example, in Outcome 1 you may be tempted to classify the content of the outcomes by all the categories for areas of change since they all are dimensions of women's empowerment; I only classified the outcome as a policy change. In Outcomes 3 and 4, however, although the end result will (hopefully) be policy change, I consider they primarily represent steps towards the State fulfilling its obligations to provide vocational education and income-generating opportunities, respectively, and I classified accordingly. In the case of Outcome 13, however, I did classify as both vocational education and policy. The danger, of course, is that since almost everything is connected to everything else, you have to be sensitive to not reducing outcome data to isolated, unconnected events. Consider that you will weave together the interrelationships in the interpretation part of this step.

Once the outcome statements are classified, you cluster the data as will be most useful for answering the evaluation questions. With only 13 outcomes, you can do this manually. When there are many numbers, using software such as Excel allows you to manage the data much better. This database has the nifty filter mechanism through which you can generate clusters of related outcome descriptions and portray them in charts and tables in order to view the outcome data from different angles and produce different stories or a meta-story. This also permits you to decide the best way to quantitatively present the data. There are some obvious disadvantages to presenting data in tables—many numbers can be mind-numbing. So either a simpler table or other types of visualizations can be more effective.

Interpretation—Using Outcome Data to Answer the Harvest Questions

Analysis provides you with information about *what* has been achieved in the form of tables, charts, graphs, and clusters of text. The interpretative function in Outcome Harvesting aims to produce answers about *so what* do the numbers and text mean. It is in the interpretation stage that you produce evidence-based (i.e., outcomes-based) judgments that answer the prime harvest questions. It is also in this step that you play more of an evaluative than a facilitative role. As the name suggests, evaluation is about making judgments of value regarding the findings.

Who makes the judgments depends on the evaluative nature of the exercise. This is tricky. The harvester's job can involve both facilitating the users' judgments in M&E and in developmental and some formative evaluations, *and* making your own judgments to answer the harvest questions in external, summative evaluations, or both. From my own experience, I know both the value and the difficulty of moving back and forth between those roles. Sometimes, however, the primary users either do not have the time or interest to be involved in the interpretation phase or believe it will be more useful to only have an external evaluator or team make these judgments. This is especially the case when they are going to use the findings to be accountable to a donor. Nevertheless, when appropriate, bringing users and internal human sources together in a workshop or two to discuss the findings can benefit their learning and your interpretation. Barbara Klugman exemplifies the potential value in Box 6.1.

BOX 6.1 SENSE-MAKING WORKSHOP

In an evaluation of a network focused on securing livelihoods for the working poor, especially women, in the informal economy, I brought together for four days 15 people—the network staff and the leaders of all of their programs—to make collective sense of the 422 outcomes harvested. While each of the leaders had reviewed their individual program's outcomes, they had not compared and contrasted them with each other nor with the network staff. For each program, I printed in big writing each of the outcomes I had identified that appeared to relate to each other over a five-year period (and the program's, or programs' contribution to them)—between 10 and 25 for each of eight programs. I asked each program lead to organize these outcomes into a chain, showing which of their activities influenced which outcome. I gave them a few hours to work on their own chains, which they then presented to the group as a whole. In doing so they usually added in activities from long before the period of this evaluation, which gave background and context to the changes they had influenced in the evaluation period. They also explained why they had made certain strategic decisions, which had turned out to be effective and which had not. The other network staff asked questions.

Through this process the entire organization gained much greater insights into programs that they were not directly involved in; they were also able to make links between some of their efforts and the outcomes of other programs. This served as a powerful learning moment for the organization, helping them to find ways of articulating some of their assumptions and of strengthening the coherence of their collective understanding of the work and of the relationships between the strategies of their various programs.

In my final report, I used these outcome chains to illustrate the harvest findings and balance the quantitative data that showed proportions of outcomes having different types of influence—on building movements of informal sector workers, on shifting debate among thought leaders, on labor policy. The outcome chains brought these numbers alive. The network's leaders found this complementary quantitative and qualitative data compelling when accounting to their funders.

In my experience, this collective sense-making is the most useful moment in the Outcome Harvesting process for the organization itself. It is here, together, that they draw out the insights that will shift their subsequent ways of working, rather than from the report which they frequently use more for accountability to funders, than for internal learning. For example, following the workshop and my report, my users reported that staff and network leaders continually quote the collective experience and the document to each other, often needling each other with humor. Thus, aside from the lessons groups draw from the findings, that is lessons about the appropriateness of their theory of change or the effectiveness of their strategies, they internalize how to distinguish activities and outputs from outcomes, and they start "thinking outcomes," so that their work becomes more strongly driven by the changes it hopes to influence than by the imperative to carry out the next training or the next protest or whatever the activities are.

Barbara Klugman, 2018

Therefore, the tendency I experience is that in a formal, independent, external evaluation, usually the harvester(s) answers the prime questions. In M&E processes or for internal evaluations, the intended users and often the human sources together participate in making sense of the outcomes. The interpretation is usually structured explicitly around the prime harvest questions but not necessarily. In the World Bank pilots, for example, the harvest question was implicit. They were clear what they wanted to know: *What outcomes has each World Bank project achieved and how?* This was so obvious and clear that we did not customize the question for each one of the projects. Therefore the most important advice I have about interpretation is to make sure, one way or another, the harvest questions are answered, even when they are implicit.

Basic Interpretation Guidelines

How primary users or you interpret the data will depend on what will be the most useful way to answer the harvest questions for the principal intended uses. Whoever is responsible for the interpretation, he, she or they need to bring to bear expertise to make sense of the numbers and of the text. Be synthetic but not superficial; see the whole without losing sight of the parts. But you do not want to lose the nuances and do want to stay true to the data and be intellectually rigorous.

This, of course, brings me back to the short and simple exemplar story with which I began in Chapter 1. Now I present it more explicitly as a result of the Outcome Harvesting process in Box 6.2. That is, I answer a harvest question by describing what I know based on the outcome data. (The numbers in brackets refer to the ID numbers of the outcomes—see first column in Table 6.1). One word of caution: Since the intervention is not located in a specific place, I cannot contextualize the interpretation, which is of course essential.

BOX 6.2 EXEMPLAR INTERPRETATION—ANSWERING A PRIME EVALUATION QUESTION

In the light of rights-based empowerment of women, what is the relative importance of the outcomes we have influenced?

Overall, in 2017 the intervention was partially successful in terms of the breadth of the outcomes it influenced but impressively successful in the depth of the change it influenced with **duty bearers**. First, on the weak side, the intervention was unsuccessful in influencing changes in women's and girls' exercise of power as rights-holders vis-à-vis primary or secondary education or health. No outcomes were registered in those areas because the intervention has not had sufficient time to influence change.

Three outcomes were achieved in the area of income generation but they are initial steps. In one, two women's organizations changed their missions to emphasize right-based empowerment to demand income-generating support from municipal government [4] and in the other two, the Ministry of Labor strengthened evaluation of its intern program for women entrepreneurs [7, 12]. The first outcome was influenced by the intervention through two open discussion forums it ran between November 2016 and February 2017 for the four leading women's rights organizations in the country, including these two. The program was designed to enhance their awareness and appreciation for the importance of a rights-based approach to gender discrimination. The second and third outcomes were influenced by the same contribution from the intervention. In January and April 2017, the intervention held press conferences on its experiences having internal/external evaluations of their capacity-building program for women's empowerment. This led to five articles in the print media, including the Ministry of Labor's in-house bulletin, and one TV interview with the intervention's program director.

In 2017, the intervention primarily influenced duty bearers in the executive branch of government to take action in the areas of income and rights-based policy for women and especially vocational education [2, 3, 5, 8–11, 13]. The intervention contributed through a combination of vocational capacity-building and advocacy activities. The capacity building included a vocational awareness-raising initiative in classrooms and a vocational counseling service for secondary school students, both boys and girls. It also involved recognition in early 2017 that the intervention's vocational training program was undermining a similar program run by the Ministry of Labor with both offering the traditional sewing, hairdressing, receptionist, and bookkeeping courses: this negative outcome was that women stopped enrolling in vocational training at the Ministry of Labor, which decreased 19% in the first half of the year [8]. As soon as the intervention realized it was unwittingly competing with the government program, the intervention suspended its courses and enrollment at the Ministry bounced back to 5% in the second semester [9].

In spite of almost three times as many outcomes in vocational education, it was in policy that the intervention achieved its greatest success, beginning with influencing the minister of women's affairs to declare in January that women's empowerment would be the keystone of the Ministry's policies [1], followed by the ministers of education, labor and women's affairs working together to submit the Empower All Women Through Crafts and Trade Education bill to the legislature on 1 June 2017 [3, 6]. The intervention then shifted gears from the executive branch and focused on the legislature culminating in two major outcomes:

> On 13 December 2017, nine members of the national legislature voiced their support before over 1,000 activists for the proposed Empower All Women Through Crafts and Trade Education bill to benefit lower income women. [11]
>
> In the first session on 5 January 2018, the national legislature passed the Empower All Women Through Crafts and Trade Education bill. [13]

To influence these outcomes, the intervention's advocacy activities built on those experiences providing girls with vocational services. The intervention also built on the intervention's lobbying of the three key ministries during 2016 to persuade them to work together for a vocational education bill to benefit lower income women. Thus, in January 2017 the intervention began advocacy training for its own staff and that of allies. This was followed by lobbying 17 key legislators in August-November to support the Empower All Women Through Crafts and Trade Education bill and collaborating with four allies to organize this mass rally with 1,000 activists petitioning legislators.

Furthermore, outcome 13 was also a combined vocational and policy outcome. One more directly influenced the advocacy process that led to the legislative victory:

> On 15 April 2017, Science for Women, Act Now and Lean on Government—experienced in research, community mobilization and lobbying, respectively—signed a memorandum of understanding agreeing to join forces in our campaign for vocational training for women entrepreneurs. [5]

In terms of changes in the behavior of rights holders, the two outcomes in 2017 are not only limited to girls (and do not include women) but are also less important in terms of the nature of the change. At the beginning of the year over 500 girls voluntarily attended half-day workshops about the importance of encouraging girls to enter into vocational training after graduation [2]. The intervention contributed by visiting in late 2016 each one of the eight schools in the lowest-income neighborhoods of the capital where these girls lived to request permission to hold half-day workshops, in the school building after class, about the importance of girls receiving vocational training after graduation. The second change in the behavior of rights holders was by the end of 2017, 125 school girls living in the five largest slums of the capital city had enrolled in the intervention's new postsecondary program for training in driving commercial motor vehicles and as plumbers and electricians [10]. The intervention influenced this outcome through a complementary activity to the one for outcome #2: since January 2016 the intervention provided vocational counseling services for secondary school students in these five communities, both boys and girls, to support the adolescents to discover their occupational vocations regardless of gendered norms and practices. As beneficial as these outcomes potentially are, however, for school girls living in relative poverty, they do not address the intervention's goal of empowering girls to make claims and hold duty bearers accountable.

In conclusion, it is in the advocacy and campaigning outcomes with the executive and legislative branches of government that the intervention registered its principal achievements in 2017.

I trust the exemplar demonstrates how the interpretation of outcomes is ripe with the potential for telling a story. You can readily imagine how I could weave in the significance and contribution of the intervention to produce an engaging narrative of relative success. Similarly, if in addition to the basic outcome, significance and contribution descriptions, you harvest information such as the history, context, and contribution of other social actors, or if each of the outcomes were classified in multiple ways, there is a possibility to develop a more bountiful story about outcomes in relation to each other in a common process of change.

Here are the nine basic pointers for interpreting outcomes that I use:

1. *Practice self-reflexivity*: I do not take the words at face value. I continue to ask myself: Did my sources of information mean something different than what I am understanding? Is what and how I am presenting the information and my reflections going to be intelligible and useful to the intended users? Do I know what I say I know? How is my "baggage" coloring my perceptions and understanding?
2. *Interpret the findings so they will be useful*: I keep in my focus the principal uses of my primary users, reviewing them as I answer each harvest question.
3. *Describe only those findings that merit explanation*: I answer the harvest question by pointing out the most salient features of the findings. I remind myself that there is no need to use all the data in my interpretation.
4. *Write the draft as if it were a final version*: This may be a personal idiosyncrasy based on my 10 years as a journalist, but I find that a halfbaked draft text will make it more difficult and time-consuming to arrive at a final version.
5. *Write in the first person*: I also find that by using the first person I own my own voice and engage the reader *tú a tú* (one on one), as we say in Spanish. Thus, I overcome the barriers of impersonal, passive narrative that, at best, refers to me in the third person, as in "the evaluator finds and judges." Communicate *tú a tú* with your primary users and you and they will be able to understand each other much more readily. I observe, I think, I believe, I feel, I conclude. This also acknowledges the subjectivity of all interpretation even when the data itself has been verified.
6. *Avoid becoming a hostage to numbers*: They are not as perfect or as meaningful as they may appear. Numbers will also contain errors. Persuade with your reasoning rather than statistics.
7. *Distinguish facts from opinions*: In Outcome Harvesting you are working with at least two sets of facts: your sources have described what

they know in the descriptions of the outcomes and of the intervention's contribution. The description of the significance of each outcome, however, is opinion. Be careful not to confuse the facts as known by your sources with what your sources feel or believe. This does not mean that facts are more important than opinions, or vice-versa.
8. *Make comparisons carefully and appropriately.* For example, in our exemplar I cannot compare the first quarter of 2018 with any quarter in 2017 simply because we only have data for the first month of 2018. A bit trickier is that all I know is what my sources of information report, not what they do not report.
9. *Cite the quantitative data in the text.* I do not assume the reader will refer to the tables, charts, and graphs. However careful I am in crafting my visuals, I remember that they are simply difficult for some people to understand.

Beyond stories, there are innumerable ways to present your interpretation to make it more useful. I will exemplify with a customized version of the *Gender at Work Framework* (Figure 6.3) to illustrate and interpret the same 13 outcomes based on the role of social institutions or rules (both formal and informal) in maintaining and reproducing women's unequal position in society. This framework is used to conceptualize how change happens in society in a way that is especially relevant to deep structures of inequality and discriminatory social norms. It is in principle applicable in almost any context, ranging from informal to formal social institutions changing individually and systemically.

> The top two quadrants are related to the individual. On the right are changes in noticeable individual conditions, e.g., increased resources, voice, freedom from violence, access to health and education. On the left, individual consciousness and capability—knowledge, skills, political consciousness, and commitment to change toward equality. The bottom two clusters are related to the systemic. The cluster on the right refers to formal rules as laid down in constitutions, laws, and policies. The cluster on the left is the set of informal discriminatory norms and deep structures, including those that maintain inequality in everyday practices. (Gender at Work Framework, n.d., para. 1)

Gender at Work argues that lasting change must occur in all four quadrants because when it does the changes reinforce each other, and they caution that activists often neglect the informal dimension of society represented by the two left hand quadrants.

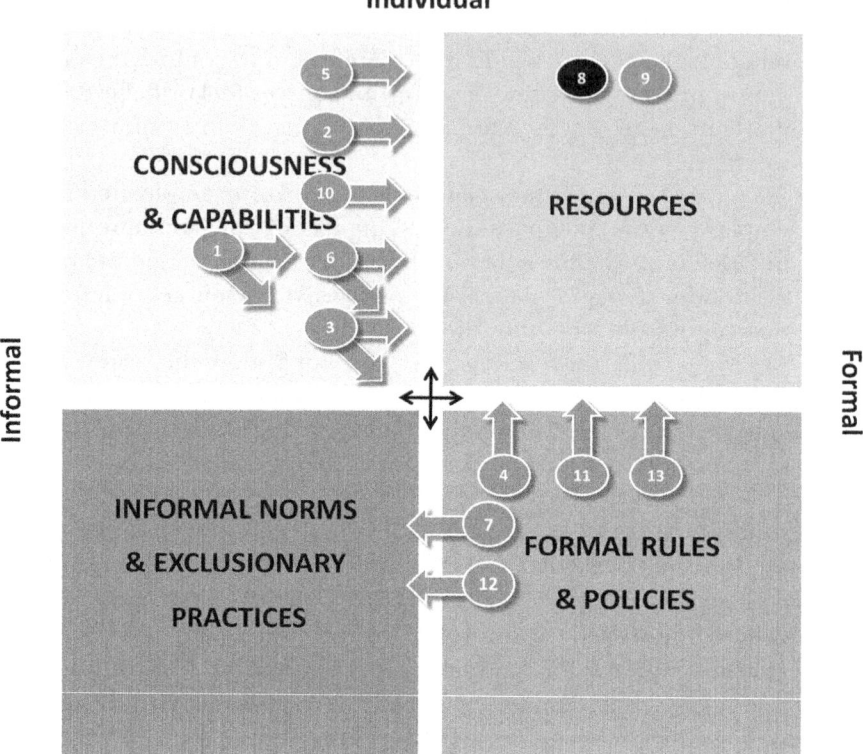

Figure 6.3 Exemplar outcomes in Gender at Work's framework.

Roughly half the outcomes are in the upper left-hand quadrant because they concern changes in the behavior of individuals, especially executive and legislative officials. These are changes in individuals that represent expressions and even shifts in power in favor of women. All of them potentially will lead to resources for individual girls and women, which is the upper right-hand quadrant. There are, however, only two outcomes in that quadrant, and they are directly related to greater resources for girls and women. And one is negative followed by another positive and both concern the enrollment of women in the Ministry of Labor's vocational training. In the lower right-hand quadrant are five outcomes that represent progress towards changing political norms, laws, and policies of formal institutions, in our exemplar, the government. Two have the potential to influence the fourth quadrant of informal institutions guided by cultural norms and practices

[7, 12]. I dare suggest that changing practices around evaluation by the beneficiaries of service programs represents a cultural change.

What potentially makes the Gender at Work framework especially useful is the potential to portray interrelationships. With our exemplar intervention's commitment to empowering women to demand access education, health, and income, the three outcomes in the upper left-hand quadrant that also point to changes in policies in the lower right-hand quadrant are especially noteworthy [1, 3, 6]. They kicked off a process of change influenced by the intervention: the national legislature passed the Empower All Women Through Crafts and Trade Education [11 and 13], which potentially will lead to greater access to education, health, and income for girls and women.

You can decide if the narrative, as in Box 6.1 or this framework with its accompanying narrative, or a combination of the two, enhances the answer to the evaluation questions. Personally, I would propose that the framework be integrated into a narrative answer of the questions. In any case, I would ask the primary users before applying it more widely.

Communicating Your Findings

Usually, although not always, the findings of an Outcome Harvest are communicated in the form of a written report. Michael Quinn Patton recommends six things that I find especially helpful for enabling me to write effective utilization-focused Outcome Harvesting reports (see Patton, 2012, pp. 369–379).

1. *Use is a process, not a report.* For an Outcome Harvesting to be useful, you engage the users from beginning to end. This process of consultation and decision-making ensures that you customize the harvest so it is maximally useful to them. Thus, at the stage of communicating the findings, I remind myself that just because something is written, does not ensure it will be read. If it is read, there is no assurance that it will be understood. And if it is understood does not guarantee it will be applied. That is, the product of an Outcome Harvest is not the report but the use of the harvest process and findings.
2. *Nonetheless, be intentional about reporting.* Know the purpose of a report and stay true to that purpose. If I have been in communication with the primary users throughout the Outcome Harvesting process, when the time comes for presenting the findings, I will have a good idea of what they need to know. Notwithstanding, I check to make sure. For example, when one of the uses of the Outcome Harvesting

evaluation is *accountability*—to present evidence of what the project, program or organization has achieved, I will discuss a draft outline with indicative weights of the different sections for a report they will be able to use in part or in whole to present to stakeholders (see Figure 6.4). In addition to adding an executive summary or striking out one or another section, we agree on the length and what annexes they need. I also find out if they need different reports for different audiences and if they do, what would be the most useful formats.

When a purpose of the outcome harvest is *learning* from the process and the findings, we often use other communication modes: I have presented findings orally, in PowerPoint summaries and through facilitated workshop discussions, as well as in periodic email updates and written reports.

3. *Stay user focused.* Focusing the report on the priorities of users and answering their questions requires customizing the reporting process. You have been consulting with your primary users through the harvesting process. You have communicated with them periodically and as fully as necessary for the decisions they have had to make as the evaluation unfolds. So as you prepare to write the report, and as you write it, consult with your primary users to ensure what you report will be useful to them.

4. *Ensure credibility.* Whether the purpose is accountability or learning, I make sure that however I communicate the findings, it will be useful but also credible. This can be subtler than it sounds because some users tend to defer to me too much or not enough. In some cases, I have to insist that there is no methodologically ideal reporting format—they know their uses; they are the ones who have to decide what will be useful. In others, because of the highly participative nature of the Outcome Harvesting process, I often have to draw the line.

For example, if my report is intended to be from an external, independent evaluator, then I will consult their views on the findings and also present them with a draft report for comments. I explain that my co-evaluators and I will accept their corrections of factual errors and we will rewrite any parts that are not readily intelligible. Nonetheless, except for internal M&E or developmental or formative evaluations in which I advise but am not responsible for interpreting the data, my co-evaluators and I reserve the right to maintain our interpretation even if the primary users do not agree. Thus, while we may have differing views on the interpretation of the data, we all must agree that it is factual. They, of course, have recourse to a management response.

5. *Use graphics and other visuals to communicate findings succinctly and powerfully.* I have found that the best way to present quantitative

outcome data is visually, as illustrated in the tables, charts, and graphs throughout this book. Two excellent sources are The American Evaluation Association's AEA365 blog (http://bit.ly/2zNAlBT) and Better Evaluation (http://bit.ly/2yMIO88). Nonetheless, visuals do not stand alone. Your narrative has to complement them.

6. *Take report writing seriously.* From the beginning, at the time of agreeing the terms of reference for an application of Outcome Harvesting, take care to talk through expectations for the deliverables. For example, seriously consider the time implications required for producing the expected report (the clock and calendar time for a report of a harvest to answer one key harvest question with 20 outcomes is significantly different than the time required to answer three questions with 100 outcomes, or five questions with 500 outcomes). Furthermore, as decisions are made during the harvesting process, keep in mind those expectations. You want to arrive at the report-writing stage able to produce what the primary users need.

Lastly, you may wonder why in Figure 6.4 I do not have a section on recommendations. It has become customary for formal evaluations to include

I	**Background:** Describe the geographical, socio-economic, political, environmental, and historical context and setting.	5%
	Also describe the organization, program, or project that was evaluated (or monitored) with Outcome Harvesting and explain the rationale for the harvest.	
II	**Harvest design:** Identify the primary intended users, the principal uses for the harvest, the prime harvesting questions that they required be answered with Outcome Harvesting, and the data that was to be collected, how and from whom.	5%
III	**Harvest methodology:** Describe how each of the six steps was customized and what the Outcome Harvesting process was that actually unfolded, including who did what, when, and where. Describe the methodological strengths and weaknesses.	5%
IV	**Key findings and conclusions:**	75%
	General findings. Introduce the evidenced-based answers to the prime harvest questions by providing an overview of the data collected	
	Question 1. In the light of rights-based empowerment of women, what is the relative importance of the outcomes we have influenced?	
V	**Conclusions and implications of findings**	10%
VI	**Annexes**—Evaluation terms of reference, biography(ies) of the harvester(s), copies of your data collection tools, the database, and any other information that would interrupt the flow of the main report.	

Figure 6.4 Exemplar—Draft outline of a harvest report.

recommendations, but in my experience to propose what action be taken based on my findings will generally be inappropriate. The exceptions are very specific circumstances in which the evaluator has special expertise—for example, a financial expert might suggest a different computerised accounting program. Or if it is an internal evaluation or an M&E exercise and the people who have the knowledge are necessarily involved in the analysis and interpretation.

Why not make recommendations as a matter of course? Well, an excellent evaluation will draw reasonable conclusions from solid evidence. The evaluators must ensure that all this information is well formulated, plausible, and verifiable, and then they must accurately interpret and make judgments about the relationships between all the data—that is, draw conclusions based on evidence. This is an awful lot to get right.

To take the next step and recommend what decisions or action the users should take, is in my experience an unreasonable expectation of an evaluation team. Surrounding the deliberations of the primary users of an outcome harvest, in addition to the findings, there will be entirely legitimate political, legal, public-perception, internal political, personality, financial, programmatic, and ethical considerations, most of which will be confidential or highly sensitive or both. We as evaluators do not have access to this information. Each one of these factors alone, and especially when combined, will be at least as important as the findings and conclusions of the evaluation when the users make decisions about what to do and not do in the future to improve their results. And this is not solely my opinion. The UK-wide Alliance for Useful Evidence promotes the use of high quality evidence to inform decisions on strategy, policy, and practice. They point out that "it has long been acknowledged that policymakers and practitioners make decisions in environments in which they are subject to multiple, often competing, influences and concerns—of which "evidence" is only one, and a highly contested one at that" (Nutley, Powell, & Davies, 2014, p. 19).

Since recommendations are so customary, I further explain my reticence with a story (Box 6.3).

BOX 6.3 LEARNING THE HARD WAY
Ricardo's Bitter Experience of an Evaluator Making Recommendations

I consider myself fortunate to have learned early-on but the hard way—by making a big mistake—the dangers of an evaluator making recommendations. It was an evaluation of an international human rights federation. My co-evaluator and I were asked by the donors, who along with the members of the federation were the primary intended users of the findings, to recommend if we thought the federation should consider transforming itself into a network. At the time, the federation had one member organization for each of seven countries, and our findings were that they had been quite successful, as evidenced by 36 outcomes, in influencing changes in civil society, multi-lateral and governmental societal actors. I had evaluated other networks and my co-evaluator was a human rights expert from one of the countries with a member in the federation. Consequently, we recommended in our report that the federation become a network because in our judgment they would have a multiplying effect if they had two, three, four or more human rights organizations per country.

This turned out to be a bombshell for the relationship of the federation with its donors. The federation had begun as a loosely organized network with numerous organizations. Early in the organizational life—and before the period we were evaluating—they had made the wrenching decision to limit membership to one organization per country for one simple reason. The human rights issue they primarily focused on was profoundly partisan and every national organization represented a different political faction. When they had more than one per country, consensual decision-making became impossible and the initiative froze. So, after much internal strife and struggle, the seven members became a federation, a decision they have basically maintained to this date. Today, over a decade later, the federation continues to prosper, now with 12 members.

Therefore, I suggest that instead of making prescriptive recommendations in an Outcome Harvesting report, you propose recommended points for discussion. These are usually in the form of questions that serve as a framework for decision makers to begin a meaningful policy debate, with you serving as facilitator or a resource person.

That said, I do not mean to imply that Outcome Harvesting evaluators do not have anything to contribute to a discussion about what to do with their findings and conclusions. They do, and so in Outcome Harvesting there is the sixth step to support use by the users that comes after you report your findings. As Michael Quinn Patton (2012) explains:

> Producing an evaluation report is not the purpose of evaluation. Evaluation is not an end in itself. The purpose is to inform thought and action. Moving from what, to so what, to now what, means moving from data to interpretation to action. Action flows from using evaluation findings. Getting evaluations used is what utilization-focused evaluation is all about. (p. 4)

I have found the sixth step to be perhaps the most difficult of Outcome Harvesting because it is unusual evaluation practice, at least in the social change and development context where Outcome Harvesting currently flourishes. I address it in the next chapter.

In Summary

During this fifth Outcome Harvesting step, the harvesters shift from the facilitating role that characterized their work in the first four steps and develop into a more predominantly evaluation role making judgments, valuing the information you facilitated collecting. This is true whether you are using Outcome Harvesting for M&E or evaluation.

As the harvester, you still facilitate the participation of primary users in making decisions about how the outcome statements best be classified in order to be able to cluster the data in the most useful way to answer the harvest question. In fact, you may even facilitate and coach them in classifying the data. But you have to make the decision whether the categories used for classification, and how the outcome statements are classified, will provide the most credible evidence with which to answer the prime questions. That is an evaluator's role.

In the interpretation of the data, there are two broad scenarios. In internal evaluations or M&E exercises in which the staff of the intervention take the lead, not solely in collecting data but in analyzing and interpreting, your responsibility is to bring hard evaluative thinking to bear to keep them honest to Outcome Harvesting principles and sound evaluative practice. The other scenario is of external, independent evaluations in which you and not the intervention staff are responsible for answering the harvest questions.

Because the first five steps are so heavily user-focused and participatory, making this shift can create tensions. Primary users and sources may find it difficult to accept that while the outcomes are theirs (i.e., the intervention's achievements), making sense of them is taken out of their hands. You will be challenged to make this shift in the most positive and constructive manner. Often a key to success is finding the most appropriate way to communicate your findings to different stakeholders. Fortunately, the process does not necessarily end when you present your findings. In the sixth and last step we will see how you can support the use of the findings after they have been received.

Notes

1. In Outcome Harvesting coding we use the term "categories" rather than "codes." This is because we do not use "codes" as commonly defined in qualitative data analysis to mean "a word or short phrase that symbolically assigns a summative, salient, essence-capturing, and/or evocative attribute for a portion of language-based or visual data." (Saldaña, 2016, p. 4)
2. I use "grounded theory" in its basic meaning of developing categories based on the data, rather than forcing the data to fit into predefined categories.

References

Gender At Work Framework. (n.d.). Retrieved from the Gender at Work website: http://genderatwork.org/analytical-framework/

Harari, Y. N. (2015). *Sapiens: A brief history of humankind.* New York, NY: HarperCollins.

Nutley, S., Powell, A., & Davies, H. (2014) *What Counts as good evidence.* Research Unit for Research Utilisation (RURU) School of Management, University of St Andrews. London, England: Alliance for Useful Evidence. www.alliance4usefulevidence.org

Patton, M. Q. (2012). *Essentials of utilization-focused evaluation.* Thousand Oaks, CA: SAGE.

Saldaña, J. (2016). *The coding manual for qualitative researchers.* Thousand Oaks, CA: SAGE.

Wilson-Grau, R. (2015, September). Evaluation of the Mercy Corps Broadening Participation Through Civil Society Programme in Iraq, 2013–2015. Retrieved from https://bit.ly/2nRUjq7

World Bank. (2014). *Cases in Outcome Harvesting: Ten pilot experiences identify new learning from multi-stakeholder projects to improve results.* Washington, DC: Author. https://openknowledge.worldbank.org/handle/10986/20015.

7

Step 6

Post-Harvest Support for Use

If stakeholders don't use your evaluation, what then was the purpose of your work?
—Marvin C. Alkin (as cited in Christie & Vo, 2015, p. xxii)

Applicability of Key Principles to Step 6

Process principles—Chapter 8
***** I. Facilitate usefulness throughout the evaluation
** III. Nurture appropriate participation
* II. Coach primary sources to formulate outcome statements
** IV. Strive for less because it will be more useful
*** V. Learn Outcome Harvesting experientially

Content principles—Chapter 9
* VI. Harvest social change outcomes
** VII. Formulate an outcome as an observable change
* VIII. Establish plausible influence of the intervention
** IX. Ensure credible-enough outcomes

Legend of Ricardo's rubrics
***** High: I always apply this principle; **** Considerable: I almost always apply it; *** Moderate: I usually apply it
** Occasional: I apply it sometimes but with quite a few exceptions; * Low: I rarely apply the principle in this step

Support for use in Outcome Harvesting begins with the predesign terms of reference and then is center stage through all five steps up to here (Chapters 2–6). This sixth step refers to use as the harvesters have answer the prime questions and present their findings, and the primary users make decisions and take action. For formal formative or summative evaluations, this is generally after the final report has been presented. For M&E and developmental evaluation, support for use can be periodic throughout the process, to support decision-making after moments of reflection and learning.

To exemplify the potential, in late 2015 I led a summative evaluation of the Mercy Corps Broadening Participation through Civil Society (BPCS) program in Iraq. The local team had been implementing the program since October 2012 with funding from USAID and was closing it down in December 2015. The program goal was to contribute to strengthening Iraq's transition to participatory democracy.

Mercy Corps pursued the goal by fostering an increasingly professional, interactive and interconnected Iraqi civil society that offers greater opportunities for citizens to contribute to and benefit from the country's development. Upon the completion of the evaluation and the program, Lorina McAdam, BPCS Chief of Party, wrote of the potential usefulness of Outcome Harvesting (Figure 7.1) for Mercy Corps.

Lorina speaks to the support for use of the Outcome Harvesting *process* and *findings*. Furthermore, on November 13, 2015, she and I presented the Mercy Corps experience at the American Evaluation Conference in Chicago to promote the *methodology* by sharing the Iraq experience as a case study.

The focus on harvest use and usefulness that guide Outcome Harvesting has a 50-year history in evaluation, with the first writing on the subject by the late Carol Weiss (1967), a North American evaluation pioneer, researcher, author, and Harvard professor. The formal emphasis on evaluation process and findings is generally considered to have been born in April, 1978, when Michael Quinn Patton (1978) published the first edition of *Utilization-Focused Evaluation*. Subsequently, the criteria of utility featured prominently in the first edition of standards in 1981 set by the Joint Committee on Standards for Educational Evaluation; utility is the first standard.[1] In 1991 the Development Assistance Committee, an initiative of the Organization for Economic Co-operation and Development, established the DAC Principles for the Evaluation of Development Assistance: impartiality, independence, credibility, and usefulness.

> The Broadening Participation through Civil Society in Iraq experience with Outcome Harvesting reveals many potential uses for Mercy Corps, particularly since its principle-based and flexible approach mesh well with many agency priorities:
>
> - *Adaptive management in complex crises:* With complexity being a constant part of our landscape, Outcome Harvesting allows us to look at what happened, even in complex situations. It also means that the outcomes of adaptations of programs can be captured, and the methodology is adaptive by nature.
> - *Campaign for impact and the 3 I's:* Outcome Harvesting lends itself well to capturing actual examples of changes that can show Impact, Influence and Innovation
> - *Evidence-based programming:* While we traditionally rely more on quantitative data, Outcome Harvesting can help serve as a qualitative evidence base with which to design future programs and iterations with more confidence.
>
> There may also be potential uses for Outcome Harvesting for measuring Mercy Corps' results in challenging and less tangible areas such as resilience, climate change adaptation, and (market) systems change. It could also be employed to identify at country-level outcomes that look beyond program-specific results. The harvest itself lends itself to internal and external communication, and results may be of interest to a wider audience than just program and technical people, but also to communications, marketing and advocacy staff.
>
> While less a use and more of a benefit, Outcome Harvesting is a practical way to include program stakeholders in program evaluation, where Mercy Corps can consult beneficiaries and other external stakeholders as experts and seek their input and opinion. This, in turn, helps Mercy Corps demonstrate accountability to those we serve.
>
> —**Lorina McAdam** quoted in Wilson-Grau, 2015

Figure 7.1 Potential uses of Outcome Harvesting for Mercy Corps.

In the last decade or so, there has been an increasing emphasis on post-evaluation use—evaluators should not stop collaborating with primary users upon the presentation of findings but facilitate post-evaluation use of what has been learned. For example, the Joint Committee on Standards for Educational Evaluation ("The Program Evaluation Standards," n.d.) standards expresses a concern for the consequences of evaluation and urges evaluators to "promote responsible and adaptive use while guarding against unintended negative consequences and misuse" (p. 1). In my experience with Outcome Harvesting, fulfilling this post-harvest supportive role has been the most difficult of the six steps because commissioners and primary users tend to see harvests as finished once the findings are reported. Therefore, make the case for an important distinction between potential utility versus actual use. A harvest that is useable falls short; the harvest must be actually used to have value and be worth all the effort.

Furthermore, Outcome Harvesting holds itself to the standard of actual use and not just usability because the purpose of the approach is to support social change. Outcome Harvesting will contribute to social change only if the harvesting process and findings are actually used and do not remain potentially useful. My expectation as a harvester is that the primary users have the responsibility to use the process and findings of a harvest, and that I have a role in supporting them to do so.

In addition to supporting my users in their use of the findings and process, as a harvester I promote the methodological lessons learned through my Outcome Harvesting experiences, beginning with the approach to evaluation itself. Twenty years ago, Weiss made an important point that echoes my experience. She cautioned:

> We cannot leave the process of evaluation utilization to chance or regard it solely as an in-house conversation among colleagues. The evaluator has to seek many routes to communication—through conferences, workshops, professional media, mass media, think tanks, clearinghouses, interest groups, policy networks—whatever it takes to get important findings (lessons learned) into circulation. And then we have to keep our fingers crossed that audiences pay attention. (Weiss, 1998, p. 32)

Alix Tiernan, a program advisor with Christian Aid Ireland, a development agency working to overcome poverty in some of the world's poorest communities in 24 countries takes utility to heart. She pioneered the use of Outcome Harvesting as a monitoring and evaluation learning tool in that organization to inform their ongoing adaptive management (Figure 7.2).

As exemplified by Mercy Corps above, I consider there are three dimensions for the support for use of an Outcome Harvest: support for use of the findings, for the process, and for the Outcome Harvesting methodology itself. I will explain in more detail the three and how each one can be used for learning or accountability or both.

Support for Use of Harvest Findings

As in evaluation, use of findings is the original and still the core use of a harvest. The nature of the requests for support for the use of findings that I receive is within the purposes that Marvin Alkin and Jean King (2017), two of the most prominent evaluators and authors on evaluation use, summarize as: (a) making decisions, (b) establishing or altering attitudes, (c) substantiating previous decisions or actions, and (d) building an individual's or an organization's harvesting capacity.

> Christian Aid does not implement projects directly but works with various local partners, both faith-based and secular, grass-roots based and advocacy organizations, local and national, who implement the project strategies. In 2016 Christian Aid redesigned its five-year Irish Aid funded Governance and Human Rights Programme, putting an emphasis on adaptive management rather than the more traditional, linear logframe-based approach. The programme design focuses on its long-term outcomes, and how well it is adapting its strategies to achieve them, rather than on delivering results against pre-determined annual targets. The main programme planning tool is the Theory of Change, which sets out the expected programme outcomes, the assumptions around how this change may come about, and then outlines the initial strategies that the programme will implement with a view to making progress towards the programme outcomes as described in the assumptions.
>
> Given the unpredictable nature of the human rights outcomes to be expected, i.e., when and how they might be achieved, and to what extent contextual factors will influence progress towards achieving them, no annual targets are set. Thus, we needed an alternate way of monitoring the programme to see whether progress was being made. Although Outcome Harvesting was conceived and designed as an evaluation tool, Christian Aid has adapted the Outcome Harvesting methodology so that it could be used for regular monitoring of progress.*
>
> During the course of 2017, we harvested, validated and substantiated outcomes. During regular reflection moments, but at least once at the end of the year, Christian Aid staff with staff from the implementing organisations analysed the outcomes as part of the process of revising the Theories of Change. In order to do this, we assessed their significance—both in narrative form and using a scale of 0–5—and the contribution by Christian Aid's partner organisation to each outcome, both narratively and using a score of low/medium/high.
>
> We combined this information with the number of outcomes achieved, and the level of the behavioural change: micro (individual or household), meso (local authority, CSO) or macro (national/international authority, state body). This then enabled us to interpret how well the programme is progressing towards the achievement of the outcomes in its Theory of Change, thus minimising the need for annual targets, and enabling nimble adaptation of the Theory of Change and the programme strategies when it seemed that the strategies are not leading to significant outcomes.
>
> —**Alix Tiernan,** 2018
>
> * Christian Aid was inspired to this adaptation by previous work by Saferworld—A Learning Paper describing their approach can be found here: http://bit.ly/2FLPt9m

Figure 7.2 Outcome Harvesting M&E for Christian Aid Ireland's adaptive management.

Once the harvest is complete, uses that were not foreseen may emerge as priorities for the primary users. For example:

- If the application of the Outcome Harvest was conceived as an exploration of the potential of the approach for the monitoring or evaluation, or both, of an intervention, accountability may not

have been the purpose. The pilot, when successful, may generate data that the primary users then decide they want to use to inform stakeholders about what was done and what is being achieved by their intervention.
- Since primary users of Outcome Harvesting are generally working in substantial uncertainty and dynamism, they often find what had been initially conceived of as a summative evaluation becomes a formative one. For example, by the time the findings are presented, the user has secured funding for the continuation of the project. Then, they decide that they want to use the findings not only for accountability but also to make decisions to modify the model or initiative based on what they learn is and is not working.
- Similarly, the primary user may receive funding for a different project and decide at the end of a summative Outcome Harvesting evaluation that they want to use the findings to plan that future work.
- Although an Outcome Harvest does not assess performance, since the contribution to outcomes will reveal information about which of their activities are delivering outcomes and which are not, primary users sometimes find that they want to use that information to evaluate the performance of departments or units, projects or programs. For example, since the harvest will identify what activities and outputs are comparatively more or less productive, or even by default those that have not generated outcomes, this information can serve as the basis for a process of analysis and reflection on performance.

Therefore, although proportionally I find that support for use of the findings is primarily about being accountable internally or externally, it can also be about learning from the findings. These new uses may demand the harvester's support. More specifically, I have been asked to perform one or more of these six tasks, sometimes by new users who emerge in the course of discussion of the report or findings. You will see that I do not consider all of these tasks appropriate:

1. *Present the findings in different formats.* I present a report of the findings of a harvest in the format that will be most useful. Usually this is a report with an executive summary and extensive annexes. (See the section "Communicating Your Findings" in Chapter 6.) The different pieces lend themselves to be used separately. For example, the executive summary may be what the primary user sends to prospective sources of funding, whereas the full report is sent to

current funders with a selection of the annexes. The annex containing the harvested outcome data—generally an Excel database—can serve as a stand-alone document for teams who want to dive deeper into the information. Commonly, I am asked to summarize the report in a PowerPoint presentation.

Nonetheless, some users only realize what they need after they have the report in hand. For example, only after reading and discussing the report do they perceive its usefulness for allies or beneficiaries. Thus, post-harvest they may ask for my co-evaluators and I to put together an oral presentation to be delivered in person or electronically, or more visual representations (a poster, for example) highlighting a process of change, how the outcomes contribute to their theory of change or the implications for their strategic plan.

2. *Further analyze the outcome data.* The original analysis of the outcomes serves to answer the prime harvesting questions. Often those answers lead to new questions that require organizing the raw harvested data into different forms. This can involve agreeing on one or more different analytical "lenses" and therefore new classification categories to insert into the Excel database.

3. *Reinterpret with different lenses.* Similarly, the initial findings can lead the primary users or other stakeholders to want to examine the findings from different perspectives. For example, a common use of the findings is to inform or reform the intervention's theory of change. As the harvester, I can play a role in facilitating or, if an external view is desired, reinterpreting the data from other conceptual perspectives.

4. *Facilitate bringing in the perspectives of others.* The outcome harvest usually challenges primary users, sometimes profoundly, in particular when it represents for them a paradigm shift in thinking about evaluation. For instance, I find that the highly participatory nature of the harvest often leads primary users to revalue *empowerment* when they have been more concerned with their own *effectiveness* in influencing change. Consequently, they may decide post-harvest that they want to include beneficiaries in interpreting the data—what is the significance of outcomes for their lives? discussing the recommended points, or making programmatic decisions, or all three.

I find all four of these tasks to support the use of Outcome Harvesting findings appropriate for me, at least as a harvester. There is another task related to the use of the findings that I have been asked to perform as an evaluator that I do not find appropriate, although this may be because of my own personal consulting ethic.

5. *Recommend action to be taken.* Once the primary users and possibly other stakeholders know *what* has been achieved and *so what* does it mean for the intervention, they are ready to decide *now what?* That is, they will need to determine the action implications of the findings. Primary users want to know what my co-harvesters and I recommend they do in the light of the findings. In the last chapter I explained why I rarely accept a request to include recommendations in a harvest report.

In addition, the late Carol Weiss (1988) explained why many years ago:

> Even when program staff know about the findings, understand them, believe them, and see their implications for improving the program, many factors can interfere with their using results for program improvement. Among the possible obstacles are conflicting beliefs within the program organization, with staff unable to agree on what the important issues are; conflicting interests between program units, so that there is a squabble over resources or clout; changes in staff, so that new people coming in have different priorities from those in force when the evaluation was begun; rigidity of organizational rules and standard operating procedures that prevent adoption of improved strategies suggested by the evaluation; shifts in external conditions, such as budget cuts or changes in the political climate that make the organization unable to respond to the need for change revealed by evaluation, and so on. (p. 5)

Moving from the principle of supporting use to actually and effectively doing so is perhaps one of the hardest challenges in Outcome Harvesting. It is a cultural change, since the common notion is that the evaluator's task ends with the presentation of the findings. Salome Tsereteli-Stephens is deputy director of research, evaluation, and learning for the American Bar Association's Rule of Law Initiative (ABA-ROLI). She has led an internal harvest exercise and explains in Figure 7.3 the lessons she learned about how to engage and support primary users after findings are reported.

Support for Uses of the Outcome Harvesting Process

Process use is common in my application of Outcome Harvesting, which is understandable since the participatory approach is not only a useful way to assess outcomes but also to monitor them as they emerge. Increasingly, colleague harvesters and I are contracted directly to advise organizations on how to develop their internal capacity to introduce Outcome Harvesting into their monitoring system. Perhaps the foremost example is that of the 25 consortia of civil society organizations (CSOs) in the Dutch Ministry

> ABA ROLI's Support to the Kyrgyzstani Legal Defense Community Program started with USAID funding in February 2012. To improve access to an impartial justice system, build public confidence in the legal system, and promote stability in the Kyrgyz Republic, ABA ROLI is using a three-pronged approach focused on enhancing the capacity, skills, and knowledge of practicing attorneys and the next generation of Kyrgyzstani lawyers. At the end of the first phase of the program in 2014, the program commissioned an internal evaluation to summarize the achievements and effectiveness of the project and use the information prospectively to inform future programming.
>
> After document review, as ABA ROLI's internal M&E coordinator, I facilitated a discussion on December 19, 2014 with the Washington DC headquarters-based staff who are deeply involved in program implementation. They have an in-depth knowledge of the program through field visits, workplan development, regular program oversight, and quarterly reporting on implementation. We discussed the program theory of change based on their history with the program and formulated draft outcomes from their perspective.
>
> I replicated this discussion in the field office in Bishkek in February 2015. Staff there reviewed the theory of change, and then compared and contrasted the outcomes identified in Washington, adjusted outcome formulations, and formulated more outcome statements. Through this hands-on exercise, field-based staff gained an in-depth appreciation for the importance of valid, high quality data and the strengths and weaknesses of the theory of change in the light of outcomes actually achieved. There was a heightened sense of commitment to improving practices for enabling collection and recording of data throughout future implementation.
>
> The result of both discussions about the importance of data and the evidence and insights generated by the outcome harvest, in addition to knowledge about more outcomes for the project, influenced managers in Washington to change program monitoring and evaluation approaches. By incorporating M&E functions explicitly into dedicated staff job descriptions almost immediately after the evaluation, they demonstrated the commitment to quality M&E.
>
> There was general agreement in ABA ROLI that this Washington-Bishkek discussion of the theory of change and outcomes improved the program monitoring processes after the evaluation, and certainly provided a consensual base as a result of the creative discussion process.
>
> The validated outcome statements proved to be a reliable foundation for a new follow-up on activities. And the useful effect is enduring. The field office has independently continued to collect data on program outcomes. They revisited the structure of the quarterly reports and elevated the role of outcome statements and supporting evidence. Several additional iterative data collection practices were also put in place, including an online survey, to regularly capture information from program beneficiaries. They significantly improved the quality of reports, with a greater focus on outcomes. As the principles of Outcome Harvesting have been integrated systematically into the program M&E system, we have also observed program staff in the field and at headquarters exploring multiple uses for outcome statements and evaluation reports—from reporting to donors and other stakeholders to using the information in communications and outreach.
>
> —**Salome Tsereteli-Stephens**, 2018

Figure 7.3 Salome Tsereteli-Stephens's ABA ROLI example of post-harvest support.

of Foreign Relations' €1 billion Dialogue and Dissent (D&D) program.[2] In 2016–2020 they are lobbying and advocating to influence development around the world. The Ministry recommended Outcome Harvesting as one approach for monitoring and evaluation.

Historically, the Netherlands has been among the world's leading aid donors and amongst the largest contributors of development assistance as percentage of gross national product. The main aim of the innovative D&D program is to contribute to sustainable inclusive development for all and fight against poverty and injustice by promoting civil society's political role. This presents a shift in focus from aid aimed directly at combating poverty through service delivery to aid aimed at tackling the root causes of poverty and (gender) inequality through lobbying and advocacy. The Ministry recognizes that when promoting civil society's political role, traditional top-down, logical framework approaches are unsuitable due to the complex and erratic nature of political processes. The Ministry says a more flexible and context-specific approach is needed, ensuring local ownership, embeddedness, and local legitimacy.

The D&D framework has two major innovations for Dutch development cooperation. First of all, the focus on promoting civil society's political role is an innovation in itself as not many donors support this role due to the greater risks, both to their reputation, since these groups may represent a wide range of political perspectives, and because of the unpredictability of outcomes. It involves promoting the advocacy capacity of CSOs and raising their voice both in their own countries and beyond. A second innovation is the choice to work with flexible theories of change that are adapted to different contexts and can constantly be updated based on contextual changes and emerging insights. To optimally feed this adaptive process, the Ministry insists that the CSOs design and implement their own planning, monitoring, evaluation, and learning systems. The Ministry recommends, however, that CSOs use "process oriented methodologies such as Outcome Harvesting" and up to 70% of the consortia have accepted the advice.

The process use purpose for an Outcome Harvest frequently pops up in the course of a harvest. It may be as early as during the review of documents that the intervention recommended as outcome-rich when we see that what they thought were "outcomes" are really outputs, or that their reporting of changes in attitudes, awareness, and consciousness turn out to be undemonstrated perceptions based on intuition or feelings but not on verifiable, demonstrated changes in behaviour. Confronting these issues leads to users recognizing that harvesting outcomes can improve communication and foment common understanding amongst their staff about what is actually understood as an "outcome."

When the use of Outcome Harvesting does not work as a carrot, some primary users realize that it can be useful when projects or programs have been going their own, dissimilar ways. Having all field staff report using the same concept of an outcome can be a soft stick to bring disparate interventions of the same organization together because "what gets measured tends to be what gets done."

The highly participatory nature of Outcome Harvesting, involving primary users in decision-making and those closest to the action in providing information, often foments greater interest and commitment to identifying outcomes and learning from them. By the time the harvest ends, there is a need to continue developing the use of the approach as an ongoing tool for M&E.

An M&E or evaluation using Outcome Harvesting often begins with a primary use to demonstrate what a project or program is actually achieving in uncertain and dynamic environments. Often it is the managers and field staff themselves who are first impressed by the operational value of a periodic, systematic review of what they have achieved and how. It is a short step then to want to more rigorously learn from what they are achieving as an ongoing activity.

One or more of these benefits of an Outcome Harvesting process lead to my co-evaluators and I being asked by users to continue to support them to adapt and integrate the practice of harvesting outcomes, and learning from them, into their work.

Use of the Outcome Harvesting Methodology

With the lessons I learned from developing and customizing the six steps for a diversity of applications, I have become much more proactive in fomenting the use of the approach. I promote the methodology in a diversity of ways, and I encourage other practitioners to do the same:

- Writing for publications about different applications of Outcome Harvesting in English, Spanish, and Portuguese, now including this book.
- Running 1-, 2- and 3-day workshops and sessions on Outcome Harvesting for colleague evaluators.
- Participating in email discussion forums, sponsoring one for Outcome Harvesting (https://dgroups.org/groups/outcome-harvesting/outcomeharvesting/), and maintaining a website (www.outcomeharvesting.net). The purpose of all these activities

includes supporting the development of a high-quality Outcome Harvesting community of practice.
- Supporting methodological use. My consultancy policy includes devoting 25% of my time to learning and sharing what I know.

Taking responsibility to share Outcome Harvesting is, for me, a means to be accountable to the numerous stakeholders with whom I have developed and used Outcome Harvesting. This, of course, includes my co-evaluators and the primary users but also many others, from the people who have served as sources of information to the intended beneficiaries of the projects, programs, or organizations I evaluate. It also includes my colleagues in the evaluation community without whom I would never have been able to become the evaluator I am today.

If support for use sounds like a straightforward challenge to facilitate primary users to see its value for them, I have to disappoint you. Use is quite problematic.

The Challenges of Use, Non-Use, Misuse, Overuse, and Abuse of Outcome Harvesting

In supporting use, the stakes are high: "Evidence has shown that decision- and policy-makers and others within the program community are more likely to embrace evaluation and to integrate it into their thinking and decision-making if they experience successful use of evaluation" (Cousins & Bourgeois, 2015). The process or the findings of Outcome Harvesting matter little if they do not serve the principal uses of the primary users. The methodological lessons only matter if they serve some useful purpose. The challenges, however, of supporting use can be messy (Figure 7.4).

The initial hurdle is ensuring that Outcome Harvesting has a useful purpose for the primary users. First, you have to guard against what Marvin Alkin (1990) defines as *symbolic purpose*: misuse "for political gain, for publicity, to obtain funding, to delay action or to avoid taking responsibility" (p. 290) in which there is no real commitment or interest to take the evaluation process or findings seriously. He considers that symbolic purpose represents *misuse* because it undermines informed decision-making. I find that the emphasis on the utilization focus of Outcome Harvesting in the terms-of-reference stage tends to flush out when the principal use of primary intended users is symbolic. These misusers have no interest in serious conceptual engagement and participation in decision-making throughout

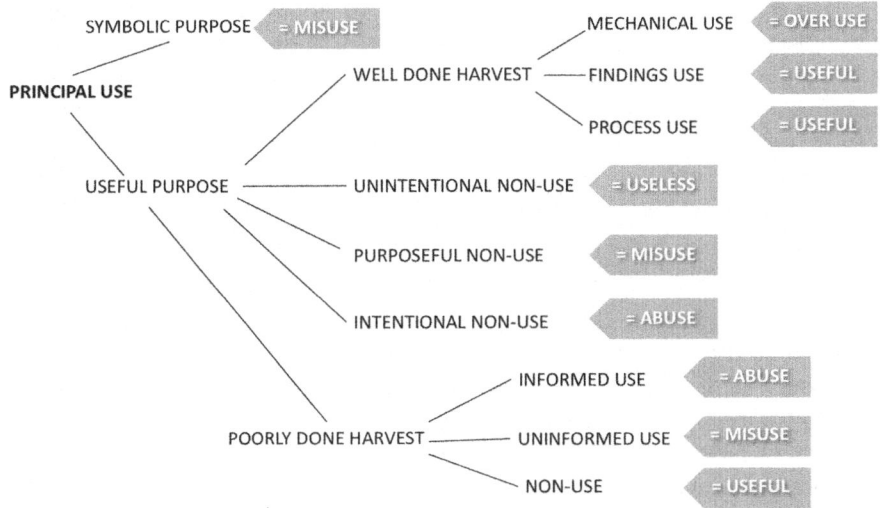

Figure 7.4 The challenges of supporting the use of Outcome Harvesting findings or process (Adapted from Alkin [1990] and Patton [2015b]).

the harvest. More than once I have nipped the harvest in the bud and declined to be contracted if it was clear to me that the purpose was symbolic.

If, however, the harvest is done with a *useful* (Alkin [1990] calls it "instrumental") *purpose* because the intended users consider there is at the least a potential likelihood of using the harvest information, then two possibilities open: well-done or poorly done harvests. A poorly done harvest can, of course, be the evaluator's fault, ranging from technical incompetence to unethical behavior. But it can also be due to unforeseen circumstances. A fundamental reason for writing this book is that I have seen poor harvests performed by other evaluators and believe the cause is a lack of information or misunderstanding about the approach. I understand how it can happen for I too have certainly committed errors and have been responsible for poor harvests because of, for example, faulty statistical analyses, not my forte.

When the findings or process of a poorly done harvest are unwittingly used, Alkin (1990) calls this misevaluation, which it is. Nonetheless, I emphasize it more as *uninformed misuse* and a mistake for which I am responsible as the evaluator and from which lessons must be drawn—once it is recognized. The more serious situation is when users know the harvest is faulty but deliberately use the findings anyway because it serves their interests. This *informed misuse* is abuse and although rarely, it has happened to me. Usually, however, either the user or I, or both of us, catch the error in time and they do not use those findings, which is, of course, regrettable but certainly appropriate.

The second possibility is the successful completion of the five steps of a well done outcome harvest, which is necessary but far from sufficient for a fruitful use of the findings. Unfortunately, I have had solid harvesting findings *intentionally not used* because the findings were not welcomed. I also consider this an abuse, as I would if I succumbed to pressures from a user to modify negative or controversial findings. More commonly, I have too often had my harvest findings *unintentionally not used*. As far as I know, this has happened when in the end the decision-makers did not require the evidence generated by the harvest; it was perceived as useless.

Of course, the desirable scenario is that a satisfactory harvest leads to the primary users using the findings and process—that is a basic purpose of Outcome Harvesting. There is, however, always a danger of overuse when weak or limited yet still valid results or process are *mechanistically used* or given too much weight. As I work more and more advising organizations on building their internal capacity in Outcome Harvesting, I quite frequently have to caution against assuming that having participated once in the application of Outcome Harvesting is sufficient for their staff to be able to supervise and support others to do the same. Assuming that one experience identifying and formulating outcomes is sufficient training to facilitate and coach others can be a case of process *overuse*. I also find users who operate in uncertain, dynamic circumstances to be under great pressure to find "best practices" that they can scale up in different times and places. This is really overuse of the findings because in their dynamic context, even when they are operating in the same place, in the future (even the near future: next year), the relationships of cause and effect often are again substantially unknown.

How to cope with these challenges for supporting use? Fortunately for Outcome Harvesting, evaluators around the world have had 40 years of experience with Utilization-Focused Evaluation. Over the four decades of experience documented in the four editions of the book of that name, plus another more recently on the essentials of the method, Michael Quinn Patton learned lessons about the importance of follow-up to enhance use (Patton, 2012, pp. 382–385). I will use nine of those lessons to frame my suggestions for how to address the messiness of use following an outcome harvest to minimize overuse, nonuse, misuse, and abuse and to enhance the harvest's usefulness.

1. *Plan for Follow-Up to Support Use*

The support for use begins with design (Step 1) when I establish that for me the purpose of Outcome Harvesting is to meet the principal intended use of primary users. Then, we discuss all six steps but only plan one at a time. Concretely, when designing the harvest, we make decisions on what documentation to review (Step 2) but only make tentative decisions on who to engage internal primary sources of information (Step 3). We discuss but delay final decisions on substantiation (Step 4) and analysis and interpretation (Step 5) until we have harvested solid outcomes. Similarly, we also entertain but postpone final decisions on how to support the use of the process and findings post-harvest (Step 6) until we get to this stage of the harvesting process. The users' participation in decision-making throughout the harvest reinforces the need to be prepared and proactive, but step by step. If successful, by the time we arrive at the sixth step, the discussion of support for use flows naturally.

2. Budget for Follow-Up to Support Use

In the Outcome Harvesting design step, users and I also discuss in principle what human resources and clock and calendar time foreseeably will be required once the findings are presented. I always propose budgeting for my time post-harvest. These are always estimates because it only makes sense to take specific decisions one step at a time. Nevertheless, foreseeing probable post-harvest support is especially palatable because I only charge a client for time actually worked. Naturally, as you progress through the harvest, the actual needs for human, financial, and time resources to support use will become clearer and clearer.

3. Offer to Adapt Findings for Different Audiences

During the course of the Outcome Harvest, primary users will understandably want to ensure that the reporting of findings will be useful to them. So I try and focus on how to report in ways also useful to their secondary users and the audiences. Some ways are obvious, such as summarizing the findings and conclusions in a PowerPoint or illustrating the executive summary with drawings, pictures, and graphs and producing it as a separate piece.

4. Keep Findings in Front of Those Who Can Use Them

In uncertain, dynamic circumstances, users and uses change often, as does the use-by-date of harvest findings. Therefore, I make the argument that I should be retained after the end of the Outcome Harvest to advise new users or on new uses that emerge post-harvest. The formal retainer agreement keeps a door open and since I only charge for my time that they actually demand, is not an expense if they do not use it.

5. Watch for Emergent Opportunities to Reinforce the Relevance of Findings

If I am engaged in supporting use post-harvest—for example, by continuing to support internal sources to hone their skills in the process of identifying and formulating outcomes or undertaking new analysis and interpretation of the findings—it is natural to be on the lookout for emerging relevance of the harvest. The significance of findings can change over time, sometimes quickly. As people react to the results, new opportunities may emerge to connect the harvest findings to unanticipated events, new decisions, emergent research, or other harvest findings. I will also seek to engage the users in promoting the methodological use of Outcome Harvesting.

6. Deal With Resistance

Rarely will there not be losers in a harvest, and sometimes the same person can win and lose from a harvest process or findings or from promoting Outcome Harvesting's use. There is always a serious risk that resistance will lead to compromises that will be unworkable, such as limiting monitoring of lower priority events. As the implications of an Outcome Harvest sink in, and especially if there are stakeholders who want to take them seriously, you can expect criticism—fair or not—of the process and the findings. Usually, those in favor of the harvest will require help in sorting out appropriate and inappropriate criticism of weaknesses and implications raised by those who oppose the harvest. You need to foster an open, frank, and informed weighing of, for example, the value of an intensely participatory exercise focusing on the results that matter most to the intervention, versus the burden of the time it takes to monitor outcomes.

7. Watch for and Guard Against Misuse

Outcome Harvesting evaluations that are highly participatory, complexity-aware, and based on qualitative data can be very political. Internal politicking between people with different vested interests is a fact of life. If you are present, however, you can head off unintentional misuse and intentional abuse of a harvest. I have found that the most common danger is simple misunderstanding due to users either seeing or not seeing what they expected to see. You can help them understand the harvest, but, of course, they have to reconcile their differences. Building time into the evaluation design in which principal users can engage with each other and the evaluation team about areas of disagreement or misunderstanding is essential. Frequently evaluations are commissioned at the last minute and findings are needed to inform funder decisions. In this context critical steps of collective sensemaking of findings can be left out, resulting in potential nonuse or misuse of findings. Thus, it can be useful to establish a simple mechanism through which adaptations of the findings for different audiences are checked with the evaluators for integrity.

8. Champion Use of the Findings, but Do Not Become a Champion for the Intervention

This has proven to be a special challenge for me, but especially for my co-evaluators who are immersed in the subject matter. We are all committed to the social change purpose of the intervention; otherwise, I will not do an outcome harvest. We believe that a rigorous assessment, however critical it may turn out to be, is positive for the intervention. Nonetheless, the challenge is to support use without sacrificing our credibility, to advocate for the harvest findings without advocating for the intervention. Eleanor Chelimsky, who in addition to having been founding director of the Program Evaluation and Methodology Division of the U.S. Government Accountability Office, is also a former president of the American Evaluation Association, concisely defines the challenge: evaluators must avoid advocating for . . .

> individual groups, particular outcomes, partisans, lobbyists, the policy makers who give us grants and contracts, in short, stakeholders in general. The problem is that once the question of evaluative honesty—that paramount value—is raised, it will tend to vitiate the persuasiveness of our work. (2010, p. 1)

9. Continue to Build Outcome Harvesting Capacity Throughout the Follow-Up Process

When the follow-up includes support for continuing to harvest outcomes as an ongoing monitoring exercise, this will be automatic. I find that this role is important when users have additional questions about the data or new questions they want answered with the data. A common request is for training in using an Excel database to cluster data or to classify the outcome descriptions with different categories. Although you can, of course, do this for them, I see it as an opportunity to build their capacity to do it for themselves.

In Summary

This sixth and final step in Outcome Harvesting can prove to be the most frustrating because success depends less on the harvester and more on the primary users. First, the users must be committed to make decisions and take action based on the harvest findings. In spite of the users' best intentions, other actors and factors may not be favorable to actually using the findings. Plus, the users have to appreciate what the harvester can provide to support action. If those two conditions are met, the harvester can provide support such as presenting the findings in different formats, further analysing the outcome data, reinterpreting the data with different lenses, and facilitating bringing in the perspectives of others. I usually, however, draw the line with support for the use of findings when the potential conflicts of interests are weighty: I do not recommend actions to be taken by the users and much less agree to implement users' decisions based on my findings.

A second area of support is in relation to the Outcome Harvesting process. This too can prove frustrating but for different reasons. Often the user who is interested in having evaluation findings, for accountability and for learning and taking action to improve the intervention, is not interested in the intervention using Outcome Harvesting for process uses. The big exception, and a growing one, is users' interest in building their intervention staff's capacity to identify, formulate, and learn from outcomes after the harvest is over. In this case, the harvesters' support for bolstering the capacity of the internal sources they have been coaching is a natural.

A third area of support for use is on something of a different order: support for the use of the Outcome Harvesting methodology by other potential users. This requires harvesters' methodological commitment because by and large this is a pro bono activity within the evaluation and social change community. It certainly can enhance the harvesters' and the users' reputations and professional profiles, as well as boost networking, but the real value is that others will learn about Outcome Harvesting. That, of course, can be a double-edged sword unless you believe, as I do, that one can be professionally more productive by cooperating than by competing with colleagues.

Lastly, supporting use runs through a number of traps and dilemmas. Users and harvesters alike may consciously or unconsciously misuse Outcome Harvesting and its findings. A poorly done harvest can lead to erroneous use or purposeful abuse. The findings of a well-done harvest may never be used, whether intentionally or unintentionally. The other danger is overuse of Outcome Harvesting, wherein the user or harvest exaggerate the process or findings. When a harvester can support a user to make decisions and actions based on the process and findings, the results, in my experience, are usually well worth the risks of misuse, mistakes, useless actions, overuse of findings, or outright unethical abuse. The prize is the realization of the purpose of Outcome Harvesting—to be useful for social change.

Notes

1. The Joint Committee on Standards for Educational Evaluation is an American/Canadian private nonprofit organization accredited by the American National Standards Institute (ANSI). The Joint Committee represents a coalition of major professional associations formed in 1975 to help improve the quality of standardized evaluation. See http://bit.ly/2yTnlwO
2. The following description of the Ministry's D&D program comes from the Ministry's report *Dialogue and Dissent Theory of Change 2.0—Supporting civil society's political role* (Kamstra, 2017).

References

Alkin, M. C. (1990). *Debates on evaluation.* Newbury Park, CA: SAGE.

Chelimsky, E. (2010, December 19). *AEA Thought Leaders Forum,* p. 1, Posted 12-19-2010 15:55, https://bit.ly/2OZiXAQ

Cousins B., & Bourgeois I. (2015). The third perspective: Uniting accountability and learning within an evaluation framework that takes a moral-political stance. In C. Christie & A. Vo (Eds.), *Evaluation use and decision making in society: A tribute to Marvin C. Alkin* (p. 91). Charlotte, NC: Information Age.

Kamstra, J. (June 2017). *Dialogue and Dissent Theory of Change 2.0: Supporting civil society's political role.* Ministry of Foreign Affairs of the Netherlands.

Patton, M. Q. (1978). *Utilization-focused evaluation.* Thousand Oaks, CA: SAGE.

Patton, M. Q. (2012). *Essentials of utilization-focused evaluation.* Thousand Oaks, CA: SAGE.

The Program Evaluation Standards—Summary Form (n.d.). Retrieved from the American Evaluation Association website: http://www.eval.org/p/cm/ld/fid=103

Weiss, C. H. (1967). Utilization of evaluation: Toward comparative study. In House of Representatives committee on government operations. In *The use of social research in federal domestic programs, Part III* (pp. 426–432). Washington, DC: Government Printing Office.

Weiss, C. H. (1988). Evaluation for decisions: Is anybody there? Does anybody care? *Evaluation Practice, 9*(1), pp. 5–19.

Weiss, C. H. (1998). Have we learned anything new about the use of evaluation? *American Journal of Evaluation, 19*(1), 32.

8

Outcome Harvesting's Process Principles

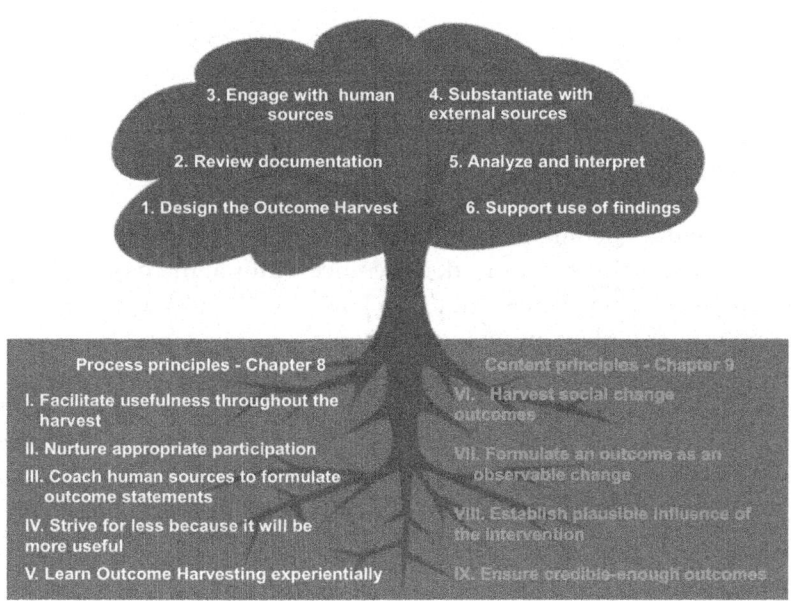

In Chapter 1, "The Guiding Principles" section, I introduced the nine core principles that I and co-harvesters have used to maintain the fidelity of the Outcome Harvesting as we customize the six steps for each harvest. I find a useful way of ordering the principles is by those that provide guidance for process and for content. The five *process principles* are those that, in my view and experience, guide *how* to apply the six Outcome Harvesting steps. The four *content principles* provide direction for *what* should be the results of the harvest. In this and the next chapter, I explain the principles one by one. You may have already referred to them because on the first page of each of the previous six chapters on the Outcome Harvesting steps, I highlight the relative importance I have found for each one of the nine principles for that specific step.

The person responsible for applying Outcome Harvesting combines the role of facilitator, coach, mentor, and evaluator. The five process principles presented in this chapter will guide you in customizing the six Outcome Harvesting steps as you perform these roles.

I. Facilitate Usefulness Throughout the Evaluation

Involve primary intended users in decision-making from the beginning to the end of the Outcome Harvest.

A basic purpose of Outcome Harvesting is to generate an evaluative process and findings that are "owned" by the users and will be applied to understand and inform their efforts at social change and contribute a little bit to a better world. Outcome Harvesting is a customized, emergent approach, for interventions that face considerable uncertainty at the moment of planning but also during implementation. This is the reason why a utilization-focus prevails from beginning to end. Design decisions must, of course, be made at the beginning of the process, but they must also be made as the process unfolds and results emerge. Users and harvesters alike accept a continuous responsibility to make certain the Outcome Harvesting process and findings correspond to emergent uses as well as the original ones, and to the prime harvesting questions derived from them.

The quantity and quality of the participation of users in decision-making throughout the Outcome Harvest can be documented and assessed if desired. This includes whether the process and findings were actually used post-harvest in the support-for-use sixth step, as explained in the last chapter. In Table 8.1, I describe how the usefulness principle applies to each one of the six steps and the degree of its applicability that I have found in my practice.

TABLE 8.1 Description and Degree of Applicability of the *Facilitating Usefulness Principle* per Outcome Harvesting Step

Outcome Harvesting Steps, Chapters 2–7	Application of the principle
1. Design the Outcome Harvest	The usefulness purpose of the harvest is to provide users with the process and findings that they need in the light of their principal uses for the Outcome Harvest. ***** **Always**
2. Review documentation	If the foreseen secondary sources turn out not to be outcome rich, then users and harvesters decide about alternatives, including the option of not using documentation as a source. ** *Sometimes*
3. Engage with human sources	These primary sources have to be motivated to share what they know about what was achieved and how the intervention contributed. Commonly they are staff reporting to one or more of the primary intended users. While at the time of reviewing and improving outcomes they may be taken aback by the amount of time it takes, by Step 5 they usually see value in the investment. *** **Usually**
4. Substantiate with external sources	Primary users must decide what verification or deepening of understanding of outcome statements is necessary so that they will be credible enough for their intended uses. *** **Usually**
5. Analyze and interpret	The analysis and interpretation of the data in the outcome statements in order to answer the prime Outcome Harvesting questions should be as useful as possible for the intended users. Therefore, even in independent, external, summative evaluations, primary users should be involved in deciding what categories make the most sense for harvesters to use to classify the outcomes in order to answer the prime harvesting questions. In M&E or other internal, developmental, or formative evaluations, primary users may, in addition, participate in making sense of the outcomes. *** **Usually**
6. Support use of findings	Primary users are responsible for deciding how harvesters will support the use of the findings post-harvest, just as they are responsible for the process and findings being used. ***** **Always**.

I accept a responsibility as a harvester to rigorously ensure the integrity of the harvesting process and products and not to impose my perception of what will be useful. Co-harvesters and I are responsible for the process and findings adhering to the standards of propriety, feasibility, and accuracy as well as utility. Nevertheless, I consider so important the American Evaluation Association (AEA) utility standard "to ensure that a harvest will serve the information needs of intended users" that I involve the people who require the findings of an Outcome Harvest to make decisions or take action throughout the process. They clarify intended uses, identify prime questions, agree with the methods to be used to collect, analyze and interpret data, participate in methodological decisions made in the course of the harvest and review drafts of findings for accuracy and legibility. As in other modes of utilization-focused evaluation, presenting the findings in the form of a written report is but one mechanism for communicating the findings and not the final one. In my experience, this involvement of users typically results in increased "ownership" and use of the harvest process and findings.

In the first design moment, if intended users, co-evaluators and I have not met face-to-face in the development of the terms of reference, we do so now. I always *actively* question the people who are commissioning the harvest to identify who will use it, for what and why. Bob Williams, the recipient of the 2014 Lazarsfeld Theory Award from the AEA for his contribution to systems approaches in evaluation, cautions that "the commissioner is only one of many agents affected by an evaluation—only one of many with a 'stake.' From a systems perspective there is no reason at all why those interests should automatically be privileged" (B. Williams, personal correspondence, July 9, 2017). I consider this initial clarity about useful for whom and why so important that I refrain from discussing even the terms of reference without it (see Chapter 2 section, "Who Will Use the Outcome Harvest?"). And I need to know what they intend to do with the findings, and perhaps the process. Why will it be useful to them?

I then *react* with what I hear they need to know in the light of their uses. If they have terms of reference in hand, the objectives or purpose will often provide insights into the questions they need the harvest to answer. I propose drafts and we then enter into a more *interactive* mode, together crafting prime harvesting questions, identifying potential sources of information, agreeing how we can best obtain information from them, and agreeing the resources necessary. This is an *adaptive* process of going back and forth to make sure that we have defined the right users, their priority uses, answerable questions, and accessible and motivated sources, all with the means at hand.

The second moment is extracting potential outcomes from secondary sources of information follows closely on the intense engagement with primary users to agree the design. Nonetheless, I find it important not to be lulled into scrubbing the agreed documentation and first look critically at whether or not these sources do have the potential outcome information. Therefore, I find it important to begin by *actively* confirming that these are the right sources. I do this quite pragmatically by either asking my users not for documents by name but for "all the documentation that you judge will have outcome rich data." I also share with them the first examples of potential outcomes that I extract, cite the sources, and if the outcome data is sparse, I let them know. "Do you have other sources?" If I can *react* with ideas of alternative sources, I do. I then *interact* with them to make sure the sources are right and worth the time and effort. The *adaptation* can range from deciding together to limit this step to only seeking illustrative examples, changing the secondary sources, or skipping the step completely.

The facilitation of *use* when engaging with human sources of information is similar to that for secondary, documentary sources. The intensity of the engagement can push usefulness to the back of the harvester's mind. I usually take the *initiative* to share with users one or more of their first final, SMART outcome statements. This is really the moment for users to make changes in the design of the data being collected and its pace. If the sources are not motivated to engage in a timely manner, I inform the users and ask for their help in stoking motivation. I am *reactive* by questioning and listening carefully to the users' satisfaction with the information they will receive. For example, are 1–2 sentence descriptions really sufficient for their intended principal uses? Do the users understand that undemonstrated changes in attitudes, feelings, beliefs, and awareness will not be harvested as an outcome, nor will their interventions activities? That is, do they understand and agree with the difference between outputs as results they control and outcomes as results they only influence? If not, I *interact* to forge understanding and *adapt* the harvesting process.

The first thing I do in the substantiation step is alert the users of the magnitude of the trove of outcomes there will be and when I will *share* with them those harvested, verifiable outcomes for review. If my facilitation is effective, they will be ready to discuss which, if any, outcomes should be verified or explored more deeply. I find that this step can lead to considerable angst on the part of users because now they must decide what will make all the outcomes credible-enough. They may also feel anxious about who to recommend—allies they worked with, or indeed those social actors they influenced—to be candidates as substantiators. It is not uncommon for users to bring in criteria from other evaluation modes with which they have knowledge or experience. This can range from traditional research criteria, including especially statistical criteria, all the way to innovative social change M&E and evaluation methodologies focused on participation and collaboration to address social injustice and the empowerment of beneficiaries. For example, I find many users expect the substantiators to be interviewed in person.

I listen hard and prepare myself to *respond* with sound evaluative advice that speaks to their concerns but based on the reality that Outcome Harvesting as a qualitative, utilization-focused approach to evaluation. For instance, if the purpose of the substantiation is to verify the accuracy of the outcome statements, we will approach substantiation differently than if they want solely to deepen understanding. The *interaction* I often engage in at this step is considering what the right criteria for "credible-enough" outcomes are in the eyes of their stakeholders—donors, beneficiaries, or their own staff. The users and I come to pragmatic decisions and *adapt* the substantiation accordingly.

In the fifth step, the facilitator must pivot primarily to the role of evaluator and if users, human sources, and others are to be involved, ensure that they perform as evaluators. So, in the analysis of the data, my task is to *actively* guide them in organizing the information. Users' tendency will often be to classify the information according to their preexisting categories. I have to *react* and insist that those categories are only acceptable to the extent that they correspond to the outcome data. *Interacting* to agree on categories that are inductively and deductively sound can be a major task. Similarly, it may be necessary to further adapt, for example, the prime harvesting questions if the data suggest it can answer other, more useful questions.

In M&E, developmental or internal formative evaluations users may be involved in making judgments in the interpretation phase. If so, I *actively* frame the task and oversee what they do. For instance, I *react* if they begin interpreting the data according to what they hoped to see, giving undue weight to some outcomes and dismissing others. Or if they answer the harvesting questions cherry-picking data, as unintentional as it may have been, I insist that they make sense of all the data, or at least seriously take it into account. This requires my *interacting*—not standing aloof in judgment—to help them *adapt* their expectations and make their judgments, taking into consideration the available information.

In external, independent evaluations, while users may contribute to the analysis tasks, they are not involved in the interpretation of the data to answer the prime harvesting questions. That is the evaluator's responsibility.

Lastly, in the sixth step of Outcome Harvesting when I step into supporting the use following the presentation of the harvest's findings, I must shift my role again because primary users are now responsible—concretely for the process and findings being used. Thus, they too decide if and when and how harvesters will support the use of the findings post-harvest. Throughout the harvest I *actively* prepare for this step. In spite of the uncertainty of how the harvest will unfold, in the design stage, I help users foresee the need to plan and budget for use. As the harvest proceeds and unanticipated and emergent needs for support for use emerge, I *react* alerting users about the implications. For example, I may detect the need for instructions and training for staff so that in the future, outcomes are properly crafted, or the expectations about the credibility of the data they report is taken into account. It is, however, usually during the analysis and interpretation of the data that it makes the most sense to begin *interacting* with users to decide on my post-harvest support. This often involves *adapting* what they and I had been thinking could be my role in supporting their use post-harvest.

II. Nurture Appropriate Participation

Depending on whether the exercise is internal or external, developmental, formative or summative, the harvester works together with primary users, human sources, and independent third parties so that they contribute to the collection, analysis, and interpretation of data in ways that enhance the harvest's rigor and credibility.

Outcome Harvesting is profoundly participatory. The reason is methodological: success depends on the involvement of primary intended users and substantiators, as well as that of the human sources of information and the harvesters responsible for carrying out the Outcome Harvesting exercise. Harvesters facilitate users to make design decisions not only initially but as the harvest unfolds. Harvesters facilitate external, knowledgeable, independent sources—the substantiators—to share their knowledge and give their opinions. Table 8.2 describes in more detail the participation involved step by step.

In the approach's utilization focus, the first group of people who participate are the primary intended users. Their participation is generally in decision-making although in some instances they may also serve as sources of information about outcomes. To begin, they are the source of the outcome-rich documentation I consulted in Step 2. This is important because in contrast to the audience that will have a passive relationship with the exercise, as in other utilization-focused approaches, the users, or their representative, are actively involved in all steps. The people in the audience will read the findings, perhaps selectively, but they do not depend on the harvesting process or findings to do their work. In contrast, the users clarify intended uses as the harvest proceeds because as findings emerge, what will be most useful may change. They review prime questions for the same reason. They agree with changes in the methods to be used to collect data. They also participate in methodological decisions made on emerging issues during the process, review drafts for accuracy and legibility, and ensure proper dissemination. This involvement typically results in increased use of the process and findings.

The second group who participate are the people—the human sources—who provide outcome data, both qualitative and quantitative. The coaching

TABLE 8.2 Description and Degree of Applicability of the *Nurturing Participation* Principle per Outcome Harvesting Step

Outcome Harvesting Steps, Chapters 2–7	Application of the principle
1. Design the Outcome Harvest	The focus on usefulness that undergirds the approach requires that primary intended users be committed to investing the time and attention right from the beginning in making decisions on what will be included in the initial design and what will be decided later. ***** **Always**
2. Review documentation	Depending on the type of evaluation, in addition to recommending what secondary sources should be consulted, users may also be involved in piloting instruments to be used in collecting data. ** *Sometimes*
3. Engage with human sources	The engagement of primary sources in identifying and formulating their outcomes is vitally important to ensure their ownership. This requires, however, hours (and sometimes days) of clock time stretched over a number of weeks and sometimes months of calendar time. ***** **Always**
4. Substantiate with external sources	The harvester's consultation with substantiators is to verify the facts of the outcome statements. Therefore, as with the primary human sources, for the core dimensions—the outcome and contribution descriptions, and probably the significance of the outcome too—the harvester supports these independent, knowledgeable, and authoritative third parties to share what they know, rather than what they think or believe. *** **Usually**
5. Analyze and interpret	The highly participative first four steps can lead to misunderstanding about responsibilities. In formative and summative independent, external evaluations, users and human sources may share their views about what the findings mean, but it is the evaluator who is responsible for making judgments about merit and worth to answer the prime harvesting questions. In M&E and other internal and developmental evaluations, the users and human sources may participate in answering the questions guiding the harvest. **** **Almost always**
6. Support use of findings	The harvester's facilitator/coach role in Steps 1, 2, 3, and 4 and evaluator role in Step 5 now become a resource role in Step 6 because here the responsibility for use of the process and findings is fully on the shoulders of the primary users. ** *Sometimes*

principle above explains how I nurture their participation. First, however, I have to decide who should serve as my primary sources. As a harvester, I quickly found that the most accurate identification and formulation of outcomes, initially at least, is best made by the project or program staff who have been closest to the action that contributed to outcomes. For example, the field workers implementing an intervention usually know better than middle managers who they are effectively influencing (and who they are not) in what ways, when and where. They also know how they influenced them to change their behavior. Equally important, the intervention's staff not only know the most, but they are highly motivated to share what they know.

They tend to be sensitive to the need to consult with others about what they do not know, including allies and the subjects themselves of their efforts to influence change. And when consulting with others does not occur to them, I have found they are responsive to the suggestion that they consult with others in order to enrich their identification and formulation of *their* outcomes. They readily recognize the reasoning of the South African Community Development Resource Association: "The complexity of social change requires participation, not only because people have the right to be central to their own change process but also for their substantial and critical inputs to offer along the way" (Reeler & van Blerk, 2017, p. 7).

The third group of participants in an Outcome Harvesting process are substantiators, who are knowledgeable about the change and authoritative in the eyes of the users but independent of the intervention. Their role is explained in Chapter 6. In addition, depending on the principal uses and the information required to answer the harvesting questions, other people may be involved: allies, participants in the intervention's activities, and really any other potential source of information about outcomes.[1]

I emphasize that the way in which participation is achieved in Outcome Harvesting is more by facilitating than following procedures. Robert Chambers of Participatory Rural Appraisal fame, in his latest book explains that "participatory methodologies can be defined as combinations of approaches and methods through which people are facilitated to do things themselves" (2017, p. 22). For an evaluator to facilitate the collection of data through a participatory mode is a challenge because of the common expectations that an evaluator does not collaborate in a mutual endeavor to identify and formulate the achievements of an intervention. I have found this to be true across the range of stakeholders—commissioners, donors, board members, managers, field staff, participants, beneficiaries. They see the harvester as someone who is making judgments about the *value* of what was done and achieved. That is the harvester's role in the fifth Outcome Harvesting step of analyzing and interpreting data. It is not, however, the role of an Outcome Harvesting evaluator during data collection and verification (Steps 2, 3, and 4). In those moments I am a *facilitator* who draws out the knowledge held by (a) primary intended users, (b) people who serve as sources of information—generally field staff of the intervention—because they are knowledgeable about what they have achieved and how, and motivated to share what they know, and (c) knowledgeable, independent third parties. I have found that this role is best performed when the engagement with my sources of information—as well as with intended users and substantiators—is also as a *coach* who facilitates mutual, evidenced based learning and not an evaluator wielding a measuring stick who arrives to make judgments about others' performance. Understandably, sources of information are challenged to accept that as my role.

III. Coach Human Sources to Formulate Outcome Statements

Provide hands-on support to people to apply what they know to craft concrete, verifiable descriptions of what has been achieved and how.

One of the key differences between my role as an Outcome Harvesting evaluator and the customary evaluator role is that when gathering data, I coach my sources in a co-learning mode rather interrogate them as an external judge of the merit, worth, or value of what they are doing and achieving. It is my responsibility that the information on outcomes be well-formulated, plausible and verifiable. I am also accountable for following a credible process of data collection, analysis, and synthesis to enable me to draw useful conclusions from solid evidence. The evaluative judgments will come later, in the fifth step (Chapter 6), once I have harvested solid, credible-enough outcomes to serve as my evidence with which to answer the harvesting questions, as you can see in Table 8.3.

I am a *coach* because I support my sources of information to perform two tasks: (a) review outcome formulations I extracted from documentation, and (b) identify and formulate the outcome statements. That is, I support them to express in succinct written descriptions what the intervention achieved, why it is important, and how the intervention contributed. I support them to share what they know. In this sense, the outcomes are theirs and not the harvesters'. Notwithstanding, once the definition is understood, identifying an outcome is straightforward; I have found it is not easy to formulate them, for one main reason. After performing this role with a wide diversity of sources running across just about every imaginable variable of diversity, I discovered that few people readily express themselves well in writing. This holds true regardless of gender, education, authority, status, language, culture, to mention some variables.

On the positive side, I am coaching people short term and it is performance driven. As soon as I have mutual satisfaction with the form and content of an outcome, the job is completed.

TABLE 8.3 Description and Degree of Applicability of the *Coach Human Sources Principle* per Outcome Harvesting Step

Outcome Harvesting Steps, Chapters 2–7	Application of the principle
1. Design the Outcome Harvest	Users must understand that in Steps 2 and especially 3 the role of the harvester is that of a coach and not an independent expert assessing performance and rendering judgments about the merit or worth of achievements. ***** **Always**
2. Review documentation	The harvester identifies and formulates of potential outcomes from documents written by human sources before approaching them which establishes the coaching role of the harvester in this and the next step. ** *Sometimes*
3. Engage with internal sources	Harvesters support people who are providing information to craft verifiable descriptions of what the intervention has achieved and how. Fulfilling this facilitation and coaching role often requires (a) overcoming the assumption that an external evaluator should be generating data if it is to be valid, (b) motivating sources who have yet to see the benefit of participation, and (c) addressing the erroneous assumption that the Outcome Harvesting evaluator is testing informants and making judgments about what they know. ***** **Always**
4. Substantiate with external sources	Harvesters make sure the outcome statements provide specific, measurable quantitative and qualitative information so the formulation can subsequently stand up to substantiation. ** *Sometimes*
5. Analyze and interpret	In independent, external formative, and summative evaluations, the facilitator/coach role pivots to the role of evaluator in this step. But in M&E, developmental and formative internal evaluations, the role of coach continues. *** **Usually**
6. Support use of findings	Once the harvest is over there can be the need for users to guard against watering down outcome statements, including non-SMART formulations. * *Rarely*

IV. Strive for Less Because It Will Be More Useful

Do only as much as necessary to achieve the desired result of answering usefully the prime harvesting questions.

The minimalist graphic designer Nicholas Burroughs (n.d.) famously defined his craft as "minimalism is not a lack of something. It's simply the perfect amount of something" (para. 1). When I add web design author Alan Smith's (2016) caution, "less is more if less *does* more . . . " (para. 1), you have the essence of this principle for Outcome Harvesting. This is not an easy technique to master and involves ethical issues, as Bob Williams explains:

By all means make things as simple as possible but what do you have to do to prevent being simplistic? One of the premises of critical systems is that you explore the consequences of the boundaries you draw and seek to mitigate any negative consequences. (B. Williams, personal correspondence, February 21, 2018)

In Table 8.4 I describe how and how often I have found myself applying the principle to each step of the Outcome Harvesting process.

TABLE 8.4 Description and Degree of Applicability of the *Less Is More Principle* per Outcome Harvesting Step

Outcome Harvesting Steps, Chapters 2–7	Application of the principle
1. Design the Outcome Harvest	The mistake that condemns many evaluations to uselessness is setting out to do too much—too many users, uses, prime questions (and sub-questions!), and sources of information. Similarly, faced with the uncertainty of a dynamic environment, trying to plan all six steps before the process unfolds and the results emerge can be a frustrating waste of time. ***** **Always**
2. Review documentation	If the application of Outcome Harvesting is for M&E or a developmental evaluation, I usually skip this step because there is no documentation. In formative or summative evaluations, often documentation will be poor in outcome data simply because no one was expected to report outcomes. On the other hand, secondary sources may prove to be surprisingly rich, which will probably mean that there will be fewer outcomes in the next step. The harvester and users should be prepared to change this documentation step, skim through it or even skip it entirely in the light of what is likely to be found in the secondary sources *** **Usually**
3. Engage with internal sources	Limiting the quantity of outcomes to be harvested and the length of the descriptions in the outcome statement, will usually motivate human sources to do everything they can to meet the goal, whereas asking them to describe *all* outcomes as *fully* as they can, dissuades most people and they do less. ***** **Always**
4. Substantiate with external sources	The tendency is to play it safe and consult more people about more outcomes than is necessary for credibility. Instead, "credible enough" means only substantiating enough outcomes and consulting with enough people so that those who use the outcome statements will trust they are solid evidence. *** **Usually**
5. Analyze and interpret	Ideally, harvesters and users negotiate the necessary detail for reporting: the number of categories of classification in the light of the prime questions and the manageability of the resulting clusters of outcome data. Similarly, when reporting, it usually is best to aggregate outcome data in charts and tables and exemplify with representative outcomes and the processes of change they represented instead of exhaustively citing all the information in the outcome statements. ***** **Always**
6. Support use of findings	Users must be helped to avoid reading more into the harvested data and interpretation than is there. ** *Sometimes*

The adage "less is more" is a great example of the danger of making an Outcome Harvesting principle a rule. I have no absolute numbers to suggest how much is "less" and how much is too much because in my experience it varies according to needs and context. I have found, however, that by and large, the fewer the users per harvest, the more agile will be the decision-making. Similarly, it is always a judgment about how few sources or substantiators per outcome, or how little detail in the outcome statements or in the harvesting report, will make it all just as useful as can be. Whether in outcome statements or in the harvesting report, the less that is written, the greater the likelihood that the reader will pay attention to the message and not skip over or skim through the text.

For example, through an evaluation using Outcome Harvesting there are crucial moments when harvesters must check that the information they are harvesting is both useful and just plentiful enough to serve as evidence with which to answer the harvesting questions. I have found that harvesting less words will generally be more productive than scything for more, as counter-intuitive as it may appear. Therefore, when designing the outcome statements, I always suggest that the descriptions of the outcome and the contribution be one or two sentences each. I do this in the spirit of William Strunk's (1918) classic advice to omit needless words: "A sentence should contain no unnecessary words, a paragraph no unnecessary sentences, for the same reason that a drawing should have no unnecessary lines and a machine no unnecessary parts" (n.p.). I then produce examples. Unless the primary intended users and I realize that what they need are explanations rather than descriptions, this amount of detail generally is as close to perfect as I can get. In addition, I also negotiate with users a realistic number of outcomes to aim for: three to five, ten to fifteen, up to thirty per internal source. Remember, however, this is not a rule. For example, in a recent evaluation we originally estimated up to five outcomes per source. After piloting we realized up to 10 was more realistic. During the actual harvest, however, some sources reported over 20. In the end, the average was a little over nine per source.

The reason for striving for less is simple: formulating outcomes is demanding and time-consuming, regardless of whether the source of information provides the data in written or verbal form. This is because writing succinct outcome formulations is not easy. As the seventeenth century French mathematician, logician, physicist, and theologian Blaise Pascal famously said, "I would have written a shorter letter, but I did not have the time." Nonetheless, I find that by limiting the number of outcome statements expected, people are usually motivated to produce more outcomes than if the length of the description and the number of outcomes is open-ended.

Furthermore, when our task is to use less words, my co-harvesters and I are certainly more motivated to follow Ernest Hemingway's (1964) advice:

> The writer's job is to tell the truth.... All you have to do is write one true sentence. Write the truest sentence that you know.... If I started to write elaborately, or like someone introducing or presenting something, I found that I could cut that scrollwork or ornament out and throw it away and start with the first true simple declarative sentence I had written." (p. 12)

V. Learn Outcome Harvesting Experientially

Learn the steps and principles of Outcome Harvesting by actively applying them, reflecting on the results, modifying the application, and repeating the process, ideally with mentoring.

Since 2010, as Outcome Harvesting became recognized as an evaluation approach, I have written extensively, given dozens of 1-, 2- and 3-day workshops and answered hundreds of questions from people who learned about Outcome Harvesting and were trying to apply it. In addition, I myself have applied the methodology with over three dozen co-harvesters who were new to Outcome Harvesting and had to develop the capacity to understand and apply the steps and principles. It is clear to me that the six steps of Outcome Harvesting and the nine principles are best learned as we learned it—through experience (Table 8.5). Equally important, with rare exceptions, I have found that learning the approach is greatly enhanced when that direct experience harvesting outcomes is supported by a mentor versed in Outcome Harvesting.

I mentor in two types of situations. One is when undertaking an *evaluation*. I customarily team up with one or more co-evaluators who are content experts whereas I am the Outcome Harvesting methodologist. Usually they do not have evaluation experience but have content or context expertise. More recently, I am carrying out evaluations with other seasoned evaluators who often take the lead but require methodological support with Outcome Harvesting. The nature of these relationships range from my mentoring them to learn how to coach, all the way to our learning together how to continue innovating the way we apply the Outcome Harvesting principles. I will let colleagues who have benefitted from, and then taken on, the mentoring or coaching role themselves explain the challenge. All are core practitioners of Outcome Harvesting with whom I have worked.

Richard Smith, based in the United Kingdom, prior to working as a consultant evaluator and provider of support to organizations wanting to use Outcome Harvesting, was a senior manager in the international not-for-profit

TABLE 8.5 Description and Degree of Applicability of the *Learning Experientially Principle* per Outcome Harvesting Step

Outcome Harvesting Steps, Chapters 2–7	Application of the principle
1. Design the Outcome Harvest	Primary users and their staff serving as human sources of information often believe that Outcome Harvesting can be taught through well-written instructions and a superb workshop. With notable exceptions, that is not true in my experience. In the design step I commonly have to caution them that their understanding will often come only in the process of actually designing the harvest, identifying and formulating outcomes, deciding on substantiation, analyzing and interpreting outcomes, and actually using the process and findings. That is the way most people develop the capacity to apply the approach. *** **Usually**
2. Review documentation	Although with exceptions, even seasoned researchers will generally require mentoring for extracting potential outcomes from secondary sources of information. *** **Usually**
3. Engage with human sources	Seasoned evaluators or M&E staff from the intervention who are new to Outcome Harvesting will usually require mentoring to engage with primary sources as facilitators and coaches and not as judgmental evaluators. Incorporating the principles into their practice, too, will require mentoring. ***** **ALWAYS**
4. Substantiate with external sources	Perhaps substantiation is the most difficult part of Outcome Harvesting to learn since it walks the fence between quantitative social science research and qualitative M&E and evaluation methodology. The rationale for credible-enough has to be constructed between harvesters and primary users, and for those new to Outcome Harvesting often the key to success is mentoring. *** **Usually**
5. Analyze and interpret	In this step, the shift away from participating for primary users (and human sources and sometimes substantiators), and from facilitating/coaching to evaluating for harvesters, is frequently difficult. Analysis ideally still requires participation of users but interpretation is fundamentally the responsibility of the harvesters. Mentoring is sometimes necessary to arrive at the proper division of responsibilities in, for example, the written presentation of findings. **** **ALMOST ALWAYS**
6. Support use of findings	Perhaps the toughest thing to learn about the Outcome Harvesting approach is how to operationalize the sixth step based on its utilization-focus that process and findings be useful and not solely useable. Engaging evaluators post-evaluation is not common practice and evaluators are not responsible for use—the primary users are. Thus, harvesters have to be creative in order to be invited to provide support. *** **Usually**

environment/natural resource management sector. Richard explains well the mentoring dynamic:

> After developing my proficiency at harvesting outcomes as a representative of an initiative being evaluated using Outcome Harvesting and then work-

ing as an evaluator applying Outcome Harvesting, I have coached co-evaluators and continued to learn as much as I taught. Being challenged with "basic questions" from those new to harvesting outcomes helps remind me of the key principles of harvesting. And, when a co-evaluator rather than I has direct access to the most suitable data sources because of language or other factors, I have learned to adapt and simplify my guidance and adjust the scope of data collection in order to ensure that the exercise results in robust, SMART outcome descriptions that can serve as evidence. (R. Smith, personal communication, October 11, 2017)

Barbara Klugman is a South African evaluator who supports civil society organizations, networks, and donors in strengthening their strategies and learning systems for promoting social change and she undertakes strategic evaluations.

I came to Outcome Harvesting serving as a co-evaluator with Ricardo. He was the methodologist and I the expert in undertaking and evaluating social justice advocacy. I then ventured off on my own to lead Outcome Harvesting evaluations but arranged to virtually discuss with Ricardo challenging issues as they arose. For example: How can not taking action—maintaining an unpopular position—be an outcome plausibly influenced by an advocacy campaign? Or, when is annually introducing something novel no longer an outcome because it is doing more of the same thing? Navigating meaning and significance as a lone evaluator is much harder than when you debate theory and practice with someone who has repeatedly faced these issues before. (B. Klugman, personal communication, May 21, 2016)

Emilia Bretan is a Brazilian lawyer and university professor who launched herself into a new career as an evaluator.

My theoretical and practical experience prior to Outcome Harvesting was in research and evaluation that cast the role of the evaluator as an independent, external judge of "pure, unadulterated" information. It has only been through the support of an Outcome Harvesting mentor that I have been able to overcome my resistance to facilitating the participation of my informants in a mutual process of establishing the content of outcomes. Now, I confidently engage with them, asking questions, clarifying doubts and questioning when an outcome is not clear or there is a lack of evidence, all without the fear that I am "contaminating the evidence." (E. Bretan, personal communication, April 4, 2016)

Goele Scheers is a Belgian evaluator with considerable experience in managing Outcome Harvesting evaluations supporting organizations to develop their own M&E capacity to use Outcome Harvesting.

> The principal challenge for someone applying Outcome Harvesting for the first time is, I believe, guiding people to understanding when something can be considered an outcome and when not and then formulating it in a credible, verifiable and succinct manner. How to do this is indeed best learned through practice, with the support of someone who is more experienced in Outcome Harvesting. (G. Scheers, personal communication, April 23, 2016)

The second type of situation in which I mentor is when I accept the task of *advising internal M&E staff* on how to use Outcome Harvesting as a monitoring and evaluation tool. They customarily do have evaluation experience and have read a lot about Outcome Harvesting, or they may even have taken a course with me, but they have little or no experience actually carrying out an Outcome Harvest. This is a special challenge and I have had bitter, fruitless experiences when I have accepted to contribute to the introduction of Outcome Harvesting in an organization on an ad hoc basis—typically a one-off training or coaching on demand. I have concluded that being brought in as an expert on Outcome Harvesting to do one-off training, but not as a mentor, is just not effective. People tend not to break old patterns nor grasp the counterintuitive rationale of Outcome Harvesting without a sustained if light engagement. Also, without timely support, people new to Outcome Harvesting tend to fall into patterns of multiplying errors that hands-on mentoring can minimize.

Outcome Harvesting is far from unique as an M&E or evaluation approach that requires learning through doing with a mentor. As colleagues and I were discovering the importance of the mentoring role for Outcome Harvesting, Ricardo Ramírez and Dal Brodhead (2013) were discovering the same for Utilization-Focused Evaluation (U-FE), one of the two methodological legs of Outcome Harvesting. They were responsible for supporting evaluation professionals using U-FE for the first time with five Asian research projects in the field of information and communication technology for development. In their excellent *Utilization Focused Evaluation: A Primer for Evaluators* (Ramírez & Brodhead, 2013), they too use mentoring as a core function:

> In our experience, utilization focused evaluation is best learned through practice and evaluation professionals using UFE for the first time require mentoring support. We call it walking the talk. The talk (theory, if you will) is all about genuine collaboration, mutual understanding, shared ownership, and engaged learning. The walk (practice) is about engaging in evaluation processes to achieve the desired outcome of intended use by intended users. Walking the talk requires knowing the theory and putting it into action through reflective practice. (p. v)

I certainly know of people who have learned Outcome Harvesting without mentoring but I cannot think of a case in which they did so successfully all by themselves. Said another way, I have found that most people learn Outcome Harvesting experientially and with the support of someone with more experience in the approach. Naturally, the need diminishes with more experience.

In either case of mentoring—co-evaluating or advising—there are of course advantages and disadvantages. For example, experience with utilization-focused, developmental, or goals-free evaluation will probably enhance your learning of Outcome Harvesting. Experience with other M&E and evaluation approaches can be positive for learning Outcome Harvesting. This is especially true if those experiences led to a recognition of the need for alternative approaches when evaluating unpredictable, dynamic situations, or behavior change. But those same experiences can be a hindrance if you have to evaluate an original plan or reconstituted theory of change to see if it was implemented and achieved the intended results.

In Summary

The task of facilitating usefulness throughout the harvest is an overarching principle because the bottom line for the other four process principles is that they serve the principal uses that the primary intended users have for the Outcome Harvesting approach. It is also a more general principle because I find that the *active-reactive-interactive-adaptive* mode is also applicable to coaching, and mentoring, and indeed evaluating. Facilitation is complemented by a hands-on coaching role with the human sources to formulate their—the sources—outcome statements. Part of the facilitation task applies to nurturing participation by users and substantiators, as well as sources and sometimes other stakeholders. The two other keys to a successful process are applying creatively the adage "less is more" and experientially learning how to do Outcome Harvesting. In the next chapter, I will explain the four complementary content principles.

Note

1. When Outcome Harvesting is used in a mixed methods evaluation, an even wider range of people may participate. For example, when the users wanted to know the opinions of academics or experts about the intervention's performance or achievements, I have complemented the Outcome Harvest with an opinion survey or interviews.

References

Burroughs, N. (n.d.). Retrieved from Quotes on Design website: https://quotesondesign.com/nicholas-burroughs/

Chambers, R. (2017). *Knowing better? Reflections for development.* Rugby, England: Practical Action Publishing. doi:10.3362/9781780449449

Hemingway, E. (1964). *A moveable feast.* New York, NY: Scribner.

Ramírez, R., & Brodhead, D. P. (2013). *Utilization focused evaluation: A primer for evaluators.* Penang, Malaysia: Southbound. Retrieved from http://bit.ly/2s8NWz4

Reeler, D., & van Blerk, R. (2017). *The truth of the work: Theories of change in a changing world.* Community Development Resource Association. Retrieved from http://www.cdra.org.za/articles-by-cdra-practitioners.html

Smith, A. (2016, April 13). *Minimalism for a successful user experience.* Retrieved from https://usabilitygeek.com/less-is-more-importance-minimalist-web-design/

Strunk, W. (1918). *Elements of style.* Ithaca, NY: Priv. print. [Geneva, NY: Press of W. F. Humphrey]; Bartleby.com, 1999. (http://www.bartleby.com/141/strunk5.html www.bartleby.com/141/. [printed out February 12, 2018].

9

Outcome Harvesting's Content Principles

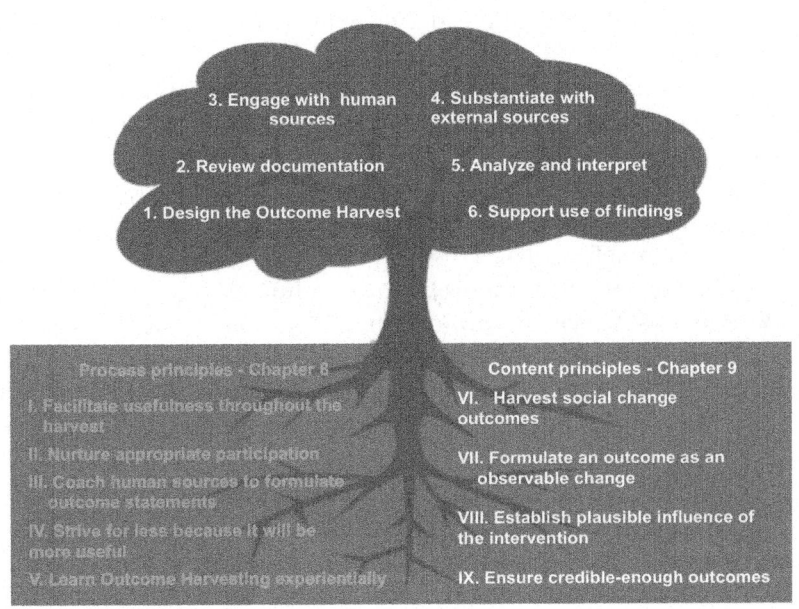

In this chapter, I will explain the last four of the nine principles that I have found to be imperative for guiding me and my colleagues in generating the content of an outcome harvest. These content principles provide you with guidance on *what* should be the results when you carry out an outcome harvest.

VI. Harvest Social Change Outcomes

Social change in Outcome Harvesting is defined as societal actors modifying the way they do things in new and significant ways (outcome) that the intervention plausibly influenced (contribution).

The bottom line of social change is societal actors changing the way they do things. It is only when individuals, groups, communities, organizations, and institutions change their actions, activities, relationships, policies, and practices that a society changes, for good or bad. The essence of an outcome in Outcome Harvesting is those societal actors demonstrably changing their behaviors in those ways. Thus, by definition, outcomes in Outcome Harvesting represent social change. Nonetheless, the multiple definitions of "outcome" that are used today can lead the harvester to misapply the Outcome Harvesting approach and collect data on results that are not outcomes. To help you focus on the results that are social change outcomes, I will explain that fistful of different types of demonstrated, observable changes in a societal actor's behavior. First, these are the changes that count:

- *Action*—In one moment, a societal actor does something different than before. The president declares for the first time his support for women's empowerment as a human right.
- *Activity*—A societal actor over time does something different than before. The president includes a declaration of support for women's empowerment as a human right into his stump speech.
- *Relationship*—Two or more societal actors change the way they interact with each other. The employers' association and the Women's League agree to meet regularly to discuss ways to improve the employment of women.
- *Policy*—A collective social actor—from a family, a group, or a community to an organization or an institution—changes the rules, norms, or laws that govern its behavior. The legislature passes the equity-in-salary law.
- *Practice*—A collective social actor behaves in accordance with or implements one or more new policies. For five years running, over

half the members of the employers' association increase the salaries of women employees by a higher percentage than they do for men.

Furthermore, outcomes are changes in behavior that contribute, actually or potentially, to *impact*, where "impact" is understood as improving (or deteriorating when negative) the conditions of people's lives or the state of the environment.

I will unpack further this notion of "social change" used in Outcome Harvesting in three different ways. They are not unique to Outcome Harvesting but the three together do characterize what is understood as social change in this approach.

First, in Outcome Harvesting, societal actors taking the initiative to do something new and significantly different generally means they *alter or modify the character or nature of their behavior*. Therefore a societal actor doing more of something or doing it better, while an important result, usually does not count as a social change outcome unless the decision to do so was influenced by another actor. That is, it is an outcome only if it represents a breakthrough, a development, doing something significantly new and different than in the past, a qualitative change. In social change, changes in quality are imprecise and a matter of judgment. Consider, for example, that a social change outcome can be preventing something from happening. Delaying a law being passed for a few days is not likely to count as an outcome but preventing a single person from being tortured or executed could be a major outcome.

Second, another way to understand the difference is contrasting social change with social service. Providing services such as health care, minimum income, employment advice, education, or housing alleviates a need or provides a benefit to someone else without necessarily influencing them to change their behavior. By and large, everyone wants to be healthy, have money for basic needs, find gainful work, obtain knowledge and skills, and have a decent place to live. (The exceptions are usually involved with mental health issues or immaturity.) Providing people those services is valuable, of course, but does not constitute what is understood in Outcome Harvesting as social change. In contrast, when the challenge is not only to provide people with expected and desired services but to persuade, inspire, facilitate, or in some other way to *influence people to change their behavior, and their lives*, then we enter into the territory of social change: take the initiative to be vaccinated, buy healthy food, change one's occupation or profession, or live in different housing.

172 ▪ *Outcome Harvesting*

Third, in Outcome Harvesting we include but go beyond individual changes in the way a societal actor does things, as important as they may be, and capture outcomes that are interrelated, meaningful pieces in a *process of societal actors changing their behavior*. Outcome Harvesting reveals a variety of interrelated processes of change in which some outcomes may be minor or preliminary compared to others but nonetheless significant. For instance, in Outcome Harvesting, "policy changes" are more than changes in laws and regulations. They are modifications of the formal or informal, written or unwritten political, economic, cultural, social, or religious norms that direct or condition the actions of individuals, groups, organizations, or institutions in the sphere of the state, the market or in civil society. To arrive at a policy change requires a series of outcomes and this is what Outcome Harvesting serves to do.

Exemplifying Social Change

In Figure 9.1, I present a sequence of interrelated social change outcomes I extracted from the pilot study of a World Bank (2014) project titled Operationalizing a Latin American Access to Information Network in 2011 (pp. 83–90). Here their interrelationship is clear and in the narrative that

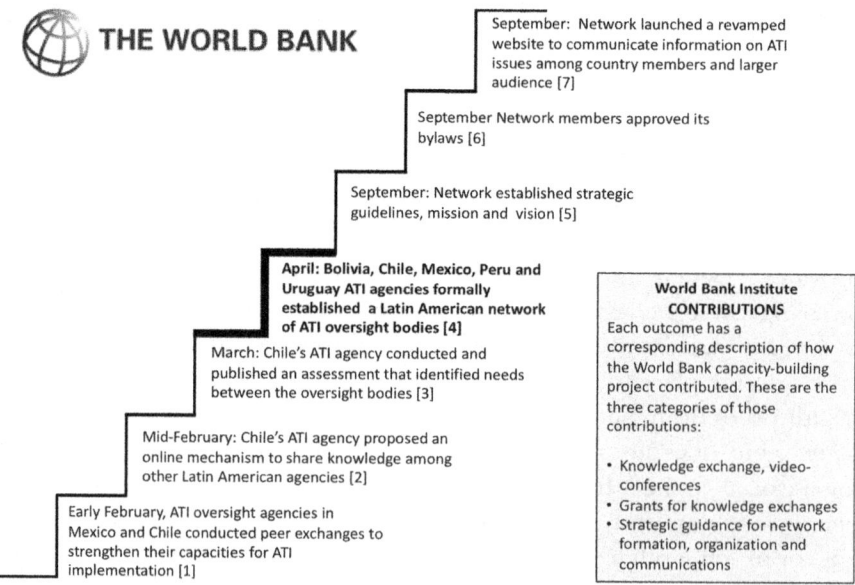

Figure 9.1 A sample process of social change represented by summaries of outcomes.

accompanies these social change outcomes in the original document, their relative importance is explained.

Since every change in behavior is potentially an outcome, how do I establish the boundaries? This is something of an art and requires judgment. But generally, if on different dates two or more societal actors do the same thing, each event is a separate outcome. Similarly, if on the same date one or more societal actors do new and different things, each event is a separate outcome. The rule of thumb that I use is to separate behaviors but aggregate dates, actors, and places according to the significance of the outcomes. For example, in outcome [1] in Figure 9.1 the team in this internal evaluation decided to consider peer exchanges as one outcome rather than as separate visits of the Mexican and Chilean ATI (access to information). On the other hand, they kept the three September outcomes separate rather than cluster them under the Network's initiatives in that month. Context in the end determines if an individual change in behavior is sufficient to qualify as an outcome.

I find that the social change principle of focusing on results that represent societal actors doing things differently is always present in four of the six Outcome Harvesting steps (see Table 9.1). This does not mean, however, that I always will use the step. For example, in an application of the approach for M&E or in developmental evaluation, there may not be documentation to review and I skip Step 2.

TABLE 9.1 Description and Degree of Applicability of the Social Change Outcomes Principle per Outcome Harvesting Step

Outcome Harvesting Steps, Chapters 2–7	Application of the principle
1. Design the Outcome Harvest	Harvesters and primary users have to decide if and which parts of the intervention to be evaluated concern social change outcomes and accordingly agree uses, questions, and sources of information. ***** **ALWAYS**
2. Review documentation	Harvesters engage the secondary sources (documentation) that are the most likely to be rich in data about potential social change outcomes. ***** **ALWAYS**
3. Engage with human sources	Users select and harvesters engage with the primary sources that are knowledgeable about social change outcomes and motivated to share what they know. ***** **ALWAYS**
4. Substantiate with external sources	The most significant social change outcomes are candidates to be substantiated. *** *Usually*
5. Analyze and interpret	The classification and interpretation of outcomes gives priority to social change categories and lenses. ***** **ALWAYS**
6. Support use of findings	Care must be taken to appropriately use findings about social change outcomes. * *Rarely*

Lastly, a societal actor not taking action or not changing course in a tumultuous situation can also be a social change outcome. And outcomes can be intended or unintended and negative or undesirable, as well as positive. I explain these instances in detail in the next principle.

VII. Formulate an Outcome as an Observable Change

To qualify as an outcome, an individual, group, community, organization, or institution must have demonstrably done something different. Also, new understanding or heightened awareness or sensitivity does not count as an outcome until evidenced in observable changes in behavior.

Clarity about the nature of the change in a societal actor's behavior that counts as an outcome must be established before deciding on using Outcome Harvesting. Thus, I find that during the first three steps I always clarify with the intended users, and then with human sources of information, that we seek evidence of concrete, perceivable changes in behavior influenced by the intervention (Table 9.2). In the fourth step I sometimes

TABLE 9.2 Description and Degree of Applicability of the Observable Change Principle per Outcome Harvesting Step

Outcome Harvesting Steps, Chapters 2–7	Application of the principle
1. Design the Outcome Harvest	Clarity about the nature of the change in a societal actor's behavior that counts as an outcome must be established before deciding on using Outcome Harvesting. Ensure there is a common understanding of what an outcome is and why it matters. ***** **ALWAYS**
2. Review documentation	The harvester seeks partial evidence of potential, concrete, perceivable changes in behavior influenced by the intervention. ***** **ALWAYS**
3. Engage with human sources	The harvester coaches people in identifying and formulating outcomes as demonstrated changes in behavior influenced by the intervention. ***** **ALWAYS**
4. Substantiate with external sources	A harvester ensures that substantiators give an informed opinion about the facts in the outcome description and do not confuse outcomes with other types of results (activities, outputs, attitudes, knowledge, or skills that the intervention controls, or impact). ** *Sometimes*
5. Analyze and interpret	The harvester guards against the tendency to draw conclusions about a societal actors' motivations behind their changes in behavior (outcome) without cause–effect evidence. ** *Sometimes*
6. Support use of findings	With the harvester's support, users also guard against the tendency to draw conclusions about the motivation behind a societal actor's change in behavior (an outcome) without cause–effect evidence. ** *Sometimes*

have to clarify with substantiators that we seek an informed opinion about the facts in the outcome description and must avoid confusion with other types of results that the intervention controls or with effects on the conditions of people's lives or the state of the environment, which in Outcome Harvesting is understood as impact. When analyzing and interpreting outcomes, and when supporting use, I also help co-harvesters and users to guard against the tendency to draw conclusions about a societal actors' motivations behind their changes in behavior when there is no evidence of a causal link between the outcome and the purported motivation.

There are three special dimensions of observable change that deserve fuller explanation.

Changes in Knowledge, Attitudes, and Skills (KAS) Are Not Necessarily Outcomes

It is customary, in international development circles at least, to talk about changes in "attitudes and behavior" as if the two terms were parallel concepts. They are not. This is especially problematic because a key strategy to influence social change is capacity-building as a means to influence beliefs, sensitivities, feelings, perceptions, opinions, as well as impart new knowledge and skills, with the rationale that these changes will lead to changes in behavior. Also, changes in attitudes, as well as in knowledge or skills, are not necessarily predictors of behavioral change. Maybe yes, maybe no.

In Outcome Harvesting we collect data on demonstrated, observable *behavioral* changes but not on the motivations or reasons for change that lie behind the outcomes. Why? The behavior of individuals can be influenced by a whole range of personal, professional, vocational, and social influences beyond the triad *knowledge, attitudes, and skills* (KAS). Similarly, changes in the behavior of groups, communities, organizations, and institutions may be influenced by a myriad of economic, political, cultural, environmental, and other factors beyond attitudinal change. Even a trained behavioral psychologist or sociologist may not be able to determine the motivating factors behind outcomes. The solution is quite straightforward: Only accept demonstrated changes as outcomes.

That is often easier said than done. For example, with capacity-building of other people and organizations such as wide-spread activity, an intervention will often have many results that are changes in KAS. Consequently, these interventions constantly face the issue of where to draw the line between the outputs and the outcomes of their work. Many training programs will propose that the changes in KAS, sometimes even demonstrated by pre- and posttests, are outcomes. Whether they are or are not outcomes as defined in Outcome Harvesting depends on the context. For instance, consider a situation in which the participants in these activities were already convinced that they wanted to know more, change their awareness, or become competent in a new area. That is, they did not have to be influenced to change their behavior; they were already convinced when they signed up for the course. Then, any changes in their KAS are outputs and not outcomes of the training programs. On the other hand, if male participants in a deeply patriarchal society had to be persuaded to attend a workshop on women's rights, then their attending would be an outcome if it indicates a shift in their interest or their recognition of the importance of an issue when previously they had shown no such interest.

Another example: An advocacy organization holds a workshop in a deeply patriarchal society and influences changes in the attitudes—as evidenced in signed pre- and post-workshop quizzes—of one or more government education officials towards, say, the importance for the rights-based empowerment of women. The result of government officials identifiably (i.e., not anonymously) demonstrating the acquisition of greater sensitivity indeed may be considered change in their behavior—they would never admit before that women were rights holders and they bearers of an obligation to provide them with equal opportunities to what men enjoy—and therefore would qualify as an outcome. Of course, I would be looking for the next outcome: the government officials taking action to provide women with greater opportunities.

That scenario contrasts to one in which a workshop takes place in a country where government officials customarily go to workshops to learn about women's rights, in which case their acknowledgement of their responsibilities as duty bearers would be an *output* of the advocacy organization and not an outcome. That is, the result is more an indicator of the high quality of the intervention's awareness-raising workshop than it is of a significant change in the government officials' behavior. In this case, an outcome would be, for example, if the officials take concrete action to launch educational opportunities that empower women, following the workshop.

Non-Action Can Be an Outcome

Influencing a social actor not to take action—that is, preventing something undesirable from happening—can be a significant outcome, but is often awkward to formulate as a change. The solution is to contextualize. For example, if an education official is persuaded not to follow a trend in other ministries to restrict opportunities that empower women, that nonaction would count as an outcome. Or, if an anti-abortion political party member does not oppose a law authorizing abortion in the case of rape or incest, that too would count as an outcome.

Negative Outcomes Are Important

Rarely will all the outcomes of an intervention be positive and, of course, everyone knows that learning from failures is a key to success. Nonetheless, I am consistently challenged to harvest negative outcomes: changes in behavior that an intervention has influenced which undermine what the intervention is trying to achieve. In my experience, people do not identify negative outcomes for three reasons. First, they do not have knowledge of negative outcomes. Second, if they do, they honestly believe that the positive outcomes are more significant. Third, they are fearful of admitting failure because then they will be held accountable, they will be blamed, for whatever they did that influenced the negative outcome.

Michael Woolcock, professor of social science and development policy, and research director of the Brooks World Poverty Institute at the University of Manchester in the United Kingdom, explains that in social change projects trying to increase the participation of marginalized groups, enhance women's empowerment, or improve the accessibility of the poor to formal legal systems, things get worse before they (hopefully, maybe) get better. This is the J-curve functional form shown in Figure 9.2. For example, in a project to empower

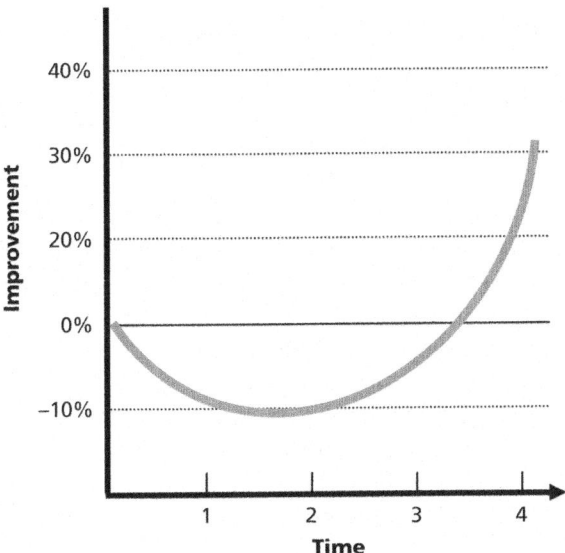

Figure 9.2 The J-curve.

women, "men initially resist ceding resources and status, perhaps violently at first, only to come around when their attitudes and/or interests change, or prevailing local norms shift" (Woolcock, 2009, p. 6). Thus, negative outcomes that undercut, weaken, impair, or otherwise undermine progress towards rights-based empowerment of women initially, at least, may suggest that the intervention is having a positive effect, as negative as it may be. Other development and social change interventions also generate outcomes that represent setbacks, retrenchment, or stagnation. For them all, the timing of a harvest is important since if I take stock halfway through (Time 2) the results would be quite different than if I do so at the end (Time 4)—see Figure 9.2.

Practically, then, how do I succeed in supporting people to identify and formulate negative outcomes? I exercise my capacity as a facilitator coach and nurture with my primary intended users and my sources of information an "enabling environment" for registering negative, as well as positive, outcomes. For example, I have found that physically separating the negative outcomes from the positive in the outcome statement format (see Figure 3.2 in Chapter 3) is necessary. Also, if sources do not register any negative outcomes, I remind them of their importance. I suggest they describe their significance in terms of the lessons learned from each negative outcome. These measures can certainly help, but it is a constant struggle to avoid negative outcomes being significantly underreported. Of course, as with positive outcomes, I can never say that what I harvest is all the outcomes that were achieved.

VIII. Establish Plausible Influence of the Intervention

To qualify as the intervention's outcome, there has to be a reasonable relationship of cause–effect between, on the one hand, the intervention's activities and outputs and, on the other, the outcome.

In Outcome Harvesting, there are two basic criteria we use for describing the causal contribution of an intervention to an outcome. First, it must be plausible enough for the intended uses of the harvest. By plausible I mean that the description of how the intervention contributed to the outcome has to hold a reasonable, probable cause–effect relationship with the outcome in the eyes of both the primary user, the harvester, and the substantiator. Second, the description of the plausible causal contribution of the intervention to each outcome must be specific and measurable enough to be verifiable. Thus, what is plausible-enough can vary greatly and the principle must be adapted throughout the first five steps of a harvest (Table 9.3).

Most of the time, I find that setting the criteria for judging plausible influence is not a major issue at the design step, although sometimes early on

Outcome Harvesting's Content Principles ▪ 179

TABLE 9.3 Description and Degree of Applicability of the Plausible Influence Principle per Outcome Harvesting Step

Outcome Harvesting Steps, Chapters 2–7	Application of the principle
1. Design the Outcome Harvest	The criteria for plausible influence has to be agreed between users and harvesters. ** *Sometimes*
2. Review documentation	The secondary source must at least suggest an implicit, possible contribution by the intervention to each outcome. *** **Usually**
3. Engage with human sources	The primary source must identify and formulate, with the harvester's coaching, a reasonable influence of the intervention on the change described in the outcome, however indirect, unintended and partial the influence may be. ***** **Always**
4. Substantiate with external sources	Harvester ensures that substantiators share what they *know* about the facts in the contribution description. Occasionally, a substantiator will confuse "influencing" with attributing the outcome solely to the intervention. ** *Sometimes*
5. Analyze and interpret	Harvesters stick to what they know and recognize the unknowns. The description of the contribution synthesizes what is known about how the intervention plausibly contributed to an outcome. Harvesters may not know if other intervention activities and outputs contributed or not to a particular outcome but seek to identify relationships between known contributions to different outcomes. **** **Almost always**
6. Support use of findings	Users must guard against exaggerating how plausibly the intervention influenced the outcomes. * *Rarely*

it has to be agreed between users and harvesters. The information extracted from a secondary source must at least suggest an implicit, possible contribution by the intervention to each outcome, although occasionally documentation will not suggest how the intervention influenced the results they report. In any case, in Step 3 the primary source always must identify and formulate, with the harvester's coaching, a reasonable influence of the intervention on the change described in the outcome. The outcome may be directly or indirectly influenced by an intervention. For example, an intervention that produces a piece of research that is then used by an ally to lobby for a change in a policy would be indirectly contributing to the outcome. Also, the outcome may be unintended—the original purpose of the research was not to influence policy. Usually, the contribution is partial, combining with other intervention activities or outputs and with additional external causal actors and factors. One contribution may influence more than one outcome. Obviously, this causal description cannot be done mechanically.

For example, one urban action-research team decided that there was no need to describe in writing how they contributed to each one of their

12 outcomes; they all knew. Instead, they decided to invest the time and energy consulting with the subjects of their outcomes (the community leaders and governmental authorities they considered they had influenced to change) to learn, first, if they had changed as the intervention understood they had, and second, what they thought the intervention team had contributed. In the process, they learned about different perceptions of their work, and they identified six more outcomes. At the other end of the spectrum, in another case the program officers of an intervention's donor for a multi-country program to influence government authorities, decided that they needed not one or two or three opinions but documentary evidence of what was described in the contribution to every outcome.

In the fourth step, sometimes the harvester has to coach substantiators to share what they know about the facts in the contribution description in order to avoid confusing "influencing" with attributing the outcome solely or primarily to the intervention. In the analysis and interpretation of the outcome data, I almost always have to remind myself and my co-harvesters to stick to what we know and recognize the unknowns. Frequently users, too, have to be reminded that I can only synthesize what they know about how the intervention plausibly contributed to an outcome. Sometimes they will want to record the intervention's activities and outputs although did not contribute to outcomes because they think so highly of what they do.

Within this highly varied customizing, how do we determine that there has been plausible contribution to an outcome? This is where the plausible influence principle provides guidance. When a development or social change intervention influences a societal actor to change, this rarely means that the change can be attributed to—was caused solely by—the intervention. In most cases the causal influence is partial, often indirect and relatively distant in time, and frequently unintended. This is because the intervention is carried out in a web of causation in concert with the influences of multiple actors and factors (Figure 9.3). Consequently, in Outcome Harvesting we focus on causal *contribution* inference rather than the more common evaluation focus on causal *attribution*. Why?

> Attribution is a research concept that involves proving that A causes B. In pharmaceutical research, for example, randomized control trials are conducted comparing a drug with a placebo to establish whether the relief of symptoms can be directly attributed to the drug. This straightforward notion of cause-effect works well for simple, bounded, and linear problems, but does not work well for understanding complex systems where a variety of factors and variables interact dynamically within the interconnected and interdependent parts of the open system. (Patton, 2008, p. 4)

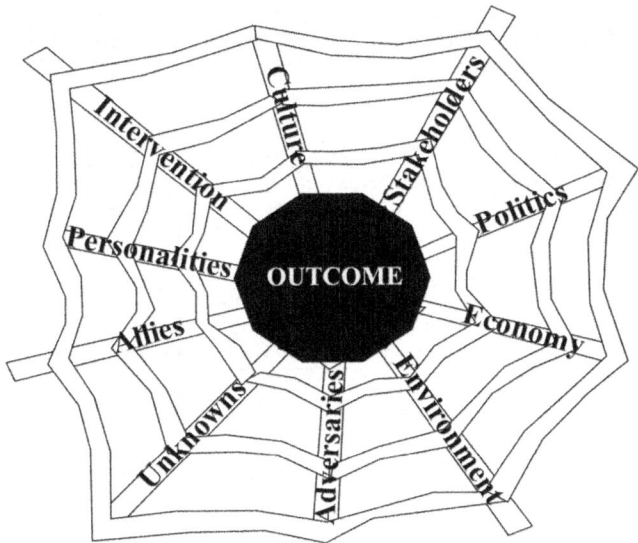

Figure 9.3 Web of causation.

In addition to being numerous, the causes of outcomes are generally nonlinear and unpredictable—the same or similar actions can have very different, unforeseeable effects in different times and contexts. Thus, we strive to establish a logical connection, a causal linkage between activities and outputs (*cause*) of an intervention that are partly responsible for one or more outcomes (*effects*). The linkages are plausible, arrived at through inductive reasoning. They are not statistically defensible relationships. Therefore the contribution inference is made with a degree of uncertainty; the conclusion is likely, but not guaranteed.

Naturally, colleagues and I have explored different approaches to establishing robust, causal contribution to enhance the likelihood and certainty of our conclusions. One interesting exercise was to use a causal inference framework adapted by the Johns Hopkins Bloomberg School of Public Health's Center for Communication Programs (Piotrow, Kincaid, Rimon, & Rinehart, 1997). Unfortunately, the framework is based on predefined intended results. So too are contribution analysis, process tracing, outcome mapping, or causal link monitoring. These four agile, complexity-aware methods to establish cause–effect relationships require theories or models of change, strategic plans, intentional designs, and other results-based management tools. So far, the approach I have found most effective for Outcome Harvesting is one derived from detective work, which starts with the effect and works backwards to infer the cause (Table 9.4). As does a detective (and other professionals

TABLE 9.4 Establishing Causal Contribution Inference Through Detective Work

Three criteria of crime solving…	…interpreted for establishing contribution inference…	…to establish the plausibility of a contribution to an outcome
Motive—The prime suspect must have had a *reason* to commit the crime.	The intervention must have had a reason to influence the societal actor, even when the result was unintended.	The outcome, whether positive or negative, corresponds to the purpose of the intervention.
Means—The prime suspect must have had a *way* to commit the crime.	The intervention must have done something that could influence the societal actor.	The intervention's activities and outputs likely influenced the outcome.
Opportunity—The prime suspect must have had the *chance* to commit the crime.	The intervention must have had the chance to influence the societal actor.	The intervention carried out those activities prior to the societal actor changing its behavior.

as varied as forensic scientists, archaeologists, and automobile mechanics) I establish a *motive* for the intervention to have influenced the outcome. Thus, a negative outcome in Outcome Harvesting is not simply one that does harm to something or somebody, but it is a change in a societal actor's behavior that undercuts, weakens, impairs, or otherwise undermines the purpose of the intervention. If there is a motive—the intervention was trying to influence the change that the outcome represents (or undermines)—then the harvester makes sure the intervention had the *means* plus the *opportunity* to influence the change. That is, I identify a verifiable act or actions of the intervention that involved the societal actor before it changed its behavior. I then infer causal contribution, which is further validated with human sources, co-harvesters, and substantiators.

There are two additional challenges in establishing causal contribution inference.

Controlling Versus Influencing Change

Drawing the line between exercising control and influencing change, vis-à-vis what the societal actor began to do differently, can be tricky because it depends on the context. For example, I do a lot of work evaluating the programs of donor agencies that fund grantees to work for social change. Rarely will changes in the grantees' behaviors count as outcomes because either the grantee had proposed the change in their grant proposal or the donor considered that what the grantee did with the grant was substantially under the donor's control through their contractual arrangement. There certainly are exceptions. A donor may persuade but not determine that grantees change the focus of their work. For example, a rural development organization in a highly patriarchal society may not have a gender equity policy. The donor's offer to fund the piloting of such a policy may tip the board decision to apply for a grant to do so, with hesitant board members reserving the right to stop the experiment. In this instance, the donor influenced the organization to experiment with a change in policy, an act that it funded but did not substantially control.

Accompanying Change Is Not Influencing It

Often a societal actor has begun to change the way he, she, or it does something before the intervention acts. While there may be changes in a societal actor's behavior that an intervention supported, it is not an outcome because the intervention did not influence the actor to change. The actor had already decided to change. In these cases, which are common with likeminded allies, the intervention conjoins with the societal actor but does not causally influence the change in behavior. The changes in the behaviors of third parties that an ally and an intervention influence together, however, are outcomes, including, for example, influencing another societal actor to become their ally and join forces. And, sometimes in the course of a joint effort, an intervention may indeed influence an ally to change its behavior, as when an ally is swayed to adopt a new tactic or strategy.

In sum, the challenge is to describe how the intervention appears to have influenced the outcome rather than prove that the intervention directly produced the observed results. Thus, when applying this principle, in Outcome Harvesting you describe specifically and measurably the activities and outputs of the intervention that establish a reasonable, probable, causal contribution. Is this credible enough? I address this question in the next and last principle.

IX. Rigorously Aim for Credible-Enough Outcomes

Apply thorough evaluative thinking to ensure that the quality of the data and of the Outcome Harvesting exercise are as trustworthy as necessary for the primary users' principal uses.

In Outcome Harvesting the principal role of a harvester is to ensure that the harvest is credible, and meets utility, feasibility, propriety, and accuracy standards. No findings have a 100% level of confidence and a 0% margin of error. Thus, the challenge is to arrive at outcomes that are sufficiently credible for the principal intended uses—no less, no more. As with truth, determining the credibility of data is not only subjective but also relative. This is an important issue because the primary sources of information about outcomes usually are internal to the intervention and thus are part and parcel of the evaluand, the "thing" being evaluated. Although there is the value and credibility when, as is often the case, internal sources are the people most knowledgeable about what the intervention has achieved and how, the subjectivity (beliefs, wishes, ingrained attitudes, perceived strengths and weaknesses, vested interests, and such) on the part of human sources may undermine credibility. Thus, there is always an issue in Outcome Harvesting of whether the data collected are credible enough, indeed, whether they are trustworthy enough for the intended users' uses. So you enhance the credibility of the data by, first, ensuring the most knowledgeable sources provide information while ensuring they understand that their accuracy can be verified. This may be in the form of multiple primary or secondary sources within the intervention. For example, if you harvest outcomes from a team, they exercise peer review, albeit internal. Second, if necessary, you substantiate select outcomes with independent but knowledgeable external actors.

The credibility concern is present right from the predesign phase when harvesters begin applying rigorous evaluative thinking as you negotiate terms of reference for an outcome harvest. Nonetheless, I raise the issue in the design step, to ensure that the Outcome Harvesting process we will not only be useful but credible (Table 9.5). Usually the concept of outcome as a change in a societal actor's behavior will not have been used by the people who generated the documentation. Therefore, in Step 2, the harvester almost always has to be especially attentive to the distinction between outputs, outcomes and impact, seek negative outcomes, and flush out outcomes of societal actors changing their behavior by not taking action. Although when coaching my sources, I may not explicitly use the SMART framework (Chapter 1, Figure 1.5), I always have to apply those criteria to make the outcome statements as credible as possible on face value. Also, I always apply this principle in the substantiation step in order to arrive at credible-enough data for stakeholders who will understandably scrutinize and question the trustworthiness of the process and the believability and accuracy of the findings. Nonetheless, credibility is always relative, and substantiation has to be negotiated by users and harvesters case-by-case.

In the fifth step of analysis and interpretation (Chapter 6), the harvester usually must ensure that the outcome data harvested is appropriately represented in the findings. Similarly, in the sixth step of support for use (Chapter 7), sometimes when supporting use of the findings it is necessary

TABLE 9.5 Description and Degree of Applicability of the Credible-Enough Principle per Outcome Harvesting Step

Outcome Harvesting Steps, Chapters 2–7	Application of the principle
1. Design the Outcome Harvest	Harvesters begin applying rigorous evaluative thinking in the predesign step of negotiating terms of reference, which continues through the design step. You address the issue of expectations about the trustworthiness of the data that will be collected. This is the initial means to ensure that the quality of the data and the Outcome Harvesting process will be credible, as well as useful. ***** **ALWAYS**
2. Review documentation	Usually the concept of outcome as a change in a societal actor's behavior will not have been used by the people who generated the documentation. Therefore the harvester has to be especially attentive to the distinction between outputs, outcomes, and impact, seek negative outcomes, and flush out outcomes of societal actors changing their behavior by not taking action. **** **Almost always**
3. Engage with human sources	The SMART framework is intended to make the outcome statements as accurate as possible and thus aids harvesters in applying rigorous evaluative thinking as they coach human sources. ***** **ALWAYS**
4. Substantiate with external sources	Because Outcome Harvesting involves human sources with a vested interest in the outcomes they report, stakeholders will understandably scrutinize and question the trustworthiness of the process and the believability and accuracy of the findings. Nonetheless, credibility is always relative, substantiation is but one part of credibility, and substantiation has to be decided by users and harvesters case by case. ***** **ALWAYS**
5. Analyze and interpret	Having credible data is necessary but when the harvester organizes it and uses it as evidence to answer the prime harvesting questions, proper weight must also be given to the different types of outcomes—incipient and full-blown, negative and positive, pieces of processes of change, and stand-alones—so that the use of the outcomes is also credible. *** **Usually**
6. Support use of findings	Misunderstanding and misuse (cherry-picking) are latent threats to post-harvest credibility that the harvester can assist in preventing when involved in supporting the use. ** *Sometimes*

to guard against users inappropriately cherry-picking the findings when using the data.

The Principles in Summary

In the previous and in this chapter, I have presented the nine principles that emerged as colleagues and I developed the Outcome Harvesting approach (Table 9.6). The five process principles will guide you in *how* to apply the six Outcome Harvesting steps. Similarly, the four content principles

TABLE 9.6 Applicability of 10 Outcome Harvesting Principles per Six Outcome Harvesting Steps

Outcome Harvesting Principles	Outcome Harvesting Steps					
	1. Design the Outcome Harvest, Chapter 2	2. Review documentation, Chapter 3	3. Engage with human sources, Chapter 4	4. Substantiate with external sources, Chapter 5	5. Analyze and interpret, Chapter 6	6. Support use of findings, Chapter 7
Process principles, Chapter 8						
I. Facilitate usefulness throughout the harvest	***** ALWAYS	** *Sometimes*	*** *Usually*	*** *Usually*	*** *Usually*	***** ALWAYS
II. Nurture appropriate participation	***** ALWAYS	** *Sometimes*	***** ALWAYS	*** *Usually*	**** Almost always	** *Sometimes*
III. Coach primary sources to formulate outcome statements	***** ALWAYS	** *Sometimes*	***** ALWAYS	** *Sometimes*	*** *Usually*	* *Rarely*
IV. Strive for less because it will be more	***** ALWAYS	*** *Usually*	***** ALWAYS	*** *Usually*	***** ALWAYS	** *Sometimes*
V. Learn Outcome Harvesting experientially	*** *Usually*	*** *Usually*	***** ALWAYS	*** *Usually*	**** Almost always	*** *Usually*
Content principles, Chapter 9						
VI. Harvest social change outcomes	***** ALWAYS	***** ALWAYS	***** ALWAYS	*** *Usually*	***** ALWAYS	* *Rarely*
VII. Formulate an outcome as an observable change	***** ALWAYS	***** ALWAYS	***** ALWAYS	** *Sometimes*	** *Sometimes*	** *Sometimes*
VIII. Establish plausible influence of the intervention	** *Sometimes*	*** *Usually*	***** ALWAYS	** *Sometimes*	**** Almost always	* *Rarely*
IX. Ensure credible-enough outcomes	***** ALWAYS	**** Almost always	***** ALWAYS	***** ALWAYS	*** *Usually*	** *Sometimes*

will advise you on *what* the results of my harvest should be during each of those steps. You have seen that the principles are not discreet; to a greater or lesser extent each one is interrelated with one or more of the other principles. In my experience I have found that step by step, some principles are more applicable than others. At the beginning of the six chapters (2–7) on the Outcome Harvesting steps, I alert you to the principles that I have found to be more or less applicable to that aspect of Outcome Harvesting. Please, however, do not be mechanical in using my advice. Principles require that you interpret and adapt the guidance they contain to context.

References

Patton, M. Q. (2008). Advocacy impact evaluation. *Journal of Multidisciplinary Evaluation, 5*(9), 4.

Piotrow, P. T., Kincaid, D. L., Rimon, J. G., & Rinehart, W. E. (1997). Impact evaluation. In *Health communication: Lessons from family planning and reproductive health* (pp. 131–172). Westport, CT: Praeger.

Woolcock, M. (2009). *Towards a plurality of methods in project evaluation: A contextualised approach to understanding impact trajectories and efficacy* (Brooks World Poverty Institute Working Paper 73), ISBN: 978-1-906518-72-1

World Bank. (2014). *Cases in Outcome Harvesting: Ten Pilot Experiences Identify New Learning from Multi-Stakeholder Projects to Improve Results.* Washington, DC: Author. Retrieved from https://openknowledge.worldbank.org/handle/10986/20015

APPENDIX A

History of Outcome Harvesting 2002–2017

The idea of Outcome Harvesting was born in the Netherlands at the beginning of this century when I was working with Novib, one of the four historical Dutch private development agencies and today the Dutch Oxfam. Beginning in 2002, while working part time but accelerating in 2007 when I began working full time as an evaluator, subject matter experts and I developed the approach that became known as Outcome Harvesting through over 50 evaluative exercises for diverse types of organizations.[1] We had the active participation of dozens of primary intended users, a number of whom served as harvesters in internal evaluations.[2] The process was basically empirical: As we faced different evaluation challenges we looked for ideas in the evaluation literature and began testing them as we evaluated. This involved a good deal of trust on the part of our commissioners and primary users, who accepted that we were entering into uncharted territory, for them as well as us. Initially, we were doing summative evaluations of international social change networks and the programs of donor agencies to support grantees. Eventually we branched out into developmental and

TABLE A.1 Topics Evaluated in 2002–2017 by Ricardo Wilson-Grau With Colleagues

Access to information in Latin America	Local, national and international **governance**, global
Art and culture in Central America	North–South **competition** policy
Blended eLearning, China	Open governmental **contracting** processes, world-wide
Children's rights in Latin America	**Organic farming** in Africa
Climate change and food security, Colombia	Pharmaceutical **procurement** and supply, Kenya, Tanzania and Uganda
Conflict prevention and **peacebuilding**, global	**Poverty** and **injustice**, Ghana and Tanzania
Constitutional **health** mandates in Latin America	**Primary health care** system, Nigeria
Competency Based Medical Education, Canada and United States	**Public sector reform**, Burundi
Deforestation, global	Solid **waste management**, Bosnia
Early child marriage, India	Strengthen international, national and local **civil societies**, global
Eco-health, global	Strengthen parliamentary oversight of national **budgets**, Africa
Education in the Philippines	**Violence** against women, global
Environmental rights in Latin America	Water, **sanitation**, and **hygiene**, Honduras and Ghana
European Union **environmental policy**	Women's **entrepreneurship**, Africa
Health rights, Costa Rica and Uruguay	**Women's rights**, global
Human rights in Central America and Asia	Local, national and international **governance**, global
ICT, Africa and Asia	North–South **competition** policy
Integrated **water** resource management, global	Open governmental **contracting** processes, world-wide

formative evaluation, with projects, programs, and organizations addressing a wide diversity of development and social change challenges, ranging across a full range of cutting-edge innovation in social change around the world (Table A.1).

In spite of this wide diversity, all the organizations we evaluated, to a greater or lesser extent, met one or more of the usefulness criteria for Outcome Harvesting described in the first chapter: Their need was for evaluation or monitoring combined with learning; the purpose of their intervention was social or political change; they wanted to evaluate primarily outcomes; and their programming context did not lend itself to more traditional evaluation.

The story developed in four stages, which I summarize here.

The Approach and This Evaluator Emerge (2002–2007)

I am often asked how I contend with evaluating interventions that do not have predefined results in a logframe, strategic plan, or theory or model of change. There were two key experiences that I believe prepared me.

From April 1990 to December 1992, I was the international campaign coordinator for the Greenpeace International campaign against toxic chemicals. I arrived at the apex of Greenpeace's astounding 10-year period of success and consequent rapid growth. Income and programs had increased on average 40% a year since 1980 and the then foremost environmental campaigning organization in the world was expanding from the North to the South, or the Third World as it was then known. I had been hired because I had over 20 years of successful management experience, a perspective on the world rooted in Latin America, and a background in the social sciences, all new qualities for a Greenpeace International senior manager.

I had 65 international and 80 national staff campaigning on a combined budget of US$10 million. I confronted what I considered to be a serious problem of fragmentation: seven international projects and autonomous national programs in 12 countries campaigning against a wide variety of toxic problems—global issues of pesticides, chlorine bleaching of pulp and paper, hazardous waste incineration, waste trade, often complemented by regional or national issues—with growing pressure from a large segment of the international council and board to shift our campaigning towards environmentally sound, economically viable, and socially just means of producing goods and services, a demand with which I strongly identified.

As a first step, I thought what was required was greater clarity about the theories of campaigning being employed within each one of the projects and national offices. When I launched the discussion, I was met with resounding silence. After a few minutes, one of the most experienced campaign managers declared, "Ricardo, it is simple. When we see environmental evil, we take direct action to stop it. We go for it. It is no more complicated than that." There were no project mission statements, campaigning assumptions, objectives or indicators, predefined inputs, activities, outputs, outcomes, or impact—no more guidance than this principle to take action to stop toxic evil.

The second experience began immediately after I left Greenpeace in early 1993 to serve as a senior advisor with Novib, a historical Dutch development funding agency, which today is Oxfam Netherlands. In the early

1990s, Novib's grantees were truly partners who participated in formulating Novib's regional strategies to guide Novib's funding decisions. A dozen or so of these grantees were considered "strategic partners." They were 1% of the 900 Novib grantees. In their societies they played as important a role as did the social democrat Novib in Dutch society. For this dozen non-governmental organizations, Novib's funding commitment was long-term. I decided to introduce the notion of a five-year rolling strategic plan as the basis of the funding relationship; the donor–grantee relationship would be based on agreement about the grantee's predefined political strategy rather than a detailed plan. The resistance of the strategic partners to the use of a strategic plan, however, following on from the Greenpeace experience, planted seeds of doubt in my mind and heart about the wisdom of exhaustive planning à la results-based management approaches that were becoming very much in vogue at the time—and indeed still are today (Wilson-Grau, 2007). It was a real "pivot" as they say nowadays in the United States.

At this time, in late 2002, I began the adventure that was to become Outcome Harvesting. I was still working as a senior adviser with Novib. I was planning to retire in 5 years. However, thanks to social democratic largesse, and my boss's support, I was able to rearrange my schedule in order to take on an independent consultancy each year as a step towards a new career.

The first consultancy was to evaluate the performance and results of an international network that grouped 50 environmental and human rights organizations in the Americas, Africa, and Asia. As was then customary in the world of international development cooperation, my co-evaluator Martha Nuñez and I were hired because of our expertise as environmentalists. Neither of us was an evaluator.

We were charged with assessing what the network had accomplished. This one did not have a detailed, predefined plan of activities and expected results (as I would learn would be the case with almost all networks). Therefore, we could not assess against a plan to what extent the resources had been efficiently used, and the activities had effectively led to predefined outputs, outcomes, and impact. Furthermore, we could not find a methodology for evaluating an intercontinental advocacy network. Consequently, we had to develop an evaluative approach for both assessing an international network's performance and its influence on the environmental *problemática*. This challenge in 2002–2003 set us on the path towards discovering the concepts used in the Canadian International Development Research Centre's outcome mapping methodology and Michael Quinn Patton's Utilization-Focused Evaluation, which became two conceptual pillars on which Outcome Harvesting stands.

Over the next 5 years, with colleague evaluators, and working part time, we carried out four more utilization-focused, outcome evaluations; three of networks and the first of a development finding agency, which were to be the sources of experience for the early development of Outcome Harvesting. I was well-positioned. My work with Greenpeace had culminated 25 years of management experience in Central America and Europe in which I ran organizations similar to the grantees of these funding agencies. And I had the insider experience with Novib. Thus, I had insights from both sides of the development cooperation relationship. And, of course, I had the good fortune of the commissioners finding excellent thematic experts to work with me as co-evaluators.

The network evaluation experiences served as a basis for an article Martha Nuñez and I wrote presenting the approach we developed to evaluate international social change networks (Wilson-Grau & Nuñez, 2007), which includes the first public explanation of the utilization and outcomes focused tool that was evolving to identify, formulate, and learn from non-predefined changes in other social actors.

In 2007 I left Novib and began working full time as an independent organizational development consultant, based in Rio de Janeiro, Brazil and Amstelveen, Netherlands, but working exclusively internationally supporting large, global networks using Outcome Mapping for planning and piloting ways to monitor outcomes and learn from them. Primary users and I were able to clarify where Outcome *Mapping* leaves off and what would soon be known as Outcome *Harvesting* begins. In Outcome Mapping you monitor the indicators of change ("progress markers") in the societal actors with whom you work directly ("boundary partners"). These indicators have been agreed in the strategic plan ("intentional design") for each one of the objectives ("outcome challenges") you aim to influence and which you develop with those actors with whom you work directly. You do monitor and learn from the achievement of progress markers but evaluation per se is limited to an evaluation plan, although in the past few years outcome mapping practitioners have worked to develop ways to evaluate the implementation of intentional designs. The international networks were using Outcome Mapping but finding the process too unwieldly for them and needed an alternative.

The Participatory, Complexity-Sensitive Approach Takes Form (2008–2010)

By the beginning of 2008, the particular way my colleagues and I were approaching M&E and evaluation was taking shape as commissioners, primary users, my co-evaluators, and I found through trial and error what made the most sense for performing the basic tasks of a useful outcome evaluation for a development or social change intervention. That year I completed three more evaluations in which harvesting outcomes was a centerpiece.

By the end of 2008, the utilization-focused, social change focused approach known as "Outcome Harvesting" had emerged; we were now talking in terms of "harvesting outcomes." A characteristic of the networks and donor agencies that we had evaluated since 2002 was that they either did not have a results-based plan or if they did, circumstances had changed so drastically during implementation that the plan had become irrelevant. We recognized that to a greater or lesser degree this was because, at the time of planning, and during implementation as well, the relationships of cause and effect between what they planned or were doing and what they achieved were unknown. Therefore they had found that evaluation methodologies that assess to what extent the planned resources were efficiently used to carry out preplanned activities that generated predefined results of outputs, outcomes, and impact were unworkable, or at least not useful to them. This led to proposing an evaluation handstand: first identify outcomes and then work backwards to understand how the intervention had contributed.

Another characteristic that emerged was that success hinged on active and often intense *participation* of the organizations and people we were evaluating. The reasons were eminently practical. First, there were very few outcomes to be found in the often numerous monitoring and evaluation reports simply because people had, by and large, not been expected to report on the changes in societal actors that they were influencing. Reports focused almost exclusively on what activities had been concluded. Second, the people who were doing the work in the field knew the most about the changes they had influenced and were keen to share what they knew about their activities and outputs. Typically, in the past, these people had only been asked to report on activities or outputs. Engaging with a harvester interested in knowing and understanding what they had achieved was motivating and useful, although time-consuming. Similarly, the utilization focus enhanced a dynamic process in which decisions about the evaluation had to be made continuously, and thus the primary users also had to participate in decision-making throughout.

Another pattern became evident: the utilization and outcome focused approach was proving to be especially useful for evaluating *advocacy*, of which I wrote a paper (Wilson-Grau, 2008).

In 2009 I led three more evaluations, and we identified the evaluation methodology as "the process of harvesting outcomes." In the evaluation teams, I served as the methodologist working with a thematic or content expert as a co-evaluator. My colleagues and I found that a team approach in which I deferred to them as content experts and they to me as the methodologist enabled us to learn together and enrich the methodology, as we constantly had to customize the process for different users and uses.

All three 2009 evaluations had process and specifically capacity-building uses. We realized that the process of harvesting outcomes enabled the primary intended users and the intervention's staff to learn from the experience and build their capacity to monitor, evaluate, and take action to improve their performance and that of the intervention. This was especially important because the approach required a level of participation that, in addition to being new, was also intense. Thus, process use emerged as an important complement to the use of findings in the utilization-focused mode.

The following year we carried out four evaluations in which harvesting outcomes was the core purpose.

"Outcome Harvesting" Is Born (2011–2012)

In 2011 we carried out three evaluations and were formally talking about the methodology as "Outcome Harvesting." In an evaluation in Ghana, we had a reminder of the limitations of the approach. The intervention was interested in assessing the return on investment: "What are the implications of outcomes for a cost-benefit analysis of the Ghana program?" They had the same cost centers for their strategies: women's rights, right to food, right to education, governance, human security, HIV/AIDS and "cross cutting activities." Thus, our rationale was that we could calculate the cost of the intervention's activities that contributed to each outcome and arrive at whether the outcomes per program strategy in each region were worth the financial resources invested in them, or if there could have been less costly ways of contributing to the results.

When we attempted to classify the activities that contributed to each outcome, we hit a two-tiered wall. First, the intervention had influenced each one of the 46 outcomes by using two or more strategies. Second, we could not accurately calculate how much each strategy had contributed to each outcome. Thus, the closest we could come to a cost-benefit analysis was comparing and contrasting the expenditure in each region per strategy with the outcomes to which each strategy had contributed. And then we hit a second, insurmountable wall: the nature of each outcome and thus their relative importance and the value of the activities that contributed to them, varied considerably. In sum, it was only possible to place a dollar value on all the outcomes achieved in each region but their relative importance required a qualitative judgment steeped in an understanding of the context. Of course, this was also a lesson in the limits to statistical analysis and of Outcome Harvesting for measuring value for money. Other methods are more appropriate.

By the end of 2011, Outcome Harvesting was increasingly seen as a tried and proven qualitative approach to evaluating development and social change interventions. In 2010, I had made my first presentation on "harvesting and interpreting outcomes" at the annual American Evaluation Conference, which I have continued to do every year since but thereafter on Outcome Harvesting. In 2011 the German Development Agency GIZ (then GTZ) invited me to make a presentation on the use of the approach in their Systemic Approaches in Evaluation conference. The same year I began giving a 3-day course on Outcome Harvesting at the Centre for International Development at the University of Bologna, which I have continued annually. The Ford Foundation then agreed to publish an Outcome Harvesting booklet, which they did in May 2012 (Wilson-Grau & Britt, 2012, revised November 2013). Beginning in 2015, these learning and sharing experiences morphed into presentations by colleague Outcome Harvesting practitioners that we have organized at the Latin American, African, European, and American evaluation conferences.

In 2012 we completed another three evaluations, including one that summatively assessed the outcomes achieved and the performance of the Global Partnership for the Prevention of Armed Conflict (GPPAC). An earlier GPPAC evaluation experience and this one and its consequences revealed Outcome Harvesting as a developmental evaluation inquiry framework. Eventually, Goele Scheers and Paul Kosterink, coordinators of planning, monitoring, evaluation, and learning at the Global Platform for the Prevention of Armed Conflict, and I wrote up the GPPAC experience as a chapter in *Developmental Evaluation Exemplars: Principles in Practice* (Wilson-Grau, Scheers, & Kosterink, 2015).

I have mentioned my co-evaluators' contribution to the development of Outcome Harvesting. Commissioners and primary intended users also contributed, albeit more indirectly. For example, Karel Chambille, responsible for evaluation at the Dutch Humanist Institute for Co-Operation with Developing Countries (Hivos), has been involved since the very beginning. His continual questioning and challenges from the demand side have been and continue to be an invaluable contribution. Indeed, Karel's 15-year history with Outcome Harvesting continues because, as I write this book, we are customizing Outcome Harvesting as an M&E tool for a 17-country program with nine internal harvesters and 80 plus internal sources of information.

Outcome Harvesting Gains International Recognition—2013 to Present

In the most recent period of the Outcome Harvesting history, the approach to M&E and evaluation has flowed into the mainstream of alternative evaluation. The year 2013 began with the U.S. Agency for International Development (USAID) choosing Outcome Harvesting as one of five approaches particularly suited for monitoring and evaluation in dynamic, uncertain situations. In August, the UNDP evaluation office selected Outcome Harvesting as a promising innovation—one of 11—in monitoring and evaluation practice (UNDP, 2013) and in 2017 invited me to run a 1-day Outcome Harvesting workshop at the National Evaluation Capacities international conference in Istanbul.

In 2013–2014, I supported Jenny Gold of the World Bank Institute, then the capacity-building arm of the World Bank group, to pilot Outcome Harvesting with 10 project teams in as many development areas. The World Bank published a booklet of the cases and now lists the tool amongst its resources for internal monitoring and evaluation (World Bank, 2014).

From 2015 onwards, our use of Outcome Harvesting has diversified into different types of organizations—from church programs to medical and public health university projects, from international consortium to slum dwellers organizations. We also devote more and more time to supporting internal evaluations and the use of Outcome Harvesting for monitoring and learning, reflecting institutional commitments to the methodology. For example, in the 2011–2014 period, the environment for evaluation of development cooperation in the Netherlands veered sharply towards the dubious "gold standard" demands of random controlled trial (RCTs). Thanks to pioneering experiences over the years with Outcome Harvesting in projects and programs funded by the Dutch Ministry of Foreign Relations—notably that of such as Goele Scheers with GPPAC, evaluations of Oxfam Novib programs, and an evaluation of the advocacy of a consortium led by Hivos in which Wolfgang Richert played a key role, in 2017 the ministry changed tack and recommended Outcome Harvesting as an M&E tool to the 25 consortia of NGOs that it supports through €1 billion (not a typo) funding in the area of lobbying and advocacy for the period 2016–2020, the so-called *Dialogue and Dissent* program (Kamstra, June 2017, pp. 11–12).

In summary, Outcome Harvesting is what it is because of a long history of trial and error of a large number of people seeking to understand the achievements of an enormous variety of social change and development interventions. This snapshot of Outcome Harvesting's history would turn into a book if I were to explain what the many primary users and evaluator colleagues, and increasingly other Outcome Harvesting practitioners, have contributed to the development of the approach. I dedicate this book to them all.

Notes

1. Over the years, my co-evaluators have been: Ahmad Alulayyan, Amrita Nandy, Ana Rubio Azevedo, Barbara Klugman, Bob Williams, Carmen Alaíde Wilson-Grau, Cate Broussard, Celena Green, Claudia Fontes, Elaine Van Melle, Fe Briones Garcia , Gabriela Sánchez, Genowefa Blundo Canto, Geoffrey Howard, Gina Solari, Goele Scheers, Grace Awantang, Jane Real, Jennifer Vincent, Jenny Gold, Joanna Durbin, Julie Lafreniere , Juliette Majot, Julie Muriuki, Kayla Boisvert, Kemly Camacho, Larry Gruppen, Lindsey Leslie, Marcie Mersky, Maria Möller, Martha Nuñez, Mike Jeger, Muhammed Lecky, Natalia Ortiz, Philip Marsden, Pinki Solanki, Sara Macfarlane, Sue Edwards, Wolfgang Richert, and Zainab Qassim Ali.
2. The primary users include: Alan Hall, Andrés Sánchez, Beris Gwynne, Chaitali Sinha, Dale Chadwick, Daniel López, Dianna James, Elizabeth Silkes, Emma Holmberg, Erika Alfageme, Goele Shheers, Hannah Tsadik, Harrie Oppenoorth, Heloise Emdon, Jaana Kovalainen, Jacqueline Hart, Jenny Gold, John Mauremotoo, Karel Chambille, Konny Rassmann, Laurent Elder, Lisa Jordan, Lorina McAdam, Luis Guillermo Pérez, Manjima Bhattacharjya , Margo Mullinax, Mary Aileen D. Bacalso, Paul Kosterink, Paul van Paaschen, Richard Smith, Sharmila Mhatre, Stella Maris Cacace, Susana Rochna, Suzan van der Meij, Teyo van de Schoot, Tilly Gurman, Tricia Wind, Tycho Vandermaesen, Wenny Ho, Yvonne Es.

References

Kamstra, J. (June 2017). *Dialogue and dissent theory of change 2.0: Supporting civil society's political role*. Ministry of Foreign Affairs of the Netherlands Social Development Department Civil society unit (DSO/MO).

UNDP, Discussion Paper Innovations in Monitoring & Evaluation Prepared for the 3rd International Conference on National Evaluation Capacities, 29 September–2 October 2013 São Paulo, Brazil 23 August 2013, page 8.

Wilson-Grau, R. (2007, August). *Capacity-building baseline and outcome challenges for GPPAC*. The Hague, The Netherlands: Global Partnership for the Prevention of Armed Conflict.

Wilson-Grau, R. (2008, December). *Evaluating the effects of international advocacy networks*. A paper presented at the Advocacy Impact Evaluation Workshop at the Evans School for Public Affairs, University of Washington. Seattle, WA: Available at http://bit.ly/2GNWFOn

Wilson-Grau, R., & Britt, H. (2012, Rev. November 2013). *Outcome harvesting*. Cairo, Egypt: Ford Foundation Middle East and North Africa Office. Retrieved from www.outcomemapping.ca/ resource/resource.php?id=374

Wilson-Grau, R., & Nuñez, M. (April 2007). Evaluating international social change networks: A conceptual framework for a participatory approach. *Development in Practice, 17*(2), 258–271. Retrieved from http://www.tandfonline.com/doi/full/10.1080/09614520701197226#.UmraqKW-qIk

Wilson-Grau, R., Scheers, G., & Kosterink P. (2015). Outcome harvesting: A DE inquiry framework supporting the development of an international social change network. In M. Q. Patton, K. McKegg, & N. Wehipeihana (Eds.), *Developmental evaluation exemplars: Principles in practice* (pp. 307–321). New York, NY: Guilford.

APPENDIX B

Developing Terms of Reference to Commission an Outcome Harvest

The practical factor to support your application of the 9 principles to the six Outcome Harvesting steps is agreeing to the terms of reference. Commissioners and managers are well-advised to involve the harvesters or other people who will be responsible for an Outcome Harvest in developing the terms of reference—a general statement of the background, objectives, and purpose of the evaluation.[1] Harvesters, too, must insist on being involved, which I realize is often easier said than done.

Since this advice for people responsible for contracting harvesters, based on my Outcome Harvesting experience, runs against the procurement procedures of many organizations, I will explain how I have found it can be done. For many years I managed organizations that were wholly or partially grant funded, and I then spent 14 years as a senior adviser with Novib, the Dutch Oxfam. And since 2007 I have been working full time as an independent evaluator. Thus, I have "triangulated" experience with the challenge of commissioning evaluations. These are the principles I have found an evaluator-centered commissioning process should embody:

1. *Recruit evaluator(s) rather than select proposals.* Describe in 500–1,000 words the evaluation you want done but not how you want it done. Mention your ballpark budget. Be clear about the deadline for completion of the evaluation (which suggests that you circulate this request for expressions of interest months ahead of time; most good evaluators I know are committed various months into the future). Ask evaluators or evaluator firms who are interested in being considered to explain why they are interested and believe they qualify. Ask that they attach their CV. If they ask questions, answer them.

    The reason to focus on the evaluator rather than the proposal is two-fold. Firstly, you need to find an evaluator skilled in Outcome Harvesting and possibly a co-evaluator skilled in your field of work. Secondly, Outcome Harvesting is always customized, and the terms of reference need to be shaped in conversation with the Outcome Harvesting evaluator. So while you can have a rough idea of the questions you want to have answered and the budget you have, the detail will be developed after you have contracted the evaluator.

    To exemplify what you need for a co-evaluator if your primary evaluator is not at all familiar with your issue or the type of strategy you are using, see my profile for a co-evaluator that would be appropriate for the exemplar I have used throughout this book (Figure B.1).

2. *Engage with the candidates based on their potential to be the best match for you.* For those interested candidates whose motivation and experience appears to best match the needs for the evaluation, ask them any questions you have from your review of their interest statement. Discuss methodological challenges and proposed approaches in general. Ask them about their financials—how do they charge and

---

1. Willingness to learn how to apply an unconventional approach to monitoring and evaluation.
2. Open to being coached and mentored.
3. Capacity to cope with uncertainty and change.
4. Demonstrated (through study or work) active and passive language competence in English (and if different, the evaluation's language), especially the ability to write synthetically in English (or the other language).
5. Comfortable with working virtually and in the field with community-based organizations.
6. Expertise in women's empowerment through service delivery, capacity-building and advocacy.
7. Experience in evaluation.

Figure B.1 Exemplar—Profile of a co-evaluator without evaluation experience.

what do you get for it? Be open to talk with them if they ask for a Skype or phone call. From this arrive at a short list of candidates.

3. *Consult with their referees before contracting.* If their answers resound with you, ask to be introduced to three or more people with whom they have worked (depending on how many questions or doubts about their suitability you have and the magnitude of the evaluation). Explain who you are interested in talking with: commissioners of X, Y, and Z evaluations the candidate has done; co-evaluators of A, B, and C evaluations. Then explore with these referees the questions you have about the candidate and any other issues you may have about the candidate.

The rationale of speaking with people who know your top candidates is that in an interview, you really only learn how well someone interviews. You want to what a commissioner learns is how well a candidate interviews. By speaking with their references you will obtain a well-rounded and more objective view of the candidate.

4. *Hire the best qualified candidate after finalizing the terms of reference together.* (Figure B.2). The ToR should specify why and for whom the Outcome Harvest is being done, what it intends to accomplish,

---

1. **Background:** Provide concise information about the project, programme or organization (i.e., the intervention).
2. **Purpose:** Explain clearly and succinctly why you are doing this Outcome Harvesting exercise.
3. **Primary intended user(s) and their principal use(s):** Identify who needs to make decisions and take actions and what processes or findings or both will the Outcome Harvest serve. The users need to be engaged in the ongoing decision-making about the harvest as it unfolds, during which uses may change.
4. **What do the users need to know?** In the light of the principal uses, agree what the primary users need to know from the Outcome Harvest. In the design stage, these needs will take the form of the prime harvesting questions that will guide the exercise.
5. **Methodology:** How will Outcome Harvesting foster a process that is useful and generate findings that will be credible enough to serve the principal intended uses? This refers to a description of the six Outcome Harvesting steps, reserving their full customization for the Design step.
6. **Roles and responsibilities:** Outline what the primary intended users and the harvesters will do (and not do) to implement the Outcome Harvesting process.
7. **Timeline and milestones:** What are the different phases of the Outcome Harvesting exercise and when will they, in principle, be accomplished.
8. **Budget:** An estimation of the fees and costs.

Figure B.2 Guidelines for Term of Reference (ToR) for an Outcome Harvesting exercise.

how it will be accomplished, who will be involved in the harvest and what resources of clock and calendar time and money are available to conduct the harvest. That said, everyone must be complexity-aware when agreeing ToR: The first-time use of Outcome Harvesting is pregnant with uncertainty, dynamism, and unpredictability. Thus, the ToR best stop short of prescribing milestones and deliverables of what will be done step by step. Depending on the commissioner, I often find that when we agree the ToR we have advanced quite a bit on the design of the harvest (Chapter 2). The difference is basically that the ToR are more general and descriptive than the design, which is more specific and explanatory.

In a harvester-centered commissioning process, the commissioner invests in developing a working relationship with a real live harvester(s) as you select one. You save time and other resources, however, because you avoid developing ToR independently of the harvester who is going to do the work. You also do not needlessly elaborate extensive check lists with scores for the different qualifications that non-harvesters may imagine are important. You also save time of an unknown number of consultants developing detailed proposals based on hypothetical ToR.

Note

1. Synonymous with scope of work, call for proposals, or request for applications.

APPENDIX C

GUIDE for Outcome Harvesting Principles

To arrive at the 9 Outcome Harvesting principles, I used Michael Quinn Patton's GUIDE framework: "an acronym and mnemonic specifying the criteria for a high quality principle statement: (1) provides guidance, (2) is useful, (3) inspires, (4) supports ongoing development and adaptation, and (5) is evaluable" (Patton, 2017, p. 36).

TABLE C.1 GUIDE's Light on the Outcome Harvesting Effectiveness Principles

Outcome Harvesting Principles	Guidance	Useful	Inspiring	Developmental	Evaluable
	A principle is prescriptive. It provides advice and guidance on what to do, how to think, what to value, and how to act to be effective. It offers direction. The wording is imperative: *Do this . . . to be effective*. The guidance is sufficiently distinct that it can be distinguished from contrary or alternative guidance.	A high quality principle is useful in informing choices and decisions. Its utility resides in being actionable, interpretable, feasible, and pointing the way toward desired results for any relevant situation.	Principles are values-based, incorporating and expressing ethical premises, which is what makes them meaningful. They articulate what matters, both in how to proceed and the desired result. That should be inspirational.	The developmental nature of a high-quality principle refers to its adaptability and applicability to diverse contexts and over time. A principle is thus both context sensitive and adaptable to real-world dynamics, providing a way to navigate the turbulence of uncertainty and dynamism. In being applicable over time, it is enduring (not time-bound), in support of ongoing development and adaptation in an ever-changing world.	A high-quality principle must be evaluable. This means it is possible to document and judge whether it is actually being followed, and document and judge what results from following the principle. In essence, it is possible to determine if following the principle takes you where you want to go.
1. Facilitate usefulness throughout the harvest	Involve primary intended users in decision-making from the beginning to the end of the Outcome Harvest.	Since Outcome Harvesting is a customized evaluation approach for uncertain and dynamic situations, design and re-design must be done as the process unfolds and results emerge. Involving users in those decisions leads to the most useful answers to the harvesting questions.	A purpose of Outcome Harvesting is to generate an evaluative process and findings that are 'owned' by the users and will be used to understand and inform social change and contribute to a better world.	Users and harvesters alike accept a responsibility to ensure the Outcome Harvesting process and findings correspond to original but also to emergent uses, and to the prime evaluation (harvesting) questions derived from them.	The quantity and quality of the participation of users in decision-making throughout the Outcome Harvest can readily be documented and assessed. This includes whether the process and findings were actually used post-harvest.

(continued)

TABLE C.1 GUIDE's Light on the Outcome Harvesting Effectiveness Principles (continued)

Outcome Harvesting Principles	Guidance	Useful	Inspiring	Developmental	Evaluable
II. Nurture appropriate participation	Depending on whether the exercise is internal or external, developmental, formative or summative, the harvester works together with primary users, human sources and independent third parties so that they contribute to the collection, analysis and interpretation of data in ways that enhance the harvest's rigor and credibility.	Harvesters, although they may be subject matter experts, serve as facilitating coaches who manage a process to arrive at mutual understanding of the facts of what was achieved and how. They are not independent experts wielding measuring sticks to make judgments about others' performance and knowledge until the analysis and interpretation step.	Those who know best what will be useful and what the intervention achieved are those responsible for implementing it. Through their participation in establishing priorities and the facts about outcomes people 'subjected' to a harvest become its true subjects with agency and the corresponding empowerment that participation brings.	Who participates, when and how depends on the information required in the Outcome Harvest, which varies case by case. This is decided in principle by primary users and harvesters in the design of the harvest but reviewed as real results emerge from those participating as primary sources.	The participating users have the final say in decisions on usefulness and the primary sources on the facts about the outcome statements that are accepted as evidence with which to answer the prime harvesting questions. The uses are theirs. The outcomes are theirs. The validation of the outcome data is the substantiators'.
III. Coach human sources to formulate outcome statements	Provide hands-on support to people to apply what they know to craft concrete, verifiable descriptions of what has been achieved and how.	The people in the intervention closest to the action learn how to recognize, register and learn from outcomes they have influenced.	The people who serve as source of information are those who have been influenced to change and how the organization's activities have influenced them. They may, however, only become inspired after they have done the hard labor of harvesting and see the results.	The final formulation of the intervention's outcomes is determined by the primary sources of information—the outcomes are their outcomes. The harvester ensures the exercise is a systematic, data-based joint inquiry that upholds the honesty and integrity of the entire harvest process and generates credible data.	With the harvester's support, the primary sources arrive at sufficiently concrete quantitative and qualitative information so that the outcome formulation can be verified.

(continued)

TABLE C.1 GUIDE's Light on the Outcome Harvesting Effectiveness Principles (continued)

Outcome Harvesting Principles	Guidance	Useful	Inspiring	Developmental	Evaluable
IV. Strive for less because it will be more useful	Do only as much as necessary to achieve the desired result of answering usefully the prime harvesting questions.	A principal function of Outcome Harvesting is to communicate to decision-makers the information they need to know, when they need to know it. Thus, you work to collect information that matters to users, not simply to those supplying the information. While other methods, such as case studies, can extrapolate a process of influencing outcomes in detail, often the users can digest more easily simply written outcomes and contribution statements.	Primary sources are more motivated to provide necessary information than exhaustive (and exhausting) information. Users understand information that is concise and elegant rather than wordy and detailed.	How few users, questions, sources, words, details, outcomes, outcome dimensions, substantiators, and categories for classification are necessary, depends on their intended use, which varies according to each intervention and its context.	Less is more if the results are sufficient to meet the intended uses. Given one is capturing multiple outcomes and then analyzing them for processes and patterns, the more simply they are expressed, the easier it is to categorize and analyze them.
V. Learn Outcome Harvesting experientially	Learn the steps and principles of Outcome Harvesting by actively applying them, reflecting on the results, modifying the application, and repeating the process, ideally with mentoring.	Since the six steps of Outcome Harvesting have to be customized to users' uses in different times and contexts, following an action-reflection-modification cycle enables the harvester to avoid the temptation of trying to learn through reading and training alone.	Outcome Harvesting can be learned by self-directed, intentional, active involvement but rarely taught to a passive learner.	Actively learning how to apply Outcome Harvesting will also change the knowledge, attitudes and skills of the developing harvester about the approach. New applications will lead to new learning.	The parameter of success of experientially learning Outcome Harvesting is the primary intended users actual use of the process and findings based on SMART data, the six steps and the 10 principles.

(continued)

TABLE C.1 GUIDE's Light on the Outcome Harvesting Effectiveness Principles (continued)

Outcome Harvesting Principles	Guidance	Useful	Inspiring	Developmental	Evaluable
VI. Harvest social change outcomes	Social change in Outcome Harvesting is defined as societal actors modifying the way they do things in new and significant ways (outcome) that the intervention plausibly influenced (contribution).	Any change in behavior of a societal actor does not count as an outcome. Actors must alter or modify the character or nature of their behavior, not simply do more or improve something they had been doing.	The 'social change' in an Outcome Harvest are outcomes that contribute, actually or potentially, to impact understood as improving the lives of people or the state of the environment.	Context in the end determines if a change in behavior is sufficient to qualify as an outcome. In a process of social change, apparently small, initial outcomes may be more important than the final outcome, while in other cases the later outcomes are more significant than the initial ones.	Harvesters define clearly with primary users what counts as an outcome and why, taking into account the context as well as the nature of the change. The application of these definitions can be evaluated.
VII. Formulate an outcome as an observable change	To qualify as an outcome, an individual, group, community, organization or institution must have demonstrably done something different. Also, new understanding or heightened awareness or sensitivity does not count as an outcome until evidenced in perceptible changes in behavior.	Since the bottom line in social change is societal actors changing their behavior, Outcome Harvesting focuses on specific and measurable evidence of the change an intervention is influencing.	As important changes in attitudes are, or changes in knowledge or skills that an intervention controls, the cutting edge of autonomous social change with the potential to be sustainable is when societal actors apply that shift in attitudes, knowledge or skills to take the initiative to do something different.	An outcome statement may or may not reveal the reasons (including changes in attitudes, knowledge or skills) why the societal actor demonstrably changed. That conclusion depends on having in hand evidence—not supposition—of the motivation for why the subject of the outcome acted as she, he or it did. But, an outcome provides a tangible base from which to explore motivation.	The *who* changed *what*, *when* and *where* in an outcome description is formulated with sufficient specificity and measurability to be verifiable.

(continued)

TABLE C.1 GUIDE's Light on the Outcome Harvesting Effectiveness Principles (continued)

Outcome Harvesting Principles	Guidance	Useful	Inspiring	Developmental	Evaluable
VIII. Establish plausible influence of the intervention	To qualify as the intervention's outcome, there has to be a reasonable relationship of cause–effect between, on the one hand, the intervention's activities and outputs and, on the other, the outcome.	Outcome Harvesting rigorously differentiates between the results that an intervention controls—its activities and outputs—and those it only influences, which are the outcomes.	An outcome can rarely, if ever, be solely attributed to one intervention because in social change so many other actors and factors are present. Social change is brought about through collective action over time, not by individual lone rangers heroically determining change that can only be attributed to them.	There must be a reasonable cause–effect relationship between what the intervention did that in a small or large way, directly or indirectly, intentionally or not, contributed to, but did not determine, the change. The influence over time of the intervention on outcomes of the same societal actor may be different since generally there will be an ebb and flow of other actors and factors contributing.	How the intervention contributed to an outcome is formulated with sufficient specificity and measurability to be verifiable.
IX. Rigorously aim for credible-enough outcomes	Apply thorough evaluative thinking to ensure that the quality of the data and of the Outcome Harvesting exercise are as trustworthy as necessary for the primary users' principal uses.	In Outcome Harvesting the goal is to generate data that is sufficiently credible — no more, no less — for the primary users' principal uses.	The reputability of the process and the believability and accuracy of the findings depends in great measure on the trustworthiness and competence of the harvesters, demonstrated through their application of rigorous evaluative thinking rather than their adherence to a standardized process or method.	The decisions on what will be credible enough, and therefore what will be internally validated or externally substantiated and how, are made once the outcomes have been harvested. In the course of validation and substantiation, new decisions may be made on additional actions to be taken to ensure credibility.	Harvesters and users agree which outcomes, if any, to substantiate through non-probability, purposive, expert sampling. The results of substantiation are formally reported.

Glossary

Terms Used by Ricardo Wilson-Grau in Outcome Harvesting

accountability: An intervention's need to justify or explain work done and results achieved according to the norms and standards agreed upon. Three hundred and sixty degree accountability involves (a) upward accountability in reporting towards the board and donors, (b) downward accountability to the intervention's staff and participants, and (c) lateral accountability to other stakeholders, typically collaborators and allies.

action: A societal actor does something different than before. The president declares his support for women's empowerment as a human right.

activity: A societal actor repeatedly does something different than before. The president includes a declaration of support for women's empowerment as a human right into his stump speech.

adaptive management: A process that integrates project design, management, and monitoring to provide a framework for testing assumptions, adaptation, and learning.

analyze and interpret: Organize outcome statements so they are manageable and then use the information to provide evidence-based answers to the prime questions.

attribution: The causal link of one thing to another; for example, the extent to which observed (or expected to be observed) changes can be linked to a specific intervention in view of the effects of other interventions or confounding factors.

baseline survey/study: An analysis describing the situation in a project area—including data on individual primary stakeholders—prior to a development intervention. Progress (results and accomplishments) can be assessed and comparisons made against it.

behavioral change: Includes, but is not solely, a change in human behavior. The change can be in organizational and institutional behavior too. Changes in behavior can consist of new actions or activities but also of new relationships, policies, or practices.

beneficiaries: The individuals, groups or organizations who, in their own view and whether targeted or not, benefit directly or indirectly from the development intervention.

capacity: The ability of individuals and organizations to perform functions effectively, efficiently, and in a sustainable manner.

causal contribution inference: Establishing a logical connection, a cause-effect linkage between activities and outputs (*cause*) of an intervention that are partly responsible for one or more outcomes (*effects*). The linkages are plausible, not necessarily statistically accurate relationships arrived at through inductive reasoning. Therefore, the inference is made with uncertainty; the conclusion is likely, but not guaranteed.

change agent: Originally the term used in the early stages of Outcome Harvesting to identify the individual or organization that influences an outcome. Currently, the term "intervention" is preferred to "change agent."

complex: Unknown relationships of cause and effect until, maybe, when outcomes emerge.

complicated: Unknown but with expertise, experience or experimentation, knowable relationships of cause and effect.

confirmation or expectation bias: The tendency to consciously search for, interpret, favor, and recall outcome information that corresponds with what was planned or intended. This bias works as blinders on a horse, focusing obedience to a predetermined path and limiting the search for outcomes to the few that could be realistically forecast.

contribution description: A plausible description of how an intervention influenced an outcome in sufficient specificity and measurability to be verifiable.

CSO: Civil society organization.

design of the Outcome Harvest: Based on the principal intended uses of the primary intended users, you agree on the prime (Outcome Harvesting) questions to guide the harvest. Users and harvesters also agree the process: what information is to be collected, how, from whom, and when in order to credibly answer the questions, and what resources of time, people, and money are required. Synonymous with harvest plan.

developmental evaluation: Informs and supports an intervention that is implementing innovative approaches in uncertain, unpredictable, and dynamic situations. The process applies evaluative thinking to project, program, or organizational development by asking evaluative questions, applying evaluation logic, and gathering and reporting evaluative data throughout the innovation process.

engage with informants in formulating outcome descriptions: Through communication with primary sources of information who review the potential outcome statements extracted from documentation, and identify and formulate additional ones, you arrive at verifiable outcome statements.

evaluand: The thing being evaluated, whether it be a project, program, policy, organization, or other type of intervention.

evaluator: Person(s) responsible for carrying out the Outcome Harvest. Synonymous with "harvester."

exemplar: A composite of an organization drawn from several real evaluations used as an example in this book.

formative evaluation: Evaluation conducted during implementation to improve performance and accountability. It is usually performed midway through a planned intervention. Commonly synonymous with mid-term evaluation.

harvest users: The people who require the findings and process of an Outcome Harvest to make decisions or take action. Synonymous with "primary intended users."

harvester: Person(s) responsible for carrying out the Outcome Harvest. Usually synonymous with "evaluator."

harvest plan: The product of the design step in Outcome Harvesting. Based on the principal intended uses of the primary intended users, you agree on the prime (Outcome Harvesting) questions that will guide the harvest. Users and harvesters also agree on the process: what information is to be collected, how, from whom, and when in order to credibly answer the questions, and what resources of time, people, and money are required. Synonymous with "design of the Outcome Harvest."

impact: The changes in the conditions of people's lives or in the state of environment to which the intervention's outcomes have contributed. "In development terms, this [impact] typically means providing evidence that a particular program has brought about a sustainable improvement in the environment or in the well-being of a large number of targeted beneficiaries. Methodologically, this requires isolating the key factors that caused the desired results and attributing them to a particular agency or set of activities." (Earl, Carden, & Smutylo, 2001, p. 5).

influence: Understood broadly, it is an effect beyond the span of control of an intervention—from inspiring and encouraging, to facilitating and supporting, to persuading or pressuring the societal actor to change her, his, or its behavior. The change in a societal actor must be influenced, however partial, indirect, or unintentional it may be for an intervention to consider it contributed to the change.

intervention: An individual, group, event, an initiative, a project, a program, a policy, a strategy, or an organization that carries out activities and generates outputs that influence outcomes.

learning: Reflecting on experience to identify how a situation or future actions could be improved and then using this knowledge to make actual improvements. This can be individual or group-based. Learning involves applying lessons learned to future actions, which provides the basis for another cycle of learning.

logical framework approach (logframe): A results-based management tool that involves problem analysis, stakeholder analysis, developing a hierarchy of objectives and selecting a preferred implementation strategy. It helps to identify strategic elements (inputs, outputs, outcomes, goal) and their causal relationships, indicators of achievement, as well as the external assumptions (risks) that may influence success and failure. It thus facilitates planning, execution, and evaluation of a project or program.

mid-term evaluation: An external evaluation performed towards the middle of the period of implementation of the project, whose principal goal is to draw conclusions for reorienting the project strategy. Usually synonymous with "formative evaluation."

mixed methods: An analytical approach that combines quantitative and qualitative data.

monitoring: The periodic and systematic collection of data regarding the implementation and results of an intervention.

monitoring and evaluation (M&E): The combination of regularly collecting data on an intervention's implementation and interpreting it for learning and timely decision-making to improve performance and be accountable.

non-probability, purposive, expert sampling: A technique where the outcomes are not selected randomly but based on specific criteria, also known as judgmental, selective, or subjective sampling of persons with known or demonstrable experience and expertise in the outcome area.

nonlinearity: Effects are not proportional to the size, quantity, or strength of the inputs.

outcome harvest: The identification, formulation, analysis, and interpretation of outcomes, usually not predefined, to answer useful questions.

Outcome Harvesting exercise: The application of the Outcome Harvesting approach to meet the needs of primary intended users and their principal intended uses that require monitoring combined with evaluation (M&E) or developmental, formative, or summative evaluation.

Outcome Mapping: An approach to planning and monitoring that puts people at the center, defines outcomes as changes in behavior and helps measure contribution to complex change processes.

outcome statement: The written formulation of (a) *who* changed *what, when,* and *where,* and (b) *how* the intervention plausibly influenced them. May include the outcome's significance, context, contribution of other actors, history, and other information if it is useful.

outcome: A change in a societal actor's behavior—in the actions, activities, relationships, policies, or practices of an individual, group, community, organization, or institution.

output: The tangible goods and services that are produced (supplied) directly by a program's activities.

participation: One or more processes in which an individual (or group) takes part in specific decision-making and action, and over which s/he may exercise specific controls. It is often used to refer specifically to processes in which primary stakeholders take an active part in planning and decision-making, implementation, learning, and evaluation. This often has the intention of sharing control over the resources and responsibility for their future use.

performance evaluation: Assessment of the degree to which an intervention operates according to specific criteria or achieves results in accordance with stated goals or plans.

policy: A collective social actor—from a family, a group, or a community to an organization or an institution—changes the rules, norms, or laws that govern its behavior. For example: The legislature passes the equity in salary law.

practice: A collective social actor behaves in accordance with or implements one or more new policies. For example: For 5 years running, over half the members of the employers' association increase the salaries of women employees by a higher percentage than they do for men.

primary intended users: The people who require the findings of an Outcome Harvest to make decisions or take action. Synonymous with "harvest users."

prime (Outcome Harvesting) question: What the primary intended users need to know in the light of their principal uses for the Outcome Harvest written in the form of queries. The prime questions must be answerable with the data in outcome statements. These questions guide the Outcome Harvest—the harvest answers these questions. The prime questions are not to be confused with the specific questions to be asked of informants through questionnaires or interviews when collecting information.

principal intended uses: The decisions and actions that the Outcome Harvesting process or findings or both will serve.

process use: When the activity of implementing Outcome Harvesting enables participants—users and human sources—to learn from the experience and build their capacity to monitor, evaluate, and take action to improve their performance and that of the intervention.

process evaluation: An evaluation aimed at describing and understanding the internal dynamics and relationships of a project, program, or institution, including their policy instruments, their service delivery mechanisms, their management practices, and the linkages among these.

program evaluation: Evaluation of a set of project interventions, marshaled to attain specific global, regional, country, or sector development objectives.

project evaluation: Evaluation of an individual development intervention designed to achieve specific objectives within specified resources and implementation schedules, or within the framework of a broader program.

project: An intervention that consists of a set of planned, interrelated activities designed to achieve defined objectives within a given budget and a specified period of time.

qualitative: Something that is not summarized in numerical form, such as minutes from community meetings and general notes from observations. Qualitative data normally describe people's knowledge, attitudes, or behaviors.

quantitative: Something measured or measurable by, or concerned with, quantity and expressed in numbers.

random probability sampling: Sometimes known as aleatory probabilistic sampling, this is a process in which the sample is drawn based on some process or procedure that assures that the different units in your population have equal probabilities of being chosen: flipping coins, drawing straws or numbered chits out of a container, or using a computer to generate a random selection of numbers.

relationship: The way two or more societal actors interact with each other. For example, The employers' association and the Women's League agree to meet regularly to discuss ways to improve the employment of women.

result: The measurable output, outcome, or impact (intended or unintended, positive or negative) of an intervention.

simple: Known relationships of cause and effect.

SMART: Specific, measurable, achievable, relevant, and time-bound.

social change: In Outcome Harvesting, societal actors taking the initiative to do something new and significantly different in any sphere of human endeavor—political, economic, cultural, social, environmental, amongst others.

societal (social) actor: Individual, group, community, organization, or institution. *Societal actors* are human individuals and collectives (groups, communities) but also organizations (from civil society organizations to government agencies or businesses) and institutions such as the judicial system or the Roman Catholic Church.

sources: Documentation (secondary) or humans (primary) that provide information about outcomes.

stakeholders: A societal actor who has a direct or indirect interest in the use of Outcome Harvesting because they stand to be affected positively or negatively.

substantiate: A select number of outcome statements are consulted with one or more independent people to ensure accuracy or deepen understanding or both so that the whole set of outcome statements are credible enough for the intended uses.

substantiation: Confirmation of the substance of an Outcome Description by an informant knowledgeable about the outcome but independent of the intervention.

summative evaluation: Consists of the same process as formative evaluation but the purpose is to judge the merit, value, or significance of the intervention and is carried out at the end of an intervention.

support use: After the prime questions are answered, facilitate the users' uses of the Outcome Harvesting process and findings.

sustainability: The continuation of benefits from a development intervention once it has been completed.

target group: The specific group for whose benefit the project or program is undertaken, closely related to impact and relevance.

terms of reference: Written document presenting the purpose and scope of an evaluative process, the methods to be used, the standard against which performance is to be assessed or analyses are to be conducted, the resources and time allocated, and reporting requirements. Two other expressions sometimes used with the same meaning are "scope of work" and "evaluation mandate."

triangulation: The use of three or more theories, sources or types of information, or types of analysis to verify and substantiate an assessment, cross checking and validating data and information to limit biases.

valid outcome statement: The description of the change in the behavior of a societal actor (outcome) *and* how an intervention contributed (contribution) accurate enough for the primary intended users' principal intended uses. If there are additional dimensions to an outcome statement (the significance of the outcome, for example), the description must also be considered accurate for the whole statement to be accepted as valid.

References

Earl, S., Carden, F., & Smutylo, T. (2001). *Outcome mapping: Building learning and reflection into development programs.* Ottawa, Canada: International Development Research Centre. Retrieved from www.idrc.ca/EN/Resources/Publications/ Pages/IDRCBookDetails.aspx?PublicationID=121

About the Author

A graduate *magna cum laude* of the Universidad de Puerto Rico, Ricardo Wilson-Grau holds an MA in the Political Economy of Development from Goddard College, Plainfield, VT. He has worked in international development since the 1960s, including as a surveyor and community development worker with the national Agrarian Reform Institute (INCORA) in Colombia, field director for the American Friends Service Committee in Guatemala, director of the Latin American Program of Experiential Friends World College, journalist and managing director of Inforpress Centroamericana, senior manager with Greenpeace International in Amsterdam, and foreign aid advisor with Novib, the Dutch Oxfam. Currently he is the principal of Ricardo Wilson-Grau Consultoria, an evaluation consultancy registered in Brazil but working internationally.

Ricardo has written for publication and lectured in English, Spanish, and Portuguese on the economy and politics of Central America in the 1980s, strategic risk management in international development, and evaluation of social change. Most recently, he has written chapters on Outcome Harvesting for *Developmental Evaluation Exemplars: Principles in Practice*, edited by Michael Quinn Patton, Kate McKegg, and Nan Wehipeihana (2015); and *Principles-Focused Evaluation—The Guide*, Michael Quinn Patton (2017). He is an active member of the American Evaluation Association, the European Evaluation Society, and ReLAC, the equivalent in Latin America and the Caribbean.

Index

A

Accountability
  use of term, 211
  communication of findings and, 121–126
  credibility and, 122
  donor accountability, 4, 88–92, 114
  monitoring and evaluation and, 214
  reporting and, 122
  stakeholders and, 131, 211, 217
  substantiation and, 87–92
  support for use, 132–136, 146
  traditional evaluation *vs.* Outcome Harvesting, 4, 18, 26, 34
  See also Evaluation standards
Accuracy
  use of term, 19
  confidentiality and, 70
  credibility and, 88, 89–90, 183–185
  evaluation standards and, 19, 151–152, 183–185
  evaluator (harvester) role in, 19
  primary intended users and, 31
  substantiation and, 8, 89–92, 95, 99–102, 153–154, 217
Action
  use of term, 170, 211
  non-action, 164, 176–177
  social change outcomes and, 170–174
  See also Societal actors

Activity
  use of term, 2, 211
  social change outcomes and, 40, 57, 170–174
  See also Societal actors
Adaptive management
  use of term, 211
  as M & E learning tool, 6, 131, 133
  See also Monitoring and evaluation (M & E)
Advocacy
  evaluating advocacy, 4–8, 10–12, 43–44, 70, 164, 194–95
  Outcome Harvesting exemplars, 74, 80, 115–117, 133, 176
Alkin, Marvin C., 129, 132, 140–141
American Bar Association's Rule of Law Initiative (ABA-ROLI), 136, 137
Analysis and interpretation
  overview of, 104, 126
  use of term, 211
  applicability of key principles to, 103
  classification categories, 47–48, 104–112, 126, 127n1, 135, 145, 154
  collective sense-making and, 112–114
  communication of findings, 121–126
  credible-enough principle and, 183–185, 211
  criteria for category definitions, 106–109
  experiential learning and, 162–166
  grounded theory and, 106, 127n2

harvester (evaluator) role, 104, 107–109, 112–114, 118–121, 126
interpretation guidelines, 115–121
learning experientially and, 162–166
less is more principle and, 159–162
logical framework approach (logframe), 214
nurture appropriate participation and, 155–158
observable change and, 174–178
organization of outcome data, 104–112
Outcome Harvesting exemplar, 115–118
outcome statements and, 9, 17, 38–39, 184, 211
plausible influences and, 178–183
prime harvesting questions and, 104, 112–114, 135, 211
recommendations and, 123–126
report writing, 112–114, 118–121, 121–126
resources and, 47–48
social change outcomes and, 170–174
Assumptions
use of term, 49
evaluative thinking and, 49, 49–50, 67, 113–114, 133
harvester (evaluator) role and, 67, 133, 159
outcomes and, 67, 133
See also Adaptive management
Attribution
use of term, 211–212
vs. contribution, 61, 180
plausible influences and, 178–183
See also Causal contribution

B

Baseline survey/study
use of term, 212
Outcome Harvesting process and, 8–10
principal use and, 33–34
See also Design process
Behavioral change
use of term, 1–2, 18, 57, 212
beneficiaries and, 1–2
capacity-building and, 176
changes in knowledge, attitudes, and skills and, 175–176
observation and, 1–2, 57, 175–176
outcomes and, 1–2, 18, 57, 176–177, 215

social change and, 170–174
substantiation and, 88–89
See also Participation
Beneficiaries
use of term, 212
behavioral change and, 1–2
effectiveness *vs.*, 5, 6–7
impact and, 7
as stakeholders and, 1–2, 5, 6, 12, 100–101, 117, 131, 135, 137, 140, 153–154
See also Impact; Participation/participatory approaches; Stakeholders
Bourgeois, Isabelle, 140
Bretan, Emilia, 164
Brodhead, Dal, 25, 31, 71, 165
Budgeting, 67, 101, 143, 154–155, 202
See also Terms of reference (ToR)
Burroughs, Nicholas, 159

C

Cabaj, Mark, 81–84
Canadian International Development Research Centre, 18, 192
Capacity building
use of term, 212
behavioral change and, 176
learning/capacity changes, 105
Outcome Harvesting as capacity-building methodology, 33–34, 67–70, 77, 132–136, 142, 145–146, 162–166, 194–195
social change and, 176
support for use and, 33–34, 67–70, 77, 132–136, 142, 145–146, 162–166, 194–195
Causal contribution
use of term, 2, 42, 212
attribution *vs.* contribution, 61, 180
behavioral change and, 1–2, 42
causal inference framework, 181–183, 212
cause-effect relationships and, 15, 26, 60, 91, 175, 178–183
complexity-awareness and, 181–182
controlling *vs.* influencing change, 182–183
inductive reasoning and, 212
logical framework approach (logframe), 214

plausible influences and, 15, 60, 178–183
societal actors and, 178–183
uncertainty/dynamism/unpredictability and, 21–23, 26, 134, 150–155
See also Attribution; Behavioral change; Contribution; Influence; Intervention; Societal actors; Substantiation
Chambers, Robert, 157–158
Chambille, Karel, 196, 198n2
Change agents
use of term, 212
See also Intervention
Christian Aid Ireland, 132–133
Civil society organization (CSO), 212
Coaching, *See* Facilitator coach
Co-evaluators
commissioning of, 201–204
impact on Outcome Harvesting approach, xix–xxxi, 162–166, 196, 198n1, xxviin1
See also Facilitator coaches; Harvester (evaluators)
Commissioning process, 201–204
Communication of findings
accountability and, 121–126
analysis and interpretation and, 112–114, 118–121, 121–126
credibility and, 121–126, 145
primary intended use and, 121–126
reporting, 112–114, 121–126
report writing, 112–114, 118–121, 121–126
See also Reporting
Complexity
use of term, 212
causal contribution and, 181–182
complexity-awareness, xxiv, 21–23, 81–84, 131, 193–195
Complicated
use of term, 212
See also Causal contribution
Confidentiality, 43–44, 68–70, 97, 124
Confirmation bias
use of term, 212
See also Substantiation
Content principles
overview of, 13–15, 169, 170, 185–186
credible-enough principle and, 183–185, 186
observable change and, 174–178, 186
plausible influences and, 178–183, 186

social change outcomes, 170–174, 186
See also Behavioral change; Social change
Contribution
use of term, 212
attribution *vs.*, 61, 180
contribution analysis, 81–84
documentation review and, 59
outcome statements and, 38, 40–42, 215
plausible influences and, 15, 60, 178–183
social change and, 182–183
societal actors and, 178–183
See also Attribution; Behavioral change; Causal contribution; Influence; Intervention; Societal actors; Substantiation
Cousins, J. Bradley, 140
Credibility
use of term, 88
accountability and, 122
accuracy and, 88, 89–90, 183–185
analysis and interpretation and, 183–185, 211
communication of findings and, 121–126, 145
credible-enough principle and, 87–89, 183–185, 186
design process and, 183–185
documentation review and, 183–185
facilitator coaches and, 183–185
harvester (evaluators) and, 183–185
participation and, 155–158
primary intended use and, 183–185
primary sources and, 14, 155–158, 183–185
prime harvesting questions and, 89
secondary sources and, 14, 91, 183–185
substantiation and, 87–89, 89–92, 93–95, 183–185
use of findings and, 87–89, 93–95, 183–185

D

Data collection
harvesting instrument and, 52–60, 85n1
See also Harvesting instrument
Data validation. *See* Substantiation
Decision-making
facilitating usefulness and, 130, 140–145, 150–155

participation and, 20, 32–33, 139, 155, 161, 215
primary intended use and, 13, 14, 18, 20, 32–33, 36
support for use and, 132
utilization-focused evaluation and, 4, 13, 14, 18, 150–155
Design process
overview of, 8–10, 29–31, 44–49, 49–50, 213
applicability of key principles to, 29–31
coaching and, 158–159
credible-enough principle and, 183–185
documentation review, 8, 45
experiential learning and, 162–166
facilitating usefulness and, 150–155
harvesting instrument, 44–45, 52, 106
less is more principle and, 159–162
nurture appropriate participation and, 155–158
observable change and, 174–178
outcome statements and, 9, 38–42, 45
plausible influences and, 178–183
primary intended use and, 8, 31–33
primary sources and, 8, 42–44, 46, 158–159
prime harvesting questions and, 17, 34–38, 53, 152–155
professional evaluation standards and, 18–19
resources needed, 48, 48–49, 213
secondary sources and, 8, 42–44, 45
SMART outcomes and, 17, 80
social change outcomes and, 170–174
substantiation and, 8, 47, 178–183
support for use and, 9, 34, 48
terms of reference (ToR) and, 29–31, 44–45, 49–50, 185, 201–204
timeline, 44–49, 213
uncertainty/dynamism/unpredictability of, 21–23, 26, 134, 150–155
use of findings and, 9, 34, 48
See also Harvest plan
Dialogue and Dissent programs (Dutch Ministry), 136, 137–138, 138–139, 197
Documentation review
overview of, 51–52, 60–62
applicability of key principles to, 51–52
contribution and, 59
credible-enough principle and, 183–185
data collection organization, 52–54, 85n1
design process and, 8, 45
extracting outcome data, 54–60
facilitating usefulness and, 150–155
facilitator coaching and, 106–109, 158–159
harvesting instruments, 52–54, 61–62
impacts, 54–60
influence and, 57, 178–183
learning experientially and, 162–166
less is more principle and, 159–162
nurture appropriate participation and, 155–158
observable change and, 174–178
outcomes, 46, 56, 58, 60–61, 68, 71, 74, 84, 152–153, 170–174
outcome statements and, 16–17, 54–60
outputs and, 54–60
primary sources and, 60
prime harvesting questions, 52–54
resources needed, 45, 123
secondary sources and, 54–60
significance and, 59–60
societal actors and, 57
software and formatting tips for, 53–54, 72, 76, 106, 112, 134–135, 145
support for use and, 150–155
terms of reference (ToR) and, 123
See also Harvesting instrument
Donors
accountability and, 4, 88–92, 114
budgeting for, 67, 101, 143, 154–155, 202
Dutch Humanist Institute for Co-Operation with Developing Countries (Hivos), 196, 197

E

Effectiveness, 5, 6–7
See also Accountability; GUIDE for Outcome Harvesting
Evaluand
use of term, 184, 213
Evaluation standards
accuracy and, 19, 151, 151–152, 183–185
design process, 18–19
Outcome Harvesting and, 18–21, 130–132, 151–152
See also Accountability
Evaluative thinking, 49, 49–50, 67, 113–114, 133

Evaluators
    use of term, 213
    external evaluators, xxv, 20–21, 113–114, 122, 154
    internal evaluators, 114, 124, 126, 189–190, 197
    See also Facilitator coaches; Harvester (evaluators); Monitoring and evaluation (M & E)
Exemplar
    use of term, xxv, 213
    See also Outcome Harvesting exemplars
Expectation bias. *See* Confirmation bias
Experiential learning, 162–166
External sources. *See* Secondary sources (external)

F

Facilitating usefulness, 130, 140–145, 150–155, 166
    See also Support for use
Facilitator coaches
    use of term, 23–25, 71–83
    confidentiality and, 43–44, 68–70, 97, 124
    credibility and, 183–185
    design process and, 158–159
    documentation review and, 106–109, 158–159
    experiential learning and, 162–166
    facilitating usefulness and, 150–155, 166
    less is more principle and, 159–162
    outcome formulation and, 73–78, 78–81, 177–178
    outcome statements and, 17, 57–58, 64, 65–67, 70, 73, 74–85, 184
    participatory ping-pong process, 65–67, 81–84, 85–86, 155–158
    Michael Quinn Patton on, 71
    plausible influences and, 178–183
    primary intended use and, 158–159
    primary sources and, 65–67, 71–73, 158–159
    roles of, 23–25, 71–73, 104, 158–159, 186
    secondary sources and, 158–159
    self-reflexivity and, 76, 77
    SMART outcomes and, 17, 57–58, 64, 65–67, 70, 73, 74–85
    substantiation and, 158–159
    support for use and, 158–159
    terms of reference (ToR) and, 201–204
    use of findings and, 158–159
    utilization focused approach and, 25, 71, 165–166
    See also Harvester (evaluator); mentoring
Feasibility
    use of term, 19
Formative evaluation
    use of term, 213, 214, 215
    Outcome Harvesting and, 89, 134, 154, 155, 156, 159, 160

G

Gender at Work Framework, 119–121
Global Platform for the Prevention of Armed Conflict (GPPAC), xix–xx, 106, 196
Gold, Jenny, 3, 197, 198n1, 198n2
GUIDE for Outcome Harvesting, 205–210

H

Harari, Y.N., 103
Harvester (evaluators)
    use of term, 2, 213
    accuracy and, 19
    analysis and interpretation and, 104, 107–109, 112–114, 118–121, 126
    assumptions and, 67, 133, 159
    confidentiality and, 43–44, 68–70, 97, 124
    credible-enough principle and, 183–185
    evaluator recommendations and, 124–126
    experiential learning and, 162–166
    facilitating usefulness and, 150–155, 166
    less is more principle and, 159–162
    mentorship and, 23–25
    outcome formulation and, 54–60, 73–78, 78–81
    participatory ping-pong process and, 65–67, 81–84, 85–86, 155–158
    plausible influences and, 178–183
    primary intended users and, 126
    primary sources and, 71–73, 158–159
    recommendations and, 123–126
    reporting and, 123–126, 136
    roles of, 18–21, 23–25, 71–73, 104, 126, 158–159
    self-reflexivity and, 76, 77

support for use and, 132–136
terms of reference (ToR) and, 201–204
See also Facilitator coach
Harvesting instrument
criteria for category definitions and, 106–109
data collection and, 52–60, 85n1
design process, 44–45, 52, 106
documentation review and, 52–54, 61–62
Outcome Harvesting exemplars, 52–54, 52–55, 54, 55, 59, 64, 72
outcomes and, 53–54, 64–65
outputs, 53–54
primary sources and, 72
prime harvesting questions and, 53
software and formatting tips, 53–54, 60, 72, 76, 106, 112, 134–135, 145
See also Data collection; Documentation review
Harvest plan
use of term, 213
See also Design process
Harvest users (primary intended users)
use of term, 213
See also Primary intended use
Hemingway, Ernest, 162
Hivos (Dutch Humanist Institute for Co-Operation with Developing Countries), 196, 197

I

Impact
use of term, 2, 39, 41, 56–57, 171, 213, 217
documentation review and, 54–60
intervention beneficiaries and, 7
Outcome Harvesting approach and, 6–8, 18, 35, 38, 175
outcomes and, 2–3, 38, 39, 41, 56–57, 171
social change and, 170–174
See also Beneficiaries
Indicators of change, 60, 176, 193, 212
Influence
use of term, 214
causal contribution and, 15, 60, 178–183
outcomes and, 57, 178–183
plausible influence and, 57, 178–183
primary intended use and, 178–183
primary sources and, 178–183
secondary sources and, 178–183
substantiation and, 178–183

Interventions
use of term, 214, 216, 218
negative outcomes and, 177–178
plausible influences and, 178–183
See also Causal contribution; Impact; Substantiation; Sustainability

K

Key principles
overview of, 13–15, 149, 150, 166, 169, 170, 185–186
of analysis and interpretation, 103
applicability of to design process, 29–31
coaching human (primary) sources, 158–159, 186
credible-enough principle and, 183–185, 186
facilitating usefulness, 150–155, 166
learning experientially, 162–166, 186
less is more principle and, 159–162, 186
nurture appropriate participation, 155–158, 186
observable change and, 174–178, 186
plausible influences and, 178–183, 186
social change outcomes, 170–174, 186
substantiation and, 87–89
use of findings and, 129–132
King, Jean, 132
Klugman, Barbara, xxi, 7, 66–67, 113–114, 164, 198n1
Kosterink, Paul, xx, xxiv, 106, 196

L

Learning
use of term, 214
Less is more principle and, 159–162
Logical framework approach (logframe)
use of term, 214

M

McAdam, Lorina, 130–131, 198n2
Mentoring
learning experientially principle and, 162–166
role of facilitator coach and, 23–25
utilization focused approach and, 25, 71, 165–166

Mercy Corps, 130–131, 132
Mertens, Donna, 67
Mid-term evaluation (formative evaluation)
  use of term, 214
Mixed methods
  use of term, 214
Monitoring and evaluation (M & E)
  use of term, xxv
  decision-making and, 4, 13, 14, 18, 150–155, 214
  learning experientially principle and, 162–166
  Outcome Harvesting approach, 4–10, 24–25, 33, 36–38, 61–62, 113, 126–127, 139, 165–166

N

Nonlinearity
  use of term, 181, 215
  See also Complexity
Novib, 191–192

O

Observable change
  analysis and interpretation and, 174–178
  behavioral change and, 1–2, 57, 175–176
  design process and, 174–178
  documentation review and, 174–178
  non-action as change, 163, 176–177
  observable change principle and, 174–178
  primary and secondary sources and, 174–178
  support for use and, 174–178
Outcome formulation
  facilitator coaches and, 73–78, 78–81, 177–178
  harvester (evaluators) and, 54–60, 73–78, 78–81
  primary sources and, 46, 78–81
  See also Substantiation
Outcome Harvesting
  use of term, 2, 215
  overview of, xviii–xix, 1–10, 18–26, 190
  budgeting for, 67, 101, 143, 154–55, 202
  capacity building and, 33–34, 67–70, 77, 132–136, 142, 145–46, 162–166, 194–195

challenges of, 20–21, 23, 33, 36, 38, 136, 140–146, 157–158, 165–166
co-evaluator impact on development of, xix–xxxi, 162–66, 196, 198n1, xxviin1
donors and, 4, 67, 88–92, 101, 114, 143, 154–155, 202
evaluation standards and, 18–19
expert sampling technique, 93, 214–215
influence of Michael Quinn Patton on, xi–xii, xxii–xxiv, 14–15, 18, 192
international recognition, 197–198
limitations of, 142–145
team approach to, 194–195
traditional evaluation *vs.*, 4–8, 13–15, 21–23, 81–84, 193–195
utilization focused approach and, 13, 18, 24, 30, 130, 142, 153–154, 192–195
See also Key principles; Outcome Harvesting exemplars; Wilson-Grau, Ricardo
Outcome Harvesting exemplars
  overview of, xxv, 10–11
  advocacy exemplars, 74, 80, 115–117, 133, 176
  analysis and interpretation, 115–118
  classification of outcome descriptions, 107–111
  co-evaluators, 202
  contribution of interventions, 107
  documentation review, 45, 58
  efficiency criteria and, 35
  evaluation report, 11–12
  facilitator relationships, 78, 79, 81
  Gender at Work, 120–121
  harvesting instruments, 52–54, 52–55, 54, 55, 59, 64, 72, 74, 75
  impact and, 35
  interpretation guidelines, 115–121
  outcomes, 58, 72, 74, 75, 107
  outcome statements, 40, 59, 64
  primary sources, 46, 58
  primary users/principal use, 32, 45
  prime evaluation questions, 36–37
  principal use, 32
  report outlines, 123
  resources needed, 48
  secondary sources, 45, 58
  SMART outcomes, 80
  substantiation and, 47, 96, 97–98
  support user of findings, 48
  timeline, 48–49

Outcome Harvesting exercise
    use of term, 215
    terms of reference (ToR) and, 203–204
Outcome Mapping
    use of term, 18, 215
    outcome mapping methodology, 18, 26, 192–193
Outcome Mapping (Earl, Cayden, & Smutlyo), 18
Outcomes
    use of term, 1–8, 2, 18, 54, 57, 215
    key concepts, 1–8
    analysis and interpretation and, 112–121
    assumptions and, 67, 133
    behavioral change and, 1–2, 18, 57, 176–177, 215
    changes in knowledge, attitudes, and skills (KAS), 175–176
    classification categories and, 47–48, 104–112, 126, 127n1, 135, 145, 154
    complexity-awareness and, 21–23, 193–195
    contribution and, 55, 59
    credibility and, 183–185
    criteria for category definitions, 106–109, 112
    design process and, 17, 170–174
    documentation review and, 46, 56, 58, 60–61, 68, 71, 74, 84, 152–153
    extracting outcome data and, 54–60
    harvesting instrument and, 53–54, 64–65
    impact and, 2–3, 38, 39, 41, 56–57, 171
    influence and, 57, 178–183
    institutional change and, 104, 215
    J-curve and, 177–178
    less is more principle and, 159–162
    negative outcomes, 54, 55, 177–178, 184, 185
    non-action as outcome, 176–177
    organization of outcome data, 104–112
    outcome formulation and, 54–60, 73–78, 78–81, 177–178
    outputs *vs.*, 81
    potential outcomes, 46, 56, 58, 60–61, 68, 71, 74, 84, 152–153
    primary intended use and, 170–174
    primary sources and, 46, 56, 58, 60–61, 68, 71, 74, 84, 152–153
    societal actors and, 170–174
    use of findings and, 170–174, 177–178
    See also Outcome statements; SMART outcomes

Outcome statements
    use of term, 2, 39, 215, 218
    analysis and interpretation and, 9, 17, 38–39, 184, 211
    classification categories for, 109–112
    contribution and, 38, 40–42, 215
    data collection and, 16–17
    description of significance, 40–42
    design process and, 9, 38–42, 45
    documentation review and, 16–17, 54–60
    exemplars, 38–39, 40
    facilitator coaches and, 17, 57–58, 64, 65–67, 70, 73, 74–85, 184
    limiting categories of, 112
    negative outcomes and, 177–178
    outcome formulation and, 54–60, 73–78, 78–81
    participatory ping-pong process and, 65–67, 81–84, 85–86
    primary intended users and, 153
    SMART criteria for, 17, 57–58, 64, 65–67, 70, 73, 74–85
    societal actors and, 40–41
    software and formatting tips for, 53–54, 72, 76, 106, 112, 134–135, 145
    substantiation and, 87–92, 217
    terms of reference (ToR), 38–42, 45–48
Outputs
    use of term, 54, 215
    documentation review and, 54–60
    harvesting instrument and, 53–54
    outcomes *vs.*, 81

P

Participation/participatory approaches
    analysis and interpretation and, 155–158
    credibility and, 155–158
    criteria for category definition process, 106–109
    decision-making and, 20, 32–33, 139, 155, 161, 215
    design process and, 155–158
    documentation review and, 155–158
    evaluator recommendations and, 123–126
    facilitating usefulness and, 150–155, 166
    interactivity and, 155–158
    nurture appropriate participation and, 155–158

outcome statements and, 65–67, 81–84, 85–86
primary intended use and, 155–158
primary sources and, 65–67, 81–84, 85–86, 155–158
prime harvesting questions and, 84–85
substantiation and, 155–158
support for use and, 155–158
Pascal, Blaise, 161
Patton, Michael Quinn
    on coaching role, 71
    communication of findings and, 121–123, 125
    on contribution *vs.* attribution, 180
    on design process, 49
    on follow-up process, 142
    GUIDE framework, 205–210
    influence on Outcome Harvesting approach, xi–xii, xxii–xxiv, 14–15, 18, 192
    on primary users, 39
    on role of facilitation, 24
Performance evaluation
    use of term, 215
Ping-pong process, 65–67, 81–84, 85–86
    See also Participation/participatory approaches
Policy
    use of term, 215
    social change outcomes and, 170–174
Practice
    use of term, 215
Primary intended users
    overview of, 1–8, 3, 216
    use of term, 2, 3, 213, 215, 216
    accuracy and, 31
    capacity building and, 33–34, 67–70, 77, 132–136, 142, 145–146, 162–166, 194–195
    communication of findings and, 121–126
    confidentiality and, 43–44, 68–70, 97, 124
    credible-enough principle and, 183–185
    criteria for category definitions and, 106–109
    decision-making and, 13, 14, 18, 20, 32–33, 36
    design process and, 8, 31–33
    experiential learning and, 162–166
    facilitating usefulness and, 150–155, 166
    facilitator coaching and, 158–159
    harvester (evaluator) and, 126

less is more principle and, 159–162
nurture appropriate participation and, 155–158
observable change and, 174–178
Outcome Harvesting approach and, 3, 31–33, 54–60, 198n2, xxviin2
plausible influences and, 178–183
prime harvesting questions and, 36–38
professional standards and, 18–21
social change outcomes and, 170–174
substantiation and, 87–89
support for use and, 132–136
terms of reference and, 31–33, 49–50, 152
utilization focused approach and, 31–33, 39
See also Support for use
Primary sources (internal)
    overview of, 63–65
    applicability of key principles to, 63–65
    confidentiality and, 43–44, 68–70, 97, 124
    credibility and, 14, 155–158, 183–185
    design process and, 8, 42–44, 46, 158–159
    documentation review and, 60
    experiential learning and, 162–166
    facilitating usefulness and, 150–155
    facilitator coaching and, 65–67, 71–73, 158–159
    harvester (evaluator) relationship and, 71–73, 158–159
    harvesting instrument and, 72
    influence and, 178–183
    learning experientially, 162–166
    observable change and, 174–178
    outcome formulation and, 46, 78–81
    Outcome Harvesting exemplar, 46, 58
    outcomes and, 46, 56, 58, 60–61, 68, 71, 74, 84, 152–153
    participatory ping-pong process, 65–67, 81–84, 85–86, 155–158
    self-reflexive interactions and, 76, 77
    social change outcomes and, 170–174
    societal actors and, 170–174
    substantiation and, 87–89, 92, 93–95, 101, 158–159
    terms of reference (ToR), 42–44
    use of findings and, 158–159
    See also Documentation review

Prime harvesting questions
  analysis and interpretation and, 104, 112–14, 135, 211
  credibility and, 89
  design process and, 17, 34–38, 53, 152–155
  documentation review and, 52–54
  harvesting instrument and, 53
  less is more principle and, 159–162
  ping-pong participation and, 84–85
  substantiation and, 89, 95
  terms of reference (ToR), 34–38
  See also Harvesting instrument
Principal intended use. *See* Primary intended users
Process principles
  overview of, 13–15, 149, 150, 166, 185–186
  coaching human (primary) sources, 158–159, 186
  facilitating usefulness, 150–155, 186
  less is more principle and, 159–162, 186
  nurture appropriate participation, 155–158, 186
Progress
  use of term, 214
Project
  use of term, 216
Propriety
  use of term, 19

Q

Qualitative data
  use of term, 216
  Outcome Harvesting approach and, 16–17
Quantitative data
  use of term, 216

R

Ramírez, Ricardo, 25, 31, 71, 165
Recommendations, 123–126
Relationships
  use of term, 216–17
  social change outcomes and, 170–174
Reporting
  accountability and, 122
  communication of findings, 112–114, 121–126
  evaluator recommendations and, 124–126
  recommendations, 123–126, 136
  support for use of findings and, 134–135
  terms of reference (ToR), 45, 123
  See also Communication of findings
Resources
  for analysis and interpretation, 47–48
  budgeting, 67, 101, 143, 154–155, 202
  design process, 48, 48–49, 213
  documentation review, 45, 123
  software and formatting tips, 53–54, 72, 76, 106, 112, 134–135, 145
  substantiation and, 101
  terms of reference (ToR) and, 44–49
Results
  use of term, 217
Richert, Wolfgang, xx, 197, 198n2

S

Sampling
  use of term, 216
  expert sampling technique, 93, 214–215
  nonprobability sampling, 93–95, 214
  random probability sampling, 216
  substantiation and, 93–95, 214
Scheers, Goele, xix–xx, xxiv, 65–66, 76, 77, 164–165, 196, 197
Secondary sources (external)
  confidentiality and, 43–44, 68–70, 97, 124
  credible-enough principle and, 183–185
  design process and, 8, 42–44, 45
  documentation review and, 54–60
  experiential learning and, 162–166
  facilitating usefulness and, 150–155, 166
  facilitator coaching and, 158–159
  influence and, 178–183
  less is more principle and, 159–162
  observable change and, 174–178
  outcome data and, 54–60
  Outcome Harvesting exemplar, 96
  social change and, 170–174
  substantiation and, 89–92, 92, 93–95, 97–99
  terms of reference (ToR), 42–44
  See also Documentation review
Sense-making workshop, 112–114

Simple
  use of term, 217
SMART outcomes
  use of term, 217
  criteria for outcome statements, 17, 57–58, 64, 65–67, 70, 73, 74–85
  design process and, 17, 80
  facilitator coaches and, 17, 57–58, 64, 65–67, 70, 73, 74–85
  Outcome Harvesting exemplars, 80
  primary sources and, 66–67
  substantiation and, 87–92, 217
Smith, Richard, xxi, 162–163, 162–164, 198n2
Social change
  use of term, 217
  action and, 170–174
  activity and, 40, 57, 170–174
  analysis and interpretation and, 170–174
  behavioral change and, 170–174
  capacity-building and, 176
  causal contribution and, 182–183
  design process and, 170–174
  documentation review and, 170–174
  impact and, 170–174
  negative outcomes and, 177–178
  Outcome Harvesting approach and, 1–8
  policy and, 170–174
  primary intended use and, 170–174
  primary sources and, 170–174
  secondary sources and, 170–174
  substantiation and, 170–174
  support for use and, 170–174, 174–178
  use of findings and, 170–174
  See also Intervention
Societal actors
  use of term, 217
  causal contribution, 178–183
  controlling *vs.* influencing causal contribution, 182–183
  documentation review and, 57
  outcomes and, 170–174
  outcome statements and, 40–41
  substantiation and, 170–174
  See also Causal contribution
Sources
  use of term, 217
  See also Primary sources (internal); Secondary sources (external)
Stakeholders
  use of term, 217
  accountability and, 131, 211, 217
  beneficiaries as, 1–2, 5, 6, 12, 100–101, 117, 131, 135, 137, 140, 153–154
  See also Primary intended use; Primary sources (internal)
Strunk, William, 161
Stufflebeam, Dan, 19
Subjective sampling. *See* Sampling
Substantiation
  overview of, 87–89, 101–102
  use of term, 217
  accountability and, 87–92
  accuracy and, 8, 89–92, 95, 99–102, 153–154, 217
  applicability of key principles to, 87–89
  behavioral changes and, 88–89
  choosing substantiators, 93–95
  confidentiality and, 97–98
  confirmation bias, 58, 212
  credibility and, 87–89, 89–92, 93–95, 183–185
  deepened understanding and, 89–90, 100–101
  design process and, 8, 47, 178–183
  experiential learning and, 162–166
  facilitating usefulness and, 150–155
  facilitator coaches and, 158–159
  influence and, 178–183
  intervention independence and, 217
  less is more principle and, 159–162
  nonprobability sampling, 93–95, 214
  nurture appropriate participation and, 155–158
  options for substantiation, 89–92
  outcome formation and, 88–89
  Outcome Harvesting exemplars, 47, 96, 97–98
  outcome statements and, 87–92, 217
  peer review and, 97–99
  primary intended users and, 87–89
  primary sources and, 87–89, 92, 101, 158–159
  prime harvesting questions and, 89, 95
  resources needed, 101
  secondary sources and, 89–92, 92, 93–95, 97–99
  social change outcomes and, 170–174
  societal actors and, 170–174
  substantiation process, 95–101
  substantiator roles, 8, 92, 93–99, 101, 153, 155, 157–158, 174–175, 180

terms of reference (ToR) and, 47
timing of, 89–90
Summative evaluation
use of term, 213, 214, 215, 217
Support for use
overview of, 130–132, 145–146
use of term, 217
accountability, 132–136, 146
applicability of key principles to, 129–132
attitude establishment/altering, 132
capacity building for primary internal sources, 33–34, 67–70, 77, 132–136, 142, 145–146, 162–166, 194–195
challenges to, 140–142
credibility and, 87–89, 93–95, 183–185
decision-making and, 132
design process and, 9, 34, 48
documentation review and, 150–155
experiential learning and, 162–166
facilitating usefulness, 130, 140–145, 150–155
facilitator coaches and, 158–159
follow-up process and, 142–145, 150, 152
harvester (evaluator) role in, 132–136
influence and, 178–183
less is more principle and, 159–162
negative outcomes and, 177–178
observable change and, 174–178
Outcome Harvesting methodology and, 136–139, 139–140
participation and, 155–158
primary intended users and, 132–136
primary sources and, 158–159
reporting and, 134–135, 134–136
social change outcomes and, 170–174
societal actors and, 170–174
Sustainability
use of term, 217

T

Target group
use of term, 217
Terms of reference (ToR)
use of term, 217
budgeting, 67, 101, 143, 154–155, 202
co-evaluators and, 201–204
deliverables, 123

design process, 29–31, 44–45, 49–50, 185, 201–204
development of, 201–204
documentation review, 123
evaluation commissioners and, 20, 29–30
evaluative thinking and, 49–50, 184
Outcome Harvesting exercise and, 203–204
outcome statements, 38–42, 45–48
primary and secondary sources, 42–44
primary intended use and, 31–33, 49–50, 152
prime harvesting questions, 34–38
reporting requirements, 45, 123
resource allocation, 44–49
substantiation and, 47
The World Bank, 3, 104–106, 114, 172–173, 197
Tiernan, Alix, 132, 133
Timeline
design process and, 44–49, 213
Triangulation
use of term, 218
Trochim, William M.K., 49, 93
Tsereteli-Stephens, Salome, 136, 137

U

Uncertainty/dynamism/unpredictability, 21–23, 26, 134, 150–155
USAID (U.S. Agency for International Development), xix, 130, 137, 197
Usefulness. *See* Support for use
Utility
use of term, 19
Utilization focused evaluation
use of term, 18
communication of findings and, 121–123, 125
follow-up process and, 142, 150, 152
mentoring and coaching roles and, 25, 71, 165–166
Outcome Harvesting approach and, 13, 18, 24, 30, 130, 142, 153–154, 192–195
participatory approach of, 155–158
primary users and, 31–33, 39
role of facilitation and, 24
utilization-focused criteria, 36–38
See also Patton, Michael Quinn

Utilization-Focused Evaluation (Patton), xxii, xxiii, 18, 30, 130, 142, 192
Utilization Focused Evaluation (Ramírez and Brodhead), 25, 31, 71, 165

W

Weiss, Carol, 130, 132, 136
Weiss, C. H., 132
Williams, Bob, xvi, xix, 43–44, 152, 159–160
Wilson-Grau, Ricardo
    evaluation practice of, xvi–xvii, 68, 70, 191–195
    evaluator recommendations and, 124–126
    social praxis of, xxvi–xxvii
Woolcock, Michael, 177–178

Made in the USA
Middletown, DE
16 February 2019